AL-KINDI:

THE PHILOSOPHER OF THE ARABS

GEORGE N. ATIYEH

Chairman, Department of Humanities
University of Puerto Rico

KITAB BHAVAN
New Delhi-110002

Kitab Bhavan
Publishers, Distributors, Exporters & Importers
1784, Kalan Mahal, Darya Ganj
New Delhi - 1100 02 (India)

Phone : (91-11) 23277392/93, 23274686, 30906494
website : www.kitabbhavan.com
Email : nasri@vsnl.com
Fax : (91-11) 23263383

First Edition 1994
IInd Reprinted 2006

ISBN : 81-7151-187-2
Code No. : A00147

Laser Typesetting at :
Laser Track
1784, Kalan Mahal, Darya Ganj
New Delhi-110002 [India]

Published in India by :
Nusrat Ali Nasri for Kitab Bhavan
1784, Kalan Mahal, Darya Ganj
New Delhi - 1100 02 [India]

Printed in India at :
Nice Printing Press
Khureji Khas, Delhi-110051

PREFACE

I have attempted here to present to the general reader and the student of Arab-Muslim thought a tolerable sketch of al-Kindi's philosophy. I thought it important and necessary to bring together in one volume the information available about his philosophy and works, and to trace his Influence down the centuries. I do not pretend to have written an exhaustive, least of all, a final study of al-Kindi and his contribution to philosophy.

Al-Kindi is the first of a galaxy of great Muslim thinkers whose humanistic and scientific works helped shape the trend of the medieval Arab renaisance. To study him is important not only for tracing the origin of the different tendencies in Arab-Muslim thought, but also for understanding the methodologies and attitudes of a great number of Muslim thinkers. His writings which include works on all current sciences of his time put him in a unique position to help establish the relations of Arab-Muslim philosophy with earlier philosophies and with following generations of Muslim thinkers who deal with metaphysical, and scientific problems.

The existence of an Arab-Muslim philosophy raises many problems. In what sense can we consider it pure Philosophy? In what relation does it stand to theology? What peculiarities of its own does it have? What contributions did it make to the discipline of philosophy as a whole? Philosophy is a technical term as we know. It is the study of reality, the search for certainty and the study of values by means of reason. In this sense philosophy is a Greek invention. The ancient Greeks established the bases and the rules for the huge and kaleidoscopic edifice of philosophy; and since then men of all nations have been adding their own contribution and insight to that edifice. One, therefore, cannot take the study of philosophy solely to mean, the rational search into reality and actions; it should be considered also as conceptual formulation of man's deeper experiences and his interpretation of the world through a peculiar vision springing from the ethos of the philosopher's own environment.

The Near East like all other areas that have contributed to philosophical thought has a manifest set of beliefs and a particular world-view. It has contributed, both in Ancient and Medieval times, an important share to philosophy by inventing new approaches, by discovering new solutions and simply by bringing in its own vision to contrast with the extreme rationalistic and humanistic attitude of the greatest of the Greek philosophers. It has been often been said that the Arab-Muslim world has no proclivity towards rationalistic philosophy and science. It is indeed a challenge to try to prove the contrary especially when one believes that philosophy cannot be as objective and rationalistic as that. In al-Kindi we have a notable case of an Arab-Muslim intellectual, representing the milieu in which he flourished. It should be interesting and enlightening to study him first as a philosopher and a product of his own genius and secondly as a product of the genius of his race. Regardless of what one thinks of al-kindi, there is no doubt that he channelised Arab-Muslim thought into new alleys. His raising the problems of the relation between philosophy and religion, his delving into the problem of the One, his attitude towards the epistemological and ethical problems single him out as the founder of Arab-Muslim philosophy.

Any extensive study of al-Kindi would have been almost impossible a few years ago. The relatively recent publication in original Arabic of a number of his philosophical treatises not only throws new light on the mode of thinking and ideas of the Philosopher of the Arabs, but also on the situation of philosophy in the Near East during the 3rd/9th century.

The publication in the early fifties of the present century by Professor M. A. Abu Ridah of Egypt of twenty-six treatises of al-Kindi generated new interest in the philosopher and his times. The works that have been published since then about al-Kindi, though not numerous, are quite extensive and indicative of this new interest.

The published works of al-Kindi range from metaphysics to astronomy. Each treatise is preceded by an outline and a brief study of the contents; the first volume opens with a general introduction which, as a whole, constitutes the best study on al-Kindi yet published in Arabic. The millenary celebrations held in Baghdad in 1962 under the auspices of the Ministry of Information, Government of Iraq, also served as a stimulus. The apparent aim of the celebrations was served well by focussing the attention of the students of Arab-Muslim thought on the first true philosopher of the Islamic world.

In English there is yet relatively very little written on al-Kindi. Professor R. Walzer blazed the trail in the recent past, and the publication by Professor Nicholas Rescher of University of Pittsburgh of a general *Annotated Bibliography* on al-Kindi (Pittsburgh, 1964) should prove most useful. With the publication of the present book and its Appendix on the works of al-Kindi, it is hoped to complete the levelling of the ground for further and more profound studies, general as well as specialized.

The Appendix is based on the list of titles of Ibn al-Nadim, the oldest that we possess. The additions and difference contained in this list are the result of investigations done in published materials without reference to extant manuscripts, which was rather a difficult task. The paucity of research facilities on Arabic and Muslim cultures at the University of Puerto Rico and the dispersion of al-Kindi's extant works over a wide area prevented me from fulfilling this essential requirement.

The title of the third Appendix is mine. The material comes from *al-Muntakhab Siwan al-Hikmah,* an unpublished work based on Abu Sulayman al-Mantiqi al-Sijistani's (d. 391/1001) famous but lost work *Siwan al-Hikmah.* Fortunately the abbreviator whose name is not mentioned in any of the manuscripts and who must have lived not later than 639/1241, made a selection *(muntakhab)* of what he thought were significant parts of al-Sijistani's original work. "I decided to set down the lives of the philosophers, their names and some of their ideas and characters, so I have selected from *Siwan al-Hikmah* an account of the ancients, and I placed at the end (of my selection) *Talimmah Siwan al-Hikmah* of the excellent scholar Zahir al Din Abu'l Hasan ibn 'Ali al-Qasim al-Bayhaqi, God's Mercy be on him."

There are several copies of this work: one in the British Museum, three in Istanbul, one in Leiden and one in Cairo. This work, one of the oldest references to al-Kindi and other Arab and Greek philosophers, contains a collection of anecdotes about al-Kindi, analects and selected passages from his writings.

To establish the text of the selection on al-Knidi, I used photostat copies of two manuscripts, the first, MS. On 9033 (fols. 60*a*-65*b*), in the British Museum (7th/14th century). On this I based my text. The second MS. 902 Koprulu in Istanbul (8th/15th century). Both seem to come from the same source. However, the manuscript in the British Museum contains an additional passage covering about fifteen lines. The Koprulu copyist could not have left that part out on purpose, but most probably he skipped over the missing lines by mistake.

Unfortunately, neither al-Mantiqi nor the abbreviator mentions the sources from which they selected their passage on al-Kindi. Except for numbers five and seven which come from the treatise *On the Soul,* we have no way of determining what specific works of al-Kindi they come from. Some of the passages are biographical in nature and consequently could not have been taken from al-Kindi's own works. The great majority could have been drawn from his ethical treatise, and there is an indication that some of the sayings have been taken from *Tahsil Subul al-Fada'il.*

The sayings in themselves correspond to a popular genre of literature common during the times of al-Kindi and frequently found in the East as a whole. Miskawayh (d. 420/1029), a friend and disciple of al-Mantiqi, put together a collection of Arab, Indian, Persian and Greek sayings in his *Jawidan Khirad* (Cairo, 1952). The *Maxims of Socrates,* which al-Kindi was possibly the first to popularize in Arabic, are to be found with minor changes in Miskawayh's work.

I hope the publication in this volume of the passages preserved by al-Sijistani would prove useful.

Finally, I would like to thank the authorities of The Carnegie Fund and the University of Puerto Rico for their financial aid. I would also like to thank Professor Lewis Richardson for correcting the language of the first draft, and Mrs. Charles Toth for correcting the second draft of this book. To Professor A. S. Bazmee Ansari, General Editor of the series, should go my deepest gratitude for undertaking to translate the *Sayings of al-Knidi* into English and for all the editorial improvements that my book needed.

GEORGE N. ATIYEH

LIST OF ABBREVIATIONS

al-Bukhala'	: *Kitab al-Bukhala'* by al-Jahiz ed. T. al-Hajiri, Cairo, 1948.
GAL (S)	: *Geschichte der Arabischen Litteratur,* Supplementband.
JRAS	: *Journal of the Royal Asiatic Society.*
al-Muntakhab	: *Muntakhab Siwan al-Hikmah.*
Die Philosophische Abhandlugen	: *Die Philosophische Abhandlungen* des *Ja'cub ben Ishaq alKindi,* ed. A. Nagy.
Rasa'il	: The edition of al-Kindi's philosophical treatises by M. A. Abu Ridah, *Rasa'il al-Kindi al-Falsafiyyah,* Cairo, 1950-53.
Ta'rikh al-Hukama'	: *Ta'rikh al-Hukama'* by al-Qifti, ed. J. Lippert, Leipzig 1903.
Uyun	: *'Uyun al-Anba' fi Tabaqat al-Atibba,* ed. A. Muller, Cairo, 1882.
ZDMC	: *Zeitschrift der Deutschen Morge landischen Gesselleschaft.*

CONTENTS

1

THE LIFE AND TIMES OF AL-KINDI

A--The Time of al-Kindi

AL-KINDI must have lived through the reigns of the 'Abbasid caliphs al-Amin (809-813 A.C.), al-Ma'mun (813-833 A.C.), al-Mu'tasim (833-842 A.C.), al-Wathiq (842-847 A.C.), and al-Mutawakkil (847-861 A.C.). Throughout this time the 'Abbasid empire was enjoying the most brilliant period of its political and intellectual life. During the early half of the ninth century, the 'Abbasid empire was at the summit of its military and political power, enjoying good relations with the Franks, at that time the enemies of Umayyad Spain. In the military field al-Ma'mun pushed the war against Byzantium to the shores of the Bosphorus. In civil administration, the connections between Baghdad, the seat of the government, and the governors of the provinces were made stronger by a net of roads, a postal system and guide books of the various provinces. Baghdad, the capital, was probably the most splendid city in the whole world with its huge palaces, gardens, public baths, places of entertainment, and markets replete with all kinds of exquisite goods.

The scientific and intellectual activities kept pace with the material splendour of Baghdad. Translations into Arabic of the Greek heritage in science and philosophy stirred up new interests and presented new problems. The Syrians had, before the coming of Islam, assimilated and preserved in Syriac a great deal of the Greek culture. In the cloisters of Syria, in the school of

Jundishahpur in Persia manned by Nestorians, and in pagan Harran in North Syria, Greek works on science, philosophy and medicine were translated and commented upon and made the bases of education. When the Muslims first appeared on the political scene of the Fertile Crescent, and as early as the end of the seventh century, several efforts were made to translate works on medicine and alchemy into Arabic, but the movement of translation did not experience its most brilliant florescence until the coming of the intellectually disposed al-Ma'mun. He established a centre of learning and translation famed in Arab history as the House of Wisdom *(Bayt al-Hikmah)*. He also sent emissaries all over the Byzantine empire to look for Greek books on various subjects. It is said that he paid for each book, translated from a foreign language into Arabic, its weight in gold. We know that al-Kindi participated in this movement, but we do not know exactly in what capacity.

As a result of the translations, and of the interest of the caliphs in science and philosophy, Greek science, medicine and philosophy rose to uprecedented heights in the Near East except during the Alexandrian period. It is during al-Ma'mun's caliphate that al-Khwarazmi wrote his famous book on Algebra. Even geodesy, the science of the calculation of the height of mountains and width of valleys, received due attention. Some of the treatises of al-Kindi on this subject must have played, along with others of the kind, a great part in the designing and construction of aqueducts, bridges, engines of war and balance.

The Greek-inspired sciences took their Arab-Muslim form in this period. The intellectual activities of Islam took two different ways, which crossed each other only occasionally. The orthodox way, inspired mostly by the Muslims, led to the rise and development of sciences such as philology, history and jurisprudence. The later and less orthodox way, influenced by Greek, Syrian and Persian cultures, led to the rise and development of disciplines such as philosophy, mathematics, astronomy, astrology, physical sciences and geography, which were later called "The Sciences of the Ancients."

Theological speculation had begun earlier in Damascus provoked by the contacts with Christians and the desire for clarification and self-interpretation. In its early stages, theology, or *kalam* was an offshoot of *fiqh* or the study of the Canon Law *(Shari'ah)*. Early in the 'Abbasid period the two had separated into what we now know as scholastic theology or *kalam*, and jurisprudence or *fiqh*. Already in the time of al-Kindi the four schools of jurisprudence, namely, that of Abu Hanifah, al-Shafi'i, Ibn Hanbal and Malik Ibn Anas had appeared. The basic difference among these schools was whether to use analogy *(qiyas)* and personal opinion *(ra'i)* for adapting the law to the demands of the times, or whether simply to base their conclusions on materials contained in the Prophetic Traditions *(Hadith)*. It was really a problem whether or not to adopt Hellenistic methods as they were commonly used in Syria or to depend solely and literally on the *Sunnah*.

Ibn Hanbal (780—855 A.C.) represents the uncompromising attitude of the champions of the *Sunnah*. Al-Ma'mun persecuted him for upholding the theory of non-creation of the Qur'an. Eventually it was the people who thought like Ibn Hanbal who in the same period must have opposed the introduction of the "Sciences of the Ancients" in Islam and hence opposed the scientific and philosophical activities of al-Kindi. Fortunately, however, and in spite of occasional persecutions prompted by the anti-intellectuals, Muslim scholars enjoyed in this period great liberty to teach in public, and to choose the subject-matter that interested them most.

In theology proper, this interval witnessed the rise and decline of Mu'tazilism. Favoured by al-Ma'mun, al-Mu'tasim and al-Wathiq, Mu'tazilism became the official creed but it suffered a great decline and persecution with the coming of al-Mutawakkil who favoured the Orthodox attitude. Al-Kindi who was inclined towards Mu'tazilism for its rationalistic tendencies, broad outlook and tolerance of Greek ideas, represents the short-lived effulgence of the "Sciences of the Ancients" in Baghdad, were they appeared suddenly, flourished, and then suddenly declined. However, they continued to thrive in the palaces of the provincial governors and men of riches.

The outstanding reason for the Orthodox opposition to the "Sciences and Ancients" was the fear that these sciences will breed impiety. There were many other reasons also which influenced the attitude of the Orthodox group. Suspicious of the Persian Manicheans, they fought them as infidels, and tried to curb their influence. Besides, the majority of those who were interested in philosophy and science were Christians, Manicheans, Sabians, Jews and the Muslims who followed the esoteric sect of the *Batinis.* The indentifying of the sciences with those who pursued them, created among the Orthodox Muslims a suspicion for all kinds of speculative activities and a misunderstanding of their values. It is no wonder that al-Kindi had to justify his activities by trying to re-establish the value of philosophy and pressing vigorously for the tolerance of foreign ideas. He had also to attack the insincerity of those religious fanatics who did not understand the importance of co-operation in the great task of searching for truth.

This is the period during the 'Abbasid rule in which al-Kindi flourished, a period in which the translation of the Greek philosophic works were nearing completion and the chief characteristics of Muslim civilization were in the process of unfolding themselves into a greater spiritual and intellectual maturity.

Al-Kindi was descended from the famous South Arabian tribe of Kindah, immortalized by the poet Imru al-Qays, who sings of a trip to far off Byzantium long before the coming of Islam. The great-grand-father of al-Kindi was a Companion of the Prophet.[1] His father, under the caliphs al-Mahdi (775—785 A.C.) and al-Rashid (786—809 A.C.) was a governor of al-Kufah. Probably he was born there during his father's stay as governor.

The Philosopher of the Arabs, as al-Kindi is generally called, was born into a high family, rich in culture and esteem. Although the exact date of his birth is not known, we can safely assume that he was born towards the end of the eighth century A.C. There is hardly anything known about his early years in al-Kufah. Probably it was there that he became interested in learning rather than in becoming a soldier or a politician thus following in the footsteps of his ancestors. His versatility and vast interest in all branches of knowledge point to an early liking for learning. It must have been this desire that actuated him to move to al-Basrah in search for more knowledge.[2]

Al-Basrah was then a great centre of learning. It was the breeding place of such intellectual movements as al-Mu'tazilah and al-Ash'ariyah, the two great currents of Muslim theological thought. It also gave birth to a great school of grammarians inspired by Greek logic. Unfortunately we do not know the details of his stay or of his achievements in this city throbbing with intellectual activity.

Later on, he moved to Baghdad where he must have completed his education, and where, one can confidently assume, he met the various Syrian and Persian scholars who then formed the backbone of the new learning in the capital of the 'Abbasid Empire. They must have been the ones who initiated him more thoroughly into the secrets of Greek philosophy and science. He quite possibly became one of the very few Muslim Arabs of his time who mastered both Greek and Syriac.[3] His knowledge of Greek, Persian and Indian literatures earned him unique respect and fame throughout his stay in Baghdad.

Because al-Kindi had acquired a reputation as an eminent man of letters[4] and probably for other reasons such as subscribing to the theology of the times, which enjoyed official support, al-Ma'mun (813—833 A.C.) invited him to join the circle of scholars who were busy collecting the Greek scientific and philosophical works and rendering them into Arabic. Al-Ma'mun was instrumental for launching a large-scale movement to put foremost the main points of the Greek and Persian philosophical thought into Arabic. His espousal of the Mu'tazilite cause led him to justify his rationalistic tendencies in the works of the Greek philosophers. It is said that Aristotle appeared to him in a dream and assured him that there was no reason for him to refrain from taking up philosophy, because philosophy and *shari'ah* led to the same truth.[5]

Al-Kindi enjoyed the generous patronage of al-Ma'mum and his brother al-Mu'tasim. All through their caliphate he held important positions as a royal teacher[6] and probably as a physician. Al-Mu'tasim entrusted him with the education of his son Ahmad. Several of al-Kindi's works are dedicated to Ahmad or to his father. These works are written in letter form and are almost always adorned with the usual Arab greetings.[7]

During the rule of al-Mutawakkil, who reacted against the unorthodoxy of al-Ma'mum and al-Mu'tasim, al-Kindi fared ill. Al-Mutawakkil could not look favourably upon his Mu'tazilite inclinations; besides, it is said that the Sons of Musa, the well-known brother=scientists in the service of al-Mutawakkil, plotted against him so successfully that al-Kindi lost favour with al-Mutawakkil and was dismissed from service. The Sons of Musa had a reputation for scheming against all those who surpassed them in knowledge or were in the confidence of the caliph. They envied al-Kindi's library called *al-Kindiyah* for the sizeable number of good books it contained, and succeeded in persuading the caliph to confiscate it and give it to them as he had already done with the library of Hunayn Ibn Ishaq. But after a while *al-Kindiyah* was restored to its original owner.[8] However, al-Kindi could never regain his lost privileges at the court; he died in the year 252/866, or possibly a little later.[9] His death must have been a quiet one, noticed only by those nearest to him. It was the death of a great man out of favour, yet at the same time that of a philosopher who loved solitude.

Al-Kindi did not entirely escape malicious gossip, or at least misunderstanding, at the hands of his biographers. Al-Bayhaqi (449/1057—565/1169) says that biographers do not agree as to the origin of al-Kindi : for some he is a Jew, for others he is a Christian. If this information is not intended to smear the reputation of a Muslim of that period, it must be attributed to the confounding of our al-Kindi with Ya'qub al-Kindi (*fl.* ninth century), the author of *Apology of Christianity*, or with some other al-Kindi. Al-Bayhaqi places Abu Yusuf al-Kindi after al-Farabi who, in reality, preceded him. Al-Farabi was born several years after the death of al-Kindi. This error in the order of the appearance of the two philosophers leads to the assumption that al-Bayhaqi was genuinely confused as to the identity of the philosopher.[10]

Avarice has been attributed to al-Kindi by more than one author.[11] He is quoted as saying. "What is honourable about avarice is that you answer the beggar with a 'No' keeping your head up, whereas what is dishonourable about open-handedness is that you answer 'Yes' with your head down."[12] Also it is said that he advised his son saying, "Money is like a bird in hand, it is yours as long as you cling to it". But we have certain evidence to the contrary in the form of maxims uttered by al-Kindi himself on the demerits of niggardliness[13] such as : "Niggardliness is a shame upon an intelligent person", or "the niggard is always servile", or the niggard is not noble", or "he whose niggardliness increases, his eating decreases". Even if this is true, it does not reflect on him as a philosopher and scientist; neither does it reflect on him as a man. It is easy to mistake thriftiness for avarice. The same authors who chided him for his niggardliness could not help but admire his sense of humour and his achievements. Al-Jahiz reports that people liked his wit in spite of his avarice.[14] Ibn Nubatah (d. 786/1366) says of him that he was a "man who pursued literature, before taking up philosophy in all its branches. He mastered philosophy and solved many a problem of the ancient sciences. He followed the path of Aristotle and wrote many remarkable books. A versatile man, he and his books were the pride and adornment of al-Mu'tasim'a reign."[15]

Al-Kindi was of a noble character unlike many of his contemporaries and conducted himself like a dignified, dedicated and disinterested person. Some of the anecdotes in *al-Muntakhab* throw new light on this side of his personality. Once a grandson of a governor of al-Kufah asked him, "How is it that you are never seen asking at the door of the Sultan, or at the gatherings of businessmen?". He answered, "These are places where the likes of you seek their fortune, I seek mine there where nobody ever dreams of taking it away from me." Insulted once by a man with whom he was having a discussion, al-Kindi did not lose his temper but smiled and said, "It is not surprising to find that truth upsets a mentally sick person and makes him insult his loving and caring physician. A good physician, however, should never forsake his patient, or stop giving him the bitter medicine." The man had to apologize.

B—The translation from theology *(kalam)* to philosophy

Al-Kindi is considered the first philosopher of the

Arabs, not only because he was the first lover of wisdom among his people, but also because of his method, his attitude and his exploring of new fields of investigation. He bridged the gap between the half-hearted intellectual approaches of his Muslim contemporaries and the rigorous discipline of philosophy. It is really his approach and attitude that earned him the title of *faylasuf,* for what he introduced in the field of pure philosophy contained only a few original ideas, in spite of his independent thinking.

In my opinion, his greatest contribution has been the opening of the doors of philosophy to Muslim scientists. How then did he jump from theology to philosophy? To answer this question, one has to consider the difficulties which al-Kindi had to overcome. These were the common opposition to Greek philosophy and science on a popular and a theological level, and al-Kinid's inability to express himself in a language then lacking the necessary technical terminology and the facilities of expressing abstract ideas.

In the first case he managed to inculcate broadmindedness in his audience; that truth is truth no matter where it comes from, and that it is the most valuable thing in the world. If the Greeks, who were not Muslims discovered the truth, there is no reason why one should not accept it from them. Furthermore the discovery of the truth is a collective enterprise of all nations. He had at times, however, to appeal to the tribal instinct of his audience by telling them that Yunan (Greece personalized) is the brother of Qahtan, the alleged ancestor of the Arabs. Greeks and Arabs are cousins; why cannot they seek the truth together, although each one of them follows his own way.[16]

When he was faced with ignorant or fanatic opposition, he resorted to subterfuge. The story of al-Kindi and his student Abu Ma'shar is fairly well known. Abu Ma'shar, who is said to have been his neighbour, used to fan the fanaticism of the populace against what he considered the mischief of philosophy. Al-Kindi secretly sent a mutual friend to demonstrate the value and validity of philosophy to Abu Ma'shar and thus win him over. It is said that Abu Ma'shar was convinced and stopped his hostile activities against al-Kindi. Later, he became a student of al-Kindi without ever suspecting that the man who had won him over to the cause of philosophy was secret messenger of the Philosopher of the Arabs.[17]

On the theological level,[18] the method of al-Kindi shows clearly his cautions approach. Sometimes he approaches his subject like a Hellenistic mathematician and at other times like a dialectician who uses Mu'tazilite methods and argumentation and resorts to the Qur'an to prove a point as he does in the case of his explanation of verses 72-81 of *Surah* XXXVI.[19] His tendency to prove the compatibility of reason and revelation, his firm belief in such orthodox tenets as the creation of the world in time, and the attribution of a providential will to God show clearly that he occupies a special position in Muslim philosophy where no abrupt break with religion has yet occurred.

As to the second difficulty, al-Kindi did his best to adapt the Arabic language to the requirements of philosophical expression. His writings show a certain linguistic strain which can only be attributed to the struggle which he was waging against the idiosyncrasies of Arabic. The translators before al-Kindi had paved the way, but it was still not smooth enough to accommodate the onrush of new concepts. Although we cannot determine exactly to what extent al-Kindi was responsible for introducing the new terminology, we can assume that he made no small contribution, because he himself worked on translations by others, if not making his own. Further, the fact that he left us the first philosophical glossary in Arabic indicates that he was deeply interested in terms and their power of expressing abstract philosophical conceptions.

Arabic was more of a poetical language than one that lends itself to scientific and philosophical expressions. And although extremely rich in synonyms it was unable to capture the varied shades of the Greek philosophical terms. The accomplishments of al-Kindi and the translators in this respect were undeniably great. They succeeded in evolving a philosophical language made up of words to which they often had to assign new meanings in order to convey the Greek significance.

This process of adaptation took a variety of forms. First, words that were similar to the Greek terms, grammatically or otherwise, were translated directly without much difficulty. For example, the Greek *hyle* was translated, at first, as *tin* (clay) and later as *maddah* (matter). The word *symbebekos* was translated as *'arad* (accident). Secondly, they took over many of the Greek terms and then explained them by using pure Arabic words; such is the case of *philosophos* (philosopher) and *philosophia* (philosophy) which became *faylasuf* and *falsafah.* They achieved with the Arabic words *hakim* (wise) and *hikmah* (wisdom), the correct and exact translation of the Greek terms *sophos* and *sophia.* Such is the case also with *fantasiyah,* a transliteration of the Greek term *phantasia* (phantasy), one of the internal senses which they explained by the word *al-musawwirah* or *al-khayal.* Thirdly, for the purpose of making abstractions, which were hard to express in Arabic, new words were coined by adding the definite article to pronouns, prepositions and interrogative terms and suffixing *iyah*. For example, the Greek *to ti esti,* or quiddity, became *al-mahiyah,* based upon *ma huwa,* what is it? The Greek *to on,* primary substance became *al-huwiyah* derived from the pronoun *huwa,* he. Finally, the translators clothed old Arabic terms with new meanings. A good example is the word *al-a'yis* for being in general. All this was an innovation which many of the Arabs who prided themselves on the "purity" of the Arabic language frowned upon.

The sources of al-Kinidi's terminology were, in the final analysis, Aristotle and Plato, although they were derived more directly from the Neoplatonists. His glossary of technical terms, *On the Definition of Things and Their Description*, betrays a dependance on the Neoplatonized concepts of these two great philosophers. Although this glossary shows a certain primitiveness of expression, it remains, nevertheless, an unparalleled document of the philosophical knowledge which al-Kindi's time and intellectual milieu possessed, and shows also that many of the terms he used were nearer to their original meaning than the oned used by the later philosophers.

One can appreciate more fully the work of the Philosopher of the Arabs when the above-mentioned two difficulties are given due consideration.

NOTES

1. V. G. Flugel, "Al-Kindi gennant des Philosoph der Araber." *Abhandlungen fuer die Kunde des Morgenlandes*, I : 2 (Leipzig. 1857). Flugel, basing his work on *'Uyun, al-Anba' fi Tabaqat al-Atibba'* by Ibn Abi Usaybi'ah, ed. A. Muller, 2 vols., Cairo, 1882, traces the genealogy of al-Kindi to his sixth ancestor on his father's side, who came from a line of knightly warriors of the royal family ruled over Kindah before the coming of Islam.

2. Ibn Juljul (d. ca. 384/994) *Tabaqat al-Atibba,' wa'l-Hukama'*, ed. F. Sayyid, Cairo, 1955, p. 73, maintains that al-Kindi was a Basrite and that he owned a village in that region. He also mentions that he left al-Basrah for Baghdad.

3. It cannot be asserted categorically that al-Kindi knew Greek and Syriac, or that he ever translated any work from these languages. Ibn al-Nadim, the first biographer of al-Kindi, says (cf. *al-Fihrist*, p. 375) that Ptolemy's work *On Geography* was translated *for* al-Kindi. Another early historian Ibn Juljul (*Tabaqat al-Atibba'*, p. 73) says, "and he translated many philosophic works and

clarified what was difficult to understand in them. Ibn Juljul lived in Spain, however. Ibn Abi Usaybi'ah, using as a source a work of al-Kindi's contemporary and disciple Abu Ma'shar, considers him as one of the four greatest translators. Al-Qifti (p. 98) asserts that Ptolemy's work was translated *by* al-Kindi. Yet neither, al-Kindi's extant works nor the titles of the non-extant ones indicate that any of them were literal translations of Greek works. Probably he revised and corrected translations of others rather than translated them himself as is known he did in the case of the *Theology of Aristotle.* Since we lack information concerning al-Kinid's education we cannot settle this question. Cf. F. Rosenthal, "Al-Kindi and Ptolemy" in *Studi Orientale in Onore di Giorgio Della Vida,* Rome, 1956, II : 445. Also I. Madkour, *L'Organon d'Aristotle dans le monde arabe,* Paris, 1934, p. 31.

4. One of the oldest references to al-Kindi is the collection of anecdotes, analects and selected paragraphs in Abu Sulayman al-Sijistani's *al-Muntakhab Siwan al-Hikmah* (Br. Mus. Or. Ms. No. 9033 fols. 60-5) where we find reported that al-Kindi's books and treatises were so famous and so widely in use that he thought it unnecessary to collect many of al-Kindi's ideas. (See also Appendix III).

5. *Al-Fihrist,* p. 339.

6. Al-Kindi served the kings, and became closer to them through his literary activities; see *'Uyun,* I : 207. He seems to have been known in the early part of his intellectual career as a *litterateur.*

7. The philosophical letter was a common literary form used by most Hellenistic philosophers and scientists and later inherited by the Arabs. *Al-Muntakhab,* (fol. 60) attributes the invention of this form to al-Kindi: "....And he was the tutor of Ahmad ibn Muhammad al-Mu'tasim, for him he wrote most of his books and to him he addressed all of his epistles (treatises) and supplied answers to his questions. He was the first to invent this method followed by the later Muslim writers."

8. *'Uyun,* I : 208.

9. As to the year of al-Kindi's death, opinions differ. L. Massignon, on very little evidence, gives the year 246/860; see his *Recueil des textes inedits concernant l'historie de la mystique,* Paris, 1929. p. 175.

On the other hand, C. N. Nallino assigns to him the year 260/873, see his *'Ilm al-Falak, Ta'rikhuhu 'inda 'l'-Arab fi'l-Qurun al-Wusta* (History of Arab Astrology in the Middle Ages), Rome, 1911, p. 117. The date I use is the one computed by M. 'Abd al-Raziq in his work *Faylasuf 'l'-Arab wa 'l-Mu'allim al-Thani* (The Philosopher of the Arabs and the Second Master), Cairo. 1945, p. 51. His thesis is based on internal evidence in al-Kindi's work *On the Duration of the Reign of the Arabs* and a reference in one of al-Jahiz's books, *Kitab al-Bukhala* in which al-Jahiz refers to al-Kindi in the past tense. Al-Jahiz wrote his book around 254/868.

10. Zahir al-Din al-Bayhaqi, *Ta'rikh Hukama' al-Islam*, ed. M. Kurd 'Ali, Damascus 1946, p. 47.

11. The oldest reference we have to al-Kindi's niggardliness is in *al-Fihrist*, p. 357. Cf. also *'Uyun*, I : 209. There is a whole chapter on the same subject is al-Jahiz's *Kitab al-Bukhala'*. ed. Taha al-Hajiri, Cairo, 1948, pp. 70-81 Cf. also the Introduction to Van Vloten's edition, Leiden, 1900. Al-Hajiri doubts that the al-Kindi mentioned in *al-Bhukhala'* is the same person as our philosopher.

12. Ibn Nubatah al-Misri, *Sarh al-'Uyun Sharh Risalat ibn Zaydun,*, Cairo. 1278/1861. p. 143.

13. *Al-Muntakhab*, fol. 61.

14. *Al-Bukhala'*, p. 71.

15. Ibn Nubatah. *op. cit.* p. 144.

16. Al-Kindi, On *First Philosophy*, in *Rasa'il al-Kindi al-Falsafiyah*, ed. M. A. Abu Ridah, Cairo, 1950-53. I : 101-4, hereafter *Rasa'il.* Al-Mas'udi cites a poem by a little-known poet, 'Abd Allah ibn Muhammad al-Nashi', criticising al-Kindi for mixing up Qahtan with Yunan. Cf. *Muruj al-Dhahab—-Les Prairies d'or*, ed. and transl.

into French by C. Barbier de Meynard and P. de Courteille, Paris, 1923, II : 244.

17. *'Uyun,* I : 207. Cf. also *Ta'rikh al-Hukama',* p. 153.

18. See below, Chapter III.

19. *Rasa'il,* I : 373-4.

2

THE PHILOSOPHY OF AL-KINDI

A—Philosophy and Religion

It is quite appropriate to start our survey of al-Kindi's philosophy by exploring his concept of the meaning and purpose of philosophy. Such an exploration will serve two purposes. First, it will tell us what al-Kindi himself understood by philosophy, and second, because al-Kindi is representative of his age, it will reveal to us to what extent this period was in possession of an adequate understanding of the science of sciences.

In his treatise *On First Philosophy,* al-Kindi says: "The sublimest and noblest of human arts is the art of philosophy, which is defined as the knowledge of things in their realities to the limit of human power. The purpose of the philospher in his knowledge is to arrive at the truth and in his action to act in accordance with the truth.[1]

First, philosophy is considered the most exalted science, it is the science of the first cause, the first divine reality which is the cause of all other realities; that is why it is given the first place in the order of learning. It is that universal knowledge which comes first in order of nobility. Unlike Aristotle or Avicenna, al-Kindi does not consider first philosophy the study of being *qua* being, nor does he always consider philosophical knowledge the most certain. The high place which al-Kindi assigns to philosophy comes from the nobility of its subject-matter which has to do with eternal and universal things.

Although the second phrase in al-Kındi's definition "to the limit of human power", is not original with al-Kindi, it is indicative of the state of mind of all Muslim philosophers in general. It is usually affixed to the definition of philosophy in order to minimize any incompatibility between the assertion that man is enabled by his reason to know with certainty the most ultimate principles of things and the assertion that these principles are known only through divine revelation. Al-Kindi seems to have wanted to say that human knowledge, is limited, that philosophy is based on human knowledge, and that, therefore, philosophy cannot reach as far as revelation can. Although philosophy aims at discovering the "haecceity, essence, and cause of the eternal and universal things" what it discovers can never go beyond the limits of the power of human mind. At first view, al-Kindi seems to have wanted from the very beginning to save religion and with it man from *hybris* by reconciling philosophy to religion.

Al-Kindi, as the pioneer of pure philosophy in the Muslim world, offers us a list of definitions of philosophy that were common just before his time as well as during the later Middle Ages. In his treatise *On the Definitions of Things and Their Descriptions,* he records six definitions which were representative of the scholars of his time.[2] Here are they:

(1) Philosophy is composed of two words, *philo,* friend, and *sophia* or wisdom. Philosophy is the love of wisdom. This definition is based on the Greek etymology of the word.

(2) Philosophy is the human emulation of divine excellence as far as such emulation is possible. This is a functional definition.

(3) Philosophy is the practice of death. Death means the separation of the soul from the body. Moreover, death involves the suppression of material concerns, which are inimical to the virtuous life or, what

is its practical equivalent, the activity of the intellect. Another functional definition.

(4) Philosophy is science of sciences and the wisdom of wisdoms.

(5) Philosophy is man's knowledge of himself.

(6) Philosophy's proper subjuct-matter is defined as the science of the haecceity, the essence and causes of things to the limit of human power.[3]

From this repertory of definitions, al-Kindi seems to have chosen that last one added to it the idea of philosophy as a practice of virtue. The philosopher, according to him, is he who seeks after truth and lives up to it, that is, who lives justly. Perfect philosophy is not merely the knowledge of the truth; it is, besides, the realization of truth in action. The truly wise combines the seeking after wisdom and its exercise.

The concept of philosophy as the practice of virtue sounds Socratic with Stoic elements. The final end of philosophy lies in its relation to morality. The philosopher's aim in philosophizing is both to know and to become wise or, to act justly. Knowledge and virtue are regarded as equal and as important activities of reason. The implication of such a concept is to minimize the role of religion in all ethical obligations, or in other words, to assert the primacy of reason over revelation in matters of morality. It is a humanistic attitude similar to that of the Stoics and the Mu'tazilites. The Mu'tazilites, with whose tenets al-Kindi's thinking was closely associated, considered that man can arrive at the knowledge of God and of right and wrong by reason, and accordingly that philosophy should not be confined only to theoretical speculation but should also be extended to the practical aspects of life.

Al-Kindi's division of philosophy includes theology and the science of the unity of God (he does not seem to consider these two sciences as one) among the theoretical sciences, whereas the practical includes ethics; that is to say, al-Kindi's division is identical with the Aristotelian, which considered theology as philosophy's proper field of investigation. However, the Aristotelian ideal of knowledge for its own sake does not appear here and in its place we have the Stoic ideal which combines knowledge with action and which lays down the role of reason as not only to speculate but to control the passions.

Unfortunately, we have no sufficient evidence for determining whether al-Kindi lived up to this ideal. At the most we have various fragments,[4] all of which seem to point in one direction. Al-Kindi's eloquent defence of philosophy against its critics, his praise of reason as an instrument of true knowledge, his esteem for the Greek genius, his disgrace at the hand of al-Mutawakkil—all these indicate that he believed both in the theory as well as the practice of philosophy. Furthermore, some of his writings, such as *On The Means of Driving Away Sorrow*, and a poem[5] attributed to him show philosophical resignation and a great nobility of spirit. All this evidence, however, does not yet amount to absolute proof.

Al-Kindi declares more than once that one of the most important functions of philosophy is to seek the truth. In his *On first Philosophy* he deals with the investigation of truth in a manner very reminiscent of Aristotle's. He first expresses his gratefulness to all those who have contributed tc the unveiling of the truth no matter how much or how little their contribution has been. In view of the brevity of life, he tells us, no one is able by himself to attain to the truth adequately. On the other hand, the truth can be attained collectively by cooperation and accumulated effort. Very eloquently he goes on to defend truth:

"We should not be ashamed of recognizing truth and assimilating it from whatever source it may reach us, even though it might come from earlier generations and foreign peoples. For him who seeks truth there is nothing of more value than truth itself. It never cheapens or abases him who searches for it, but ennobles and honours him."[6]

His defence of the truth is followed by that of philosophy. This, however, brings him face to face with the complicated problem of the relation between reason and revelation. Al-Kindi approaches the subject on two different levels: the first is based on the identity of aims of both religion and philosophy, the second is epistemological.

In the first case and before he unfolds his point of view, al-Kindi, regarding the identity of the moral aims of religion and philosophy, argues for the necessity of philosophy and its compatibility with religion. Against the attack of those religious fanatics who were opposed to any kind of philosophical activities, he maintains that philosophy is a necessity and not a luxury. He tell the fanatics that they must declare philosophizing either necessary or unnecessary. If they say it is necessary, they must be willing to go in search of it. On the other hand, if they declare that it is unnecessary, they must give reasons and arguments to prove their contention. Now, to give reasons and arguments implies an act of philosophizing and hence philosophy is necessary in either case.[7]

This defence proposed by al-Kindi assumes great importance not only because it was made in the face of religious opposition, but also because it reveals to us that al-Kindi did not mean to undermine revelation by it; on the contrary, his main purpose seems to be to place religious concepts on what he considered stronger and sounder foundations, the use of demonstrative proofs.

However, the main "argument" he uses to defend philosophy is an assumption that both philosophy and religion have identical aims, namely, the knowledge of the unity of God and the pursuit of virtue. He substantiates this by maintaining that philosophy counts "theology, the science of the unity of God, ethics and every useful science that leads man to practice good and shun evil"[8] among its branches. Religion, he claims, does the same thing: the substance of all true prophetic messages is simply to affirm the unique divinity of God, and to enjoin upon us the election and pursuit of those virtues most pleasing in the eyes of God.[9]

In other words, al-Kindi sees that on a theoretical level both religion and philosophy deal with a similar problem, the unity of God. Also on a practical level they have identical aims, to urge man to achieve a higher moral life. On both levels, therefore, al-Kindi's thinking makes it appear that there is no essential difference between religion and philosophy since they both aim at the same thing.

Al-Kindi's inclusion of theology in philosophy confronts us with a problem. If philosophy's main purpose is to strengthen the position of religion, philosophy should be a handmaid to theology and not vice versa. What strikes one particularly is that this inclusion of theology in philosophy is a direct Aristotelian borrowing and therefore points towards a higher esteem for philosophy than for religion. This very evident implication, however, does not seem to constitute any intellectual problem for al-Kindi. As a matter of fact, there is no palpable proof that he himself was fully conscious of this point of view which one so easily derives from his writings.

This attitude of al-Kindi towards philosophy is understandable. He was introducing a new discipline into the world of Islam. Besides, although al-Kindi did not differ with the main metaphysical solutions of Islam as regards the creation of the world and its finitude, he was a believer *sui generis;* that is, he was not an orthodox Muslim in the full sense of the word. His background of Mu'tazilite thought with its attitude towards the positive role of reason in the knowledge of good and evil, would have made it easy for him to value reason above religion in its function of promoting the higher moral life of man.

On the other level, the problem that arises from the relationship that al-Kindi posits between religion and philosophy, is epistemological. Now, if philosophy and religion aim at the same thing in the moral field, does it mean that philosophy is on a par with religion when it comes to determining the more basic problem of knowledge? Which knowledge is more certain, the rational or the prophetic? Is the prophetic included in the rational? Or, do both types of knowledge arrive at the same truth by different means?

Al-Kindi does not take a consistent stand on this problem. In one place he maintains the equal certainty of both rational and prophetic knowledge; in his psychological writings, one can argue, though on slender evidence that he includes the prophetic in the rational; and in a third place he declares that human knowledge is inferior to the prophetic.

To understand the true position of al-Kindi, one has to consider the intellectual atmosphere of his age and the knowledge the Arabs then had of the discipline of philosophy. In spite of the great freedom which the intellectuals enjoyed, it was still impossible for a Muslim to place philosophical knowledge openly above the religious as did al-Farabi and Averroes a little later. That al-Kindi's purpose was probably to introduce the head of the proverbial Bedouin's camel into the tent of knowledge without really meaning to push out theology, can be easily inferred from his upholding the theory of creation in time and the finitude of the world.

Furthermore, the Muslims had not yet developed a critical approach to philosophy, or, as a matter of fact, to learning in general. The inconsistency of al-Kindi can be explained in the light of this fact. Al-Kindi's mind was not analytical but synthetical. He saw the problem of the relationship between religion and philosophy in its general context without stopping to analyze the different ramifications of the problem. In the several places where he tried to establish a harmony between religion and philosophy, he seems to entertain no doubts as to the validity of this harmony and as to the facility of its establishment once one seeks it with understanding and goodwill. He clearly states that "the utterances of Muhammad the truthful, and the message that he transmitted from the Almighty are ascertainable by intellectual arguments. Only people deprived of sound reason and enshrouded in ignorance would reject it."[10] Furthermore, Ibn Juljul tells us that al-Kindi wrote two books of an essentially religious nature—*On the Unity of God,* and *On Affirmation of Prophecy*— in which he used, as no other did before him, the methods adopted by the logicians to arrive at demonstrative truth.[11]

The attitude of al-Kindi towards the rational ascertainability of Muhammad's message is substantiated further by al-Kindi's reduction of the conflict between reason and revelation to a problem of allegorical interpretation *(ta'wil).* He attributes any contradiction between the word of the Qur'an and philosophy to our misunderstanding of the real meaning of the Qur'an.

The allegorical method was used previously by the Stoics, Philo, many of the Christian Fathers, and by the Mu'tazilites. We will illustrate al-Kindi's use of this method in order to gain an insight into his mind and his approach. However, it should be made clear that al-Kindi's method is one of exegesis based on linguistic and grammatical principles, and therefore very different from the Stoic method of interpreting the Greek myths. It is the method used by the Mu'tazilites and not by the philosophers.

The first illustration is taken from his treatise *On the Bowing of the Outermost Sphere and its Obeisance to God.*[12] Al-Kindi's disciple, Ahmad, the son of al-Mu'tasim, asked his tutor to explain the meaning of the verse والنجم و الشجر يسجدان "And the stars[13] *(al-najm)* and the trees *bow* (prostrate) themselves" (LXV : 5).

Instead of the ordinary and literal approach which would have been taken by most Muslim interpreters of his time, al-Kindi took a completely different view by adopting the method of allegorical exegesis and by trying to find a philosophical content in the meaning of the Qur'an that would enable him to establish harmony between religion and philosophy.

Now, it is a characteristic of the Arabic language that it can use the same word for two diametrically opposed meanings. Al-Kindi explains the word "prostration, bowing *(sujud),*" which appears in the verse as having a double meaning : the act of inclining one's body and head in prayer, or, making obeisance. Obviously, the stars and trees do not bow themselves in the same sense as a praying Muslim does. Bowing, therefore, must mean obeisance to God's will, the only other explanation which one can give to the word.[14]

The Philosopher of the Arabs goes on to explain how the outermost sphere *bows* to God. Al-Kindi's scheme of the universe, as we shall see a little later, is based on the Aristotelian. The heavens are a series of concentric spheres arranged around our earth as a central body. Beyond the sublunary and even beyond the celestial spheres, is the sphere whose divine harmony causes the circular revolution of the whole celestial system, that is, the planets and the fixed stars. These, in turn, through their revolution, cause generation and corruption in the physical world, or in other words, cause life and death in the vegetable and animal worlds in accordance with an established divine pattern. This, according to al-Kindi, implies that the heavenly bodies by fulfilling their functions as the proximate efficient cause *bow* to God's will, moving regularly within that established pattern and causing life and death on earth.

Besides, the outermost sphere and consequently the heavenly bodies bow, that is obey, voluntarily.[15] Al-Kindi, like Aristotle, believes that the heavenly bodies are endowed with life and reason. To prove his assertion, he uses self-evident principles such as the following. The cause pertains to a higher order than the effect. Now, if the life and reason of human beings are properties immediately caused by the heavenly bodies, then these bodies as causes, must likewise be endowed with life and reason, or they would be inferior to their effects.

Given that the heavenly bodies are endowed with life and reason, it remains to be proved whether or not life and rationality in them serve the same purpose as they do in man. Al-Kindi says "no". (We well explain his reasons later when we discuss his scheme of the universe). The function of the two properties of life and reason is to *bow* to God's will, i.e., to accomplish voluntarily what that will demands.

This is then the philosophical meaning in the light of which one should explain the above-quoted Qur'anic verse. It is not difficult, by any means, to discern the wide margin of difference between this philosophical elaboration of the meaning of *bowing* and the literal connotation of the same word.

The other illustration which we shall use is taken from another treatise, *On the Number of Aristotle's Books*......... Al-Kindi, in elaborating the differences between human knowledge and prophetic knowledge, realizes that there is a difficulty in verse انما امره اذا اراد شيأ ان يقول له كن فيكون : "But His command, when He desires a thing, is to say to it: 'Be', and it is" (XXXVI: 81). The problem which this verse raises is both linguistic and metaphysical. How can one order "something" to be which has no being? Al-Kindi justifies the linguistic use of the imperative *be* by the fact of its being metaphorical. Metaphors, similes and allegories are of common usage among the Arabs, he maintains, and it is completely justifiable to describe a thing by using qualities which that thing does not possess. Following the tradition of the Arabs to look for *corroboration* of their linguistic hypotheses in pre-Islamic poetry, he uses two verses of Imru' al-Qays'a famous *mu'allaqah,* or suspended poem: *Here Halt and Weep*

قفا نبك من ذكرى حبيب و منزل

> Till I have cried to Night, as his loins stretched out Long as his thighs, and still his breast seemed never-coming :
>
> O Night, Night, Long Night! Brighten to dawn, Though comfortless as thou dread the coming of day.[16]

Night is personified in this poem. It is described as having loins, thighs, and breasts. The indisputable fact is that neither can night be addressed as a person, nor does it have any of the above-mentioned limbs. Nevertheless the Arabs used personification in expressing a wish which otherwise would not have been stated so forcefully. The imperative *Be* maintains al-Kindi, is to be understood, therefore, metaphorically, as symbolic of God's will, and not simply as an address to something that does not exist.

The metaphysical problem implied in this imperative *Be!* will be dealt with later. It will suffice to say here that al-Kindi believes in *creatio ex nihilo* and the will of God; if God wills non-being to be,[17] it will be without further ado.

We have dealt so far with what al-Kindi thinks of the relationship between religion and philosophy according to which he maintains the absence of any incompatibility between the two. His other view is diametrically opposed to the first one, although it might appear to be different only in methodology.

Al-Kindi declares at the very beginning of his treatise *On First Philosophy* that the intellectual power of man to know the ultimate truth is limited.[18] Again when he compares human knowledge with prophetic knowledge he states clearly that human knowledge is inferior to the prophetic.

Here is how he compares both types of knowledge.

".....Like the knowledge of the Apostles which God has given a high position, a knowledge which is not the outcome of a desire (for its acquisition), of research and pain and trouble as well as study and exercise and dialectics and which does not require any time. It is the outcome of the Will of God through the purification and illumination of their souls for the (sake of) the truth by God's grace (and) His guidance, His inspiration and His messages. This knowledge is the prerogative of the Apostles over the rest of the human beings, and it is one of their unusual trances *(khawalij)*, i.e., their prodigious signs which distinguish them from the rest of the ordinary men. Human beings who are not Prophets have no way of attaining to the higher knowledge of the secondary true substances, or to the primary sensible substances and their accidents without research, or the help of logic and mathematics, as we have said; and for this a period of time is required. But the Prophets attain to this knowledge without recurring to nothing of that kind but through the Will of His Who sent them, without needing any time in reaching what they are after or anything else. The minds gain the conviction that that knowledge is from God, because He is existent, when ordinary human beings fail by their very nature to do the same, as it is beyond their nature and temperament. Thus they submit themselves and let themselves be guided. Their sound understanding is directed towards the belief in the truth of the messages of the Prophets."[19]

One may contend that the difference between philosophical and prophetic knowledge is simply one of clarity and methodology and that both come to know the same truth by taking different ways. But al-Kindi insists that there is more to it; there is a difference in comprehensiveness *(ihatah)* besides the difference in clarity and methodology.

"If one sets out to consider the answers which the Prophets have given to questions about hidden and essential things, he will find out this: should a philosopher intend to give an answer to these questions employing all the effort which has provided him with knowledge through his prolonged study and application of a rigorous discipline, we should not find that he could produce a similar answer as succinct and clear and simple and *comprehensive* as the Prophet gave to the infidels who refused to believe in the resurrection of the body; one of them, a Meccan, had brought a dry bone to Muhammad and asked him whether Allah could restore it to life. He asked, 'Who will revive the dry bones when they are decayed?' Then God, the One, the True sent him the following revelation. 'Say: He will revive them Who originated them the first time.....; Is He, Who has created the heavens and the earth, not able to create their like....?قال من يحى العظام وهى رميم - قل يحييها الذى انشاها اول مرة - - - اوليس الذى خلق السموات و الارض قدر على ان يخلق مثلهم" (XXXVI: 77-81).

Implied in this answer are the theories of creation out of nothing and the omnipotency of God which the Prophet arrived at instantly and expressed in a succinct, clear and comprehensive form.

Human knowledge, on the other hand, being derivative, depends on syllogistic reasoning which in turn depends on the senses and cannot be so comprehensively or so forcefully clear as the divine knowledge which embodies explicit and implicit aspects of truth bestowed by God upon his Prophets. However, we would be making too much of the comprehensiveness of prophetic knowledge. Yet the general trend of what al-Kindi has said about prophetic knowledge points towards its superiority.

If this is true, the problem which confronts us now is how to explain the difference between the two views of al-Kindi. One explanation would be that al-Kindi changed his mind by the time he wrote his treatise *On the Number of Aristotle's Books......* thus taking it for granted that he wrote this treatise later than *On First Philosophy.*[20] The other explanation is that he is logically inconsistent. I am inclined to take the latter view. Al-Kindi's desire to remain a conformer very likely prompted him to enthrone prophetic knowledge above the philosophical; and it is just as probable that he remained unaware of the difficulty that this step brought about in his system.

B — Logic, method, and the classification of the philosophical sciences

After having expounded al-Kindi's conception of philosophy and its relation to religion, we will try to describe his knowledge of logic, his philosophical method his classification of the philosophical sciences.

Unfortunately, none of his authentic logical works have come down to us and therefore it is impossible to reconstruct his logical system from the fragmentary information that we posses. We will concentrate instead on his knowledge of logic.

Arabic logic is Aristotelian in general outline, but it acquired many additions from Stoic sources; also there are Peripatetic and Neoplatonic influences. Arab Muslim philosophers were greatly attracted to logic, which was among the first of the Greek sciences to be translated into Arabic. In fact logic had occupied a place of honour in most Muslim academic circles during the greater part of the Middle Ages. However, Aristotelian logic was not always accepted as the best instrument for arriving at certainty. Some of the theologians rejected Aristotelian logic and took up instead Stoic logic. Others also did not accept it but tried to establish a new logic based on different principles.[21]

Al-Kindi does not tell us what is the relation of logic to philosophy. He does not say in his extant writings whether it is a part of philosophy, or simply an instrument of it, although it is implied that logic is propaedeutic to philosophical inquiry. Nor does al-Kindi give us a *clear* definition of logic and its object, although one can gather that it is the study of syllogistic arguments in descending degrees of strength. Logic is necessary for the preparation of a philosopher, he maintains, but it is not so necessary as mathematics. His treatise on the eight books of Aristotelian logic wherein he discusses the object of each of them,[22] is our only important source on his logic, yet we cannot get much out of it.

According to al-Qifti, al-Kindi also wrote commentaries on Aristotle's books.[23] Ibn al-Nadim, furthermore, mentions several works on logic written by al-Kindi himself. Among the latter were several Introductions *(Eisagoge)*, the titles of which indicate that some of them were detailed works, whereas others were short and concise. He wrote, moreover, a treatise on the *Ten Categories* and another on the *Five Categories*.

His other writings on logic include a commentary of *On Sophistical Refutations* entitled *How to Guard Against Sophistical Crafts*, and different treatise on demonstration *(apondexis-al-Burhan)*. This makes al-Kindi the first logician in Arabic. We possess a spurious work, *Liber Introductorius in Artem Logicae Demonstrationis*, which most probably is written by one of his students,[24] but which also reflects rather faithfully the ideas of al-Kindi.

According to this treatise, there are four different classes of beings into which all that exists can be reduced. Three of these classes are substances *(a'yan)* which include the individual, the species and the genera; the remaining is class is a notion *(ma'nd)*, consisting of the differentia, which distinguishes the different species from others of the same genus.[25]

The methods of teaching and investigation used by

the philosophers, he maintains, are four in number: division, analysis, definition, and demonstration. Demonstrative reasoning *(qiyas)* is considered the most important method since the knowledge one acquires by it is the most comprehensive and is used by all kinds of people. People who use demonstrative reasoning are of different types: there are the children whose reasoning is egocentric; the adults whose reasoning is based on analogy and who, profiting from their experience, deduce the unknown from the known; the scholars who are versed in dialectical reasoning and whose premises can be either true, false or absurd; and last, there are the initiates in geometrical proofs and logic who use syllogistic reasoning in order to arrive at the knowledge of those things which cannot be known by the senses or by induction. This knowledge of the initiates is called apodictic; that is demonstrative. The rest of the treatise deals with wrong conclusions, or logical errors in all their aspects and the necessity of mathematics for the study of philosophy. The author then proceeds to give examples of demonstrative reasoning by proving such theories as the following: that there is no void; that out side the universe there is neither void not plenum; and that the world was created in time. The finale is a mystical conclusion that the aim of logic is identical with that of ethics.

By assigning the *individual* to a separate class of being, this work is in fact adding a sixth "voice" to the five "voices" of Porphyry and thus makes a significant departure from the system of the latter. In one of the works authentically attributed to al-Kindi we find a reference to a sixth voice,[26] a fact that strengthens the theory that the *Liber Introductorius* was written by the philosopher himself, nevertheless, we need much stronger evidence to affirm this theory.

However, what makes us believe that *Liber Introductorius* was at least inspired by al-Knidi are the similarities found in this book to al-Kindi's solutions of the problem of creation in time, the problem of the void, and the problem of the presence or absence of void beyond the outermost sphere, apart from the theory of the six voices propounded and maintained in Arab Philosophy by al-Kindi and the Brethren of Purity only. Besides, the book makes the self-evident Euclidean principles the bases of syllogistic reasoning, a methodology probably unique with al-Kindi among all the Arab Muslim philosophers.

This scanty information hardly tells us anything about al-Kindi's logic. One can infer from it, however, that he discarded the Aristotelian forms of demonstration in favour of the hypothetical and disjunctive syllogisms preferred by the Stoics and Neoplatonists. Al-Qadi Sa'id al-Andalusi criticized his logical approach in the following words:

"His works on logic, which attained a wide range of popularity among the public, were never considered authoritative on the science. They lacked the analytical method without which there is no way of discerning the true from the false in any problem. As to the synthetic approach which al-Kindi employed in his works, it is hardly of any use except to those who possess the premises. It is only then possible to proceed to synthesis. The first premise of any problem cannot be found without analysis."[27]

This criticism of Sa'id is, without doubt, exaggerated and seems to be prejudiced.[28] Al-Kindi, in the first place, knew his Aristotelian logic well, as the list of his commentaries on the First Master's *Organon* indicates.[29] In the second place, he favoured a different approach because he was assuming that mathematical knowledge leads to the first intelligibles and that it is more certain than syllogistic reasoning.

Al-Kindi considered that universals do not have concrete existence; they are only objects of thought comprehended by the intellect after having passed from potentiality into actuality. Equally, the essence of a thing is known by the intellect, whereas its concrete existence is known by the senses. Knowledge as well as being are hierarchical. Therefore in order to know the secondary substances, that is, the intelligibles, one has first to know the primary substances. Mathematics, al-Kindi maintains, is the only way that leads us to the knowledge of the primary substances, hence to the knowledge of the things in their true realities. According to him nobody should aspire to know the first principles of things, without having mastered the sciences of mathematics.

On the whole, we can conclude that al-Kindi must have known both the Aristotelian and Stoic logics; that he must have dealt with the problem of the categories of beings, the problem of essence and accident, as well as with terms, propositions, syllogisms, opinions and error[30]; and that he must not have considered Aristotelian logic as the only means that leads to philosophical certainty. Mathematical reasoning was for him more fundamental than logic, and we know that he wrote a book *That Philosophy cannot be Attained Except by the Science of Mathematics,* the title of which points unequivocally towards this attitude to logic.[31]

Let us now turn to al-Kindi's method : how did he approach the solutions of the various problems of philosophy that confronted him?

Al-Kindi describes his method in the following manner:

It is well for us—if we are desirous of bringing our task to a successful conclusion—to hold to our ordinary practices of citing in full what the Ancients have said on the subject under discussion and of using the easiest and most economical ways toward the ends that we pursue. Furthermore, what they have left incomplete we should complete to the best of our ability, in accordance with the best usages of our language and the customs of our age.[32]

However, al-Kindi himself, in most of his extant treatises does not appear either to quote or to examine the doctrines of preceding philosophers. His dialectical method consists in taking certain self-evident definitions relevant to the subject under discussion, and then in proving by logical means the validity of his premises in the light of these self-evident definitions. Another feature common to al-Kindi's method is that he demonstrates the truth of a definition by the application of the law of the excluded middle. All alternatives that show absurdities or contradictions are eliminated until one definition remains and is taken as the true one.

As for the classification of the sciences, al-Kindi follows more or less the Aristotelian division. However, it is interesting to note that in his treatise *On The Number of Aristotle's Books...* he arranges the sciences in order of their decreasing relation to matter as we shall see. The Arab-Muslim philosophers and theologians in general were greatly interested in this problem of classification and the development of a hierarchy in which either philosophy or theology would occupy the place of honour according to the predilection of the philosopher. Al-Kindi, however, does not seem to have been very much involved in this issue of classification. He simply follows Aristotle in dividing philosophy into theoretical and practical. Just as man's existence, according to him, is two fold, intellectual and sensible,[33] so philosophy should be divided into an intellectual science and a practical science.

The intellectual science corresponds to the Aristotelian theoretical, and is divided by a dual classification into the science of divine things and the science of "artificial" things, that is, created things. From another point of view, intellectual science may be divided into three branches, each corresponding to a different class of being. First there are those objects which are not separable from matter, in fact, they are nothing but matter; and they include what al-Kindi denominates as the "corporeals" *(al-jismaniyat)*. The second class includes the objects associated with matter but which are not matter in themselves, such as the soul. Third there is that class of beings which include only those objects which are divine and absolutely separable from matter.[34] It will be noted that this third class is equivalent to the "divine things" of the former dual classification and that the first and second classes of "corporeals" and of "objects associated with matter" fall neatly into place as subdivision of the "artificial" things of the dual classification.

Ibn Nubatah, in describing al-Kindi's "philosophy" (meaning the theoretical only) also gives a double and a tripartite classification. He says:

"The science of philosophy are three: first there are the mathematical sciences which come in the middle by nature. Secondly there is the science of physics, which is lowest by nature. Thirdly there is theology, which is highest by nature. The sciences are three in number because the knowables are three. We have a science of the sensibles, or material objects. We have a science of the immaterial objects. This last is divided into the science of those objects which are absolutely separable from matter, and those that are associated with matter. The material objects are investigated by physics. Those objects that are separable by themselves but are associated with matter like the science of numbers, geometry, astrology, and musicology which are investigated by mathematics. The immaterial objects which are absolutely separable from matter are investigated by theology."[35]

Although al-Kindi dismisses practical philosophy without any discussion of its classification,[36] we may surmise that he would have followed the lines laid down by Aristotle. Thus he would have included ethics and politics under practical philosophy.

If this assumption is correct, then al-Kindi's only

deviation from the Stagirite's classification is simply linguistic and almost unnoticeable. He divides philosophy into the study of divine things and "artificial" things. The divine things are identical with the Aristotelian immovables and the "artificial" with the movables. The use of the word "artificial" is to make clear that he does not share Aristotle's opinion concerning the eternity of matter.

NOTES

1. *Rasa'il,* I : 97.

2. *Ibid.,* 172-3.

3. See F. Uberweg, *Grundriss der Geschichte der Philosophie,* Basel, 1953, I : 5, where we find a list of definitions of philosophy common to all introduction to philosophy in the fifth and sixth centuries A.C. The first four of al-Kindi's definitions are among those listed by Uberweg, which means that al-Kindi was repeating what was contained in these introductions. The origin of each of these definitions is easy to trace back to one or another of the Greek philosophers. The first goes back to Pythagoras. The second goes back to Plato's *Theaetetus* 176. Al-Farabi mentions this second definitions in his treatise *What Must Precede the Study of Philosophy,* ed. Dietrici, Leiden, 1890. p. 53. The third goes back to Plato's *Phaedo,* 64a. The fourth originated with Aristotle. The fifth (not mentioned by Uberweg) is based on the famous Socratic maxim "know thyself". The last is probably al-Kindi's own elaborations, although there is some Platonic inspiration in it. Missing from al-Kindi's list are the Aristotelian definitions of philosophy as the study of being *qua* being, and the Stoic definition : the knowledge of human and divine things.

4. *Al-Muntakhab,* fols. 60-1.

5. Ibn Nubatah al-Misri, *op. cit.,* pp. 146-7.

6. *Rasa'il,* I : 102.

7. This argument is favour of philosophising appears throughout history. Aristotle was the first to use it. It appears in a fragment

of his *Proptrepticus* (frag. 50), a book in which he justifies the need for philosophising and the place of philosophy in the totality of human life. Cicero imitated this work in his *Hortensius* and Clement of Alexandria used the same argument to defend his use of philosophy.

8. *Rasa'il,* I : 104.

9. *Ibid.*

10. *Ibid.,* 224.

11. Ibn Juljul, *op. cit.,* p. 74.

12. Appendix I, No. 124.

13. There is some difference between the interpreters of the Qur'an whether the term *"najm"* should be understood as stars or herbs. Among recent translators Blachere accepts "herbs".

14. *Rasa'il* I : 246.

15. *Ibid.,* 167. To obey implies compliance with command of the Commander, which presupposes responsible decision.

16. Translated by Eric Schroeder, *Muhammad's People,* Portland, Main, 1955, p. 3.

17. Al-Kindi does not use the term 'non-being' in the Platonic sense.

18. *Rasa'il,* I : 97.

19. *Ibid.,* 372-3.

20. This surmise is hard to substantiate because our knowledge of the lateness of the treatise *On the Number of Aristotle's Books....* is not definite. Besides, the text on the problem of religion and philosophy is not clear.

21. Ali Sami el-Nashar, *Les Methodes chez les penseurs musulmans : et leur critique de la logique Aristotelicinne,* Cairo, 1947, p. 15.

22. The Arabs considered the *Organon* of Aristotle to consist of eight books : *Categories, On Interpretation, Prior Analytics, Posterior Analytics, Topics, On Sophistical Refutations, Poetics* and *Rhetorics.*

They always prefaced Aristotle's eight books with the *Eisagoge* of Porphyry.

23. *Ta'rikh al-Hukama'*, pp. 34-8.

24. See Appendix I, No. 35.

25. *Rasa'il Ikhwan al-Safa'*, ed. by Khayr al-Din al-Zirikli, 4 vols., Cairo, 1928, I : 395.

26. *Rasa'il,* I : 126.

27. Said al-Andalusi, *Tabaqat al-Umam,* ed. L. Sheikho, Beirut, 1911, p. 52.

28. This is also the opinion of Ibn Abi 'Usaybi'ah, *'Uyun,* I : 208.

29. Al-Kindi followed the traditions of the Alexandrian Aristotelians in considering logic and mathematics as propaedeutic to philosophy.

30. These problems are either mentioned or defined in his different writings. We have definitions of substance, quality, quantity, relation, the impossible, opinion, etc. in *On the Definition of Things.......* See also R. Walzer, "Islamic Philosophy" in *History of Philosophy : Eastern and Western,* London, 1953, II : 132.

31. *Al-Fihrist,* 358. This attitude towards mathematics is made clear in *Rasa'il,* I : 378.

32. *Rasa'il* I : 103.

33. The Arabic word *"wujud"* is related to the root *w'j'd,* originally meaning *to find*. This meaning later developed into *to comprehend,* and thence, by an easy transition into the idea of *existence*. As al-Kindi uses the term *"wujud,"* it still retains much of the earlier connotation of comprehension. He says, *"wa bi-haqq ma kana'l-wujud wujudan, wujud hissi wa wujud 'aqli* (and it is true that the comprehension of things is twofold, sensible and intelligible). The context, however, fully justifies the assumption that the philosopher is speaking not only of two types of comprehension but also, in effect, of two types of *being*.

34. *Rasa'il,* II : 8-10; Aristotle, *Metaphysics,* 6, 1025b ff.

35. Ibn Nubatah, *op. cit.*, p. 146. There is a slight difference between the classification of al-Kindi as reported in his *Rasa'il* and that reported by Ibn Nubatah concerning the second class of beings. Whereas *Rasa'il,* II : 10, gives the soul an example of the science of those objects which are immaterial but associated with matter, Ibn Nubatah gives mathematics.

36. *Rasa'il,* II : 11.

3

THE THEORETICAL PHILOSOPHY

A—The Metaphysics of Being

The already mentioned classification of the sciences suggests a convenient approach to a staisfactory understanding of al-Kinid's conceptual philosophy. We shall examine first his metaphysical doctrines and then pass to his anthropological ideas and lastly to his ethics.

Metaphysics was of the essence of Arab-Muslim philosophy. It was in this field that the Muslims made their chief contribution to the history of ideas. However, the main source of Arab-Muslim metaphysics is the Plotinian system of philosophy, especially his doctrine of emanation.

Al-Kindi differed from other Arab-Muslim philosophers by drawing upon Aristotle rather than Plotinus for his approach to the fundamental problems of metaphysics. He was acquainted with the *Metaphysics* of Aristotle which was translated for him by Ustath,[1] and he seems to lean upon this work to the exclusion of the so-called *Theology of Aristotle* (Plotinus' *Enneads*, Bks. iv-vi), of which he is supposed to have corrected the Arabic translation.

For al-Kindi, metaphysics was the "science of that which does not move," or the science of divine things. He describes it as the noblest and highest of all kinds of philosophy because the object of its investigation is the highest and noblest of all beings.

The first philosophy, for this is the name which al-Kindi, follwoing Aristotle, gives to metaphysics, is the

"Science of the First Truth, which is the cause of all truth". This science deserves to be placed first because the science of the cause is prior to the science of the caused. By knowing the cause one comes to know all subordinations to it.

This definitions of first philosophy is based upon the earlier of Aristotle's two definitions, which was later superseded by his famous dictum that metaphysics is the study of being *qua* being.[2]

The problems which the metaphysics of al-Kindi entail do not include the same problems of the metaphysics of being *qua* being which was basic in the philosophy of Aristotle and which was the landmark of Avicenna's metaphysics. Al-Kindi's problems were limited to the classes of beings, God and His nature, His creative actions, and His relationship to the world.

In the second chapter of his treatise *On First Philosophy,* al-Kindi speaks of "being" as either sensible by nature and subject to sensible knowledge, or intellectual by nature and subject to intellectual knowledge. The first kind of being is transient, changeable and mutable in respect to position, quantity and quality. In terms of knowledge, its form is represented *(yatamaththalu)* in the Imaginative Faculty and not in the intellect. This limitation means that it is impossible to know the essence of material objects, although they are nearer to us in respect of concrete existence.

The second kind of being (from which God is excluded) cannot either be known by the senses not does it have a metarial existence. Genera and species, for example, are comprehended only by the intellect because they do not possess a sensible existence. They are intellectual notions in the human mind; they have reality *per se* but no extramental existence.

Thus whereas universals (genera and species, beings of the second class) are comprehended by the intellect, individuals (beings of the first class) are comprehended by the senses. Al-Kindi says:

> No universal notion or nay notion beyond the universal such as that of God will be represented in the soul. All representations *(muthul)* are of sensible things, whereas the intelligibles are assented to by the soul and certified by virtue of their being innately comprehended as one would necessarily comprehended such first principles as the law of the excluded middle.[3]

Al-Kindi reiterates this essential difference between universals and individuals on a gnoseological level. Universals are real as individuals, but they do not have a world of their own. They exist as common qualities of a class of individuals : "Things are either universals or particulars. By "universals" I mean genera in respect to species, and species in respect to individuals. And I mean by "particulars" individuals in respect to species."[4] Al-Kindi is saying here that there is a necessary relation between universals and individuals. Without universals, there can no individuals and without individuals no universals. He thus eliminates the problem as to which comes first, universals or individuals.

On an ontological level, al-Kindi distinguishes three kinds of created beings : those that are corporeal, those that are separable from matter by virtue of their finer nature, and those that are spritiual in which there is nothing corporeal whatsoever. Individual bodies are of the first kind, the soul of the second, "divine things" of the third. Mathematics would go into second category since it belongs by nature to the incorporeal realm but is associated with matter. It consists, according to al-Kindi, of abstractions of sensible objects which are comprehended by the intellect without any representation. The reality of mathematics does not obtain assent by innate intuition, as is the case of the intelligibles. Neither does mathematics involve a representation in the

Imaginative Faculty such as is peculiar to material objects. Rather mathematics procures assent by a process of intellectual abstraction.

As to the substantiality of these three kinds of beings, al-Kindi maintains that universals as well as individuals are substances. The most important characteristic of substantiality is self-subsistence. Universals, he declares in his work *That Threre Exist Substances Without Bodies,* are substances because they are self-subsistent. However, he fails to make a clear distinction between primary substances, or particulars according to Aristotle, and secondary substances or universals. He possibly implies such a distinction in another context[5] ; nonetheless, the implication is not clear. Now, as for the second class of being on the ontological level, the soul is considered a substance but mathematical entities are not. Mathematical concepts are not in reality either sensible or incorporeal; they float on the border line between the two kinds of beings and may be thought of as substances but they are not.

The inclusion of the universals among substances raises many questions of great importance. First of all, it raises the question of substantial forms which was one of the greatest controversial problems in the thirteenth century Europe. If the soul is a substance, it must be a composite of matter and form, and it will not be the form of the human body as Aristotle had maintained. What then will its relation to the body be? Also this inclusion raises the problem of the relation between essence and existence of which al-Kindi seems not to have been aware.

Al-Kindi does not deal with either of these two problems. His main concern is to prove that the soul is an incorporeal substance by proving that incorporeal substances do exist in the form of universals. Although al-Kindi conceives of the universals as substances, he does not, however, conceive of them as Platonic Ideas.

He is a conceptual realist rather than a realist except for his idea of the soul which he invests with a unique dignity.

To sum up, we may say that al-Kindi conceives of a duality of beings. On the one hand, there is God, whose being is beyond our descriptive capacity and to whom the definition of substance as self-subsistent does not apply. On the other hand, there are the three kinds of beings which we have discussed and which fall under the category of created being. This kind of dualism is closer to that of Aristotle whose Unmoved Mover occupies a sepatrate category, than to that of Plato who assigns to God the hightest place among His likes, the Ideas. Nevertheless in reality al-Kindi conceives of a duality different in spirit from both Plato's and Aristotle's. It is a duality between the absolutely eternal and the created-out-of nothing, between God and His creation. True, Plato and Aristotle's God is eternal *a parte ante,* but He shares eternity with matter. Al-Kindi's God is the only being who possesses absolute eternity. Al-Kindi believes that some created beings such as the soul, are indestructible, but the soul's eternity is a *parte poste,* and it is by the will of God that this is so.

B—Creation

Since the most important argument for God's existence in the philosophy of al-Kindi is based on his conception of creation, we will discuss the problem of creation before discussing the existence of God and His attributes.

One of the most crucial problems in Arab-Muslim philosophy is that of creation, and indeed it is a crucial problem in all religious philosophies. In Islam, it acquired a special interest because of its relationship to the doctrine of the unity of God, one of the deepest preoccupations of Islamic thought. To many Muslims it represents the crossroads leading either to piety or to heresy. Those who affirm the eternity of the universe are to be classfied as heretics while those who believe in its creation are deemed to deserve the bliss of paradise and the respect of the community. The philosophers, therefore, all of whome except al-Kindi believed in the eternity of the universe and matter, took great pains to disguise their real opinions and to arrive at some apparent reconciliation between the dictates of reason and those of the revealed doctrine.

The treatment of this theme by al-Kindi assumes a special importance. For although he remained in the camp of the pious, he was the first one in Islam to approach the problem of creation from a new angle and with a new methodlogy. He used mathematical and logical reasoning instead of the dialectial favoured by the theologians.

The problem of creation is dealt with chiefly[6] in his treatise *On First Philosophy* and one entitled *On the Unity of God and the Finitude of the Body of the Universe.* We will, therefore, examine the main arguments that appear in both treatises. But before we do that, a glance at the history of this problem will help us understand better the attitude of al-Kindi and his position.

The theory of creation had a diversified development before it reached the Mulsims. The Greeks as a whole never thought of creation as being out of nothing. *Ex nihilo nihil fit* was a deeply embedded theory in their culture. Whether it was Ariastotle, Plato or Plotinus, they all maintained that creation was a making of one thing out of another through either movement, formation or emanation. Christianity was responsible for bringing to maturity the idea of *creatio ex nihilo,* already found in the Old Testament. During the Byzantine period, the controversy between Proculus and Philopponus, the first maintaining staunchly the eternity of the universe and the second its creation in time, was nothing else but the culmination of the encounter between the pagan Greek and the Christian points of view before the advent of Islam.

But before we can appreciate fully the contribution of al-Kindi, a special reference must be made to the Aristotelian statement of the problem. The Stagirite holds that the universe is eternal and has no beginning in time. It is impossible, he maintains, that movement should have started by itself : God is the prime mover, but movement itself is eternal. Of the various arguments that Aristotle uses to prove the eternity of the universe, three are of particular importance. First, the world cannot have come to be because there is no such thing as absolute becoming. Everything that becomes comes from something, that is what is actually existent must have come from what was potentially existent. Matter, therefore, must be eternal, since in the thesis that matter (potential being) endowed with form becomes actual being, matter is the substratum, the indespensable condition of the passage from potentiality to actuality. The second argument is based on the eternity of time and motion. God cannot be prior to time because *priority* implies time. God's priority is of a hierarchical nature and consists in His being the simultaneous cause of time. To think of time as having a beginning is tantamount to imagining a time before time, and so on *ad infinitum*. And since time is the measure of motion and we cannot think of time without thinking of motion, the latter likewise must be eternal. The third argument is based on his dictum that what has no beginning has no end. "Every baby must have had a father, but that father must also been a baby before he was a full-grown man. Hence the perpetuation of unchanging species must be without beginning and without end."[7]

In other words, Aristotle's God is not a creatot but a mover. He merely brings, what is in potentiality. into actuality, a conception not acceptable to any religious minded person.

Apart from maintaining the eternity of the universe, matter, time, and motion, Aristotle upheld the idea that this universe is finite in respect to the magnitude of its body. The universe as a magnitude is a body because like all bodies it is bounded by a surface, and from this he concluded that there cannot be an infinite body in actuality.[8]

Contrary to Aristotle, al-Kindi consistently upheld the theory of creation out of nothing *(creatio ex nihilo)*. God is the one, the Creator out of nothing *(al-mubdi')* who maintains in existence what he has created out of nothing.[9] He uses the word *"ibda'"*, unlike later philosophers,[10] to denote creation in time out of nothing. Abu Hayyan al-Tawhidi was aware of this attitude of al-Kindi "when he introduced him as adding *ibda'*, to the traditional four Aristotelian kinds of change, being a change without substratum."[11]

Al-Kindi, with a bias towards philosophy yet positively religious, found no intellectual difficulty in rejecting the Aristotelian theory of the eternity of the universe, while at the same time he used its particular instruments to formulate his own theory.[12] He combined two main Aristotelian principles and certain self-evident propositions to prove that the creation of the universe is a motion, that motion is not etetnal, and hence, the universe itself is not eternal.

The two principles which al-Kindi made use of are: (1) The infinite cannot become actual; that is, there can be no infinite body; (2) body, time and motion are concomitants; they exist simultaneously.

The self-evident propositions that al-Kindi employed in conjunction with the above-mentioned Aristotelian principles are the following:

(1) All homogeneous bodies, none of which is greater than the other, are equal.

(2) The distance between the extremes of equal bodies is the same in actuality and potentiality.

(3) Finite bodies cannot be infinite.

(4) If either of the two equal and homogeneous bodies is increased by another homogeneous body, the two become unequal. (The increased body will be the greater of the two and greater than what it was before).

(5) If a body is decreased the remainder is smaller than the original body.

(6) If a part is taken from a body and then restored to it, the resultant, is the same body we had before.

(7) Neither of the two infinite homogeneous bodies can be smaller than the other.

(8) Of the two homogeneous bodies, the smaller is so in relation to the greater of the two, or in relation to a part of the greater.

(9) If homogeneous bodies, all of which are finite, are added together, their sum will also be finite.

Most of the proofs which al-Kindi uses to demostrate the finitude of the universe rest on the above-mentioned Aristotelian principles and self-evident prepositions. Here is how he proceeds to demonstrate his point of view.

He starts with saying that if we assume that the universe had no beginning in time, that is, that it is infinite, we have to assume an infinite body of the universe which is a contradiction in terms.

Now, if we take away a part of a supposedly infinite body, the remainder is either finite and the whole was infinite (No. 9), or the remainder is infinite and the whole was infinite. If the whole is infinite and then we add to it what was taken away, the resultant will be the same body as before (No. 6), that is an infinite one. This would imply that the infinite is greater than the infinite, which is absured. And it would also imply that the whole is indentical with the part, which is contradictory. A body, therefore, which exists in actuality must of necessity be finite. The body of the universe actually exists; therefore, it is finite, which means that it is created.

Having proved that the body of the universe is finite and created, al-Kindi, who following Aristotle, connects body, time, and motion, proceeds to prove the creation of time and motion. If "past time" without a beginning to be possible, it cannot arrive at the "present time" since this would imply that the infinite comes into actuality. But the infinite cannot come into actuality, for the infinite cannot be traversed; and to say the "present time" has passed through an infinite number of instants would imply that the infinite has been traversed. Therefore, time is finite and created. This same reasoning applies to motion.

Al-Kindi then connects his conclusion regarding the creation of time and motion with "body". Time, according to him, is the duration of the body; motion is the measure of the duration of the body. Now, if the body of the universe is finite and motion is necessarily concomitant to the body, being the measure of its duration, it follows that where there is a body there is motion. But he has already shown that where there is motion there is creation in time. Thus all three—body, time, and motion— are created.

The Philosopher of the Arabs then attacks the problem of creation in time with a corroborative argument based upon motion. We have to assume, he says, that the body of the universe is either created or eternal. If created, its generation out of nothing is a motion. Now creation is a motion; motion is not eternal but created as it has been shown before. The body of the universe, therefore, has been created in time out of nothing.

If, on the other hand, the universe is eternal, or as al-Kindi puts it, was at rest *(sakin)* and then it moved, motion is a change. This means that what is eternal has passed from a state of rest to a state of movement, which is absurd since what is eternal does not change. The universe is, therefore, created in time *(muhdath)*.

It is clear from this exposition of al-Kindi's arguments that he parts sharply from Aristotle and the Hellenistic tradition in Islam and approaches more closely the theologians.

Aristotle affirms the existence of matter as an indispensable condition of production of things, whereas al-Kindi reaffirms the religious principle of creation out of nothing overlooking completely the arguments of Aristotle against such a principle.

Furthermore, al-Kindi differs from Plato who upheld a theory of creation in time; for whereas Plato believes that matter is eternal, al-Kindi believes it was created. However, al-Kindi and Plato coincide in their conception of the relation between motion and time. Both maintain that time is concomitant with motion and change and that where there is no change there is no time. God being changeless is also timeless. Only with creation did change and, therefore, time begin.

Al-Kindi tried in his *On First Philosophy* to demonstrate that an actual body cannot be the cause of itself, it connot be infinite, nor can it be one. He thought that once he had established these three points he had proved that God is the Creator of the universe and the only eternal being. All his efforts were directed, in effect, towards this goal.

The theologians as a whole had advocated, before al-Kinidi, a theory of creation in time. To them, the universe consists of atoms and vacuum, both of which are accidents and are devoid of any self-subsistence. The atoms cannot endure for two moments of time because they are in continuous recreation. According to them, a body is inseparable from its accidents *(a'rad)*,[13] and does not precede them. Now, whatever is inseparable from its accidents and does not precede them is created in time. The body of the universe, therefore, is created in time. Al-Ghazali (1059-1111 A.C.), the most important theologian in Islam, later advocated the atomic theory of the earlier theologians, but besides adduced in support of the thesis that the world must have been created in time, the concept of the impossibility of an infinite regress.[14]

Later some of the philosophers, like al-Farabi and Avicenna, upheld a theory based upon the idea that whatever exists by virtue of causation, that is, which is not self-causing, must necessarily come into being simultaneously with the cause *(musawiq)*. Creation did not take place *in* time but *with* time. Any priority that exists between cause and effect is in the nobler nature of the cause and not in the time of creation.[15]

Al-Kindi rejects both the approach of the theologians and their atomic theory which destroys the idea of natural causality. He affirms with them, however, a voluntary creation out of nothing, which affirmation is not consonant with his partial determinism. Against the philosophers, he maintains the theory that God is prior to His creation in time as well as in nature.

As to the source to al-Kindi's particular approach and argument, one must look for it in his keen mind and in the writings of John Philopponus, who held similar views regarding the doctrine of the creation of the world and whose works were well known to the Arab-Muslim thinkers. John defended the theory of creation against Proclus by using arguments and an approach similar to those used by al-Kindi. His main argument is based on the impossibility of traversing the infinite. If the world were eternal we would not have arrived at the present moment. He maintains also with al-Kindi the voluntary creation of the world and its coming to being out of nothing. God's will, according to him, can manifest itself without need of time or body.[16] And lastly both al-Kindi and Philopponus believe in the finitude of time and space.[17] The note of difference between the two is one of methodology rather than content.

C—God: the Proofs of His Existence

Now having proved that the universe is created in time *(muhdath)*, al-Kindi proceeds to demonstrate that it has a creator *(muhdith)*. He advances five proofs, four of which are variations of the cosmological argument based upon the idea of *a novitate mundi (dalil al-huduth)*,[18] and not directly upon the argument from causality. The last proof is teleological.

The first proof is based upon the premise that the universe was created in time. It has been shown that the universe is finite in respect to body, time and motion, which means that it must have been created. According to the law of caulality everything created in time must have a creator. God, therefore, is its creator and He is consequently existent. Al-Kindi also invokes the principle of logical relation to prove the same point. According to this principle there is a necessary relation between cause and effect, or between creator and created. If it has been proved that the universe is created, what is created, must necessarily have a creator.

This proof of God's existence was frequently used by the theologians who, accepting the creation in time as a premise, tried to prove the necessity of the existence of a creator by recourse to the "principle of determination". This principle meant that prior to the existence of the universe it was equally possible for it to be or not to be. In order to make the possibility of being prevail over not - being a "determining principle," *(murajjih)* was required, and this "determining principle," they argued, was God.[19]

The second proof of al-Kindi is based upon the highly cherished Islamic idea of God's unity coupled with the assumption that all earthly beings are composite and multiple. However, the proof is basically cosmological.

Its approach is more sophisticated than the previous one, although the inspiration is Islamic.

Before he starts his argument, al-Kindi explains the equivocal meaning of the term "one". This is attributed to the "single" objects of the world of creation and also it is attributed to the One, the Creator. Inspired by an Aristotelian distinction between oneness as a number and oneness as referring to simplicity, he affirms that *one* as a number may apply both to God and to "single" objects. But as referring to simplicity it cannot be attributed to any being except God. All "single" beings are composite in themselves, that is, divisible into component parts. Only God is indivisible; He is one in essence as well as in number. Oneness is essential in God, but in "single" objects it is accidental. In the case of God, oneness is absolute unity; in the case of all other beings, it is relative and *dependent* on God.

Everything other than God, then, is in some way composite which means it is multiple. Multiplicity is by necessity a group formation of several "singles" or "ones". It follows, therefore, that where there is no oneness there is no multiplicity; and also it follows that unless the "one" proceeds the composite or muliple there is no coming to be either material or temporal. Ultimately, everything that acquires material and temporal existence must emanate from that One which precedes all other "ones", and which is, therefore, the eternal cause of all coming to be. The one is the cause of all other "ones"; He is the Creator by whose actions everything comes to be, and everything lasts as long as He wills it to last.

The third proof is advanced in both his *On First Philosophy* and *On the Unity of God and the Finitude of the Body of the Universe.*[20] It is based upon the principle that a thing cannot be the cause of itself for in order to be so, it would have to exist before itself. He means by a "thing", of course, a created one and not God. His argument for maintaining that a thing cannot be the cause of itself is established by examining all possible situations that arise when a thing is assumed to be the cause of itself, and by trying to prove their absurdity. Here are the possible situations:

(1) The thing which is the cause of itself may be non-existent and its essence non-existent. In this case there is no cause or caused because cause and effect are attributed only to what exists.

(2) A thing may be non-existent and its essence existent. But this would mean that the thing does not exist and that which does not exist is nothing. Furthermore, if a non-existent thing is the cause of itself, it is at the same time itself and different from itself, which is contradictory.

(3) The thing may be existent and its essence non-existent. Here also we meet the same contradiction as above.

(4) The thing may be existant and its essence also existent. In this case, either the essence would be different from the thing itself (which is impossible); or the same thing would be both cause and effect (which is likewise a contradiction in terms). Therefore, to say that a thing which is existent and whose essence also exists, is the cause of itself, is absured.

These arguments of al-Kindi seem to be simple and self-evident. They are so to the extant that they are based upon the law of identity (if a thing is *A*, it is *A*), and upon the law of contradiction (no proposition can be both true and false). But they are not mental exercise—they hit upon a very crucial problem. Can an already existent thing be the cause of itself? or can a thing be before itself?

The fourth proof is analogical and is really a restatement if an old Stoic argument. The analogy is between the macrocosm and the microcosm. Just as the orderly and smooth running of the human body points towards an invisible intelligent administrator, which is the soul, so do the orderly and harmonious workings of the universe point towards an invisible and all intelligent administrator, which is God. But if someone asks how we come to know this administrator, al-Kindi answers that just as we know that the soul exists by the effects we observe in the body, so we should be able to know that God exists by the effects of His wise administration manifest in the visible world.[21]

The fifth and last proof is based upon the teleological argument *(dalil al-'inayah)* frequently used throughout the ages. It is even consedered the most effective proof by such a distinguished philosopher as Immanual Kant. The presentation of this proof is not organically administered as the other proofs. It is, however, alluded to on several occasions in al-Kindi's writings. Al-Kindi points out that the orderly and wonderful phenomena of nature could not be purposeless and accidental. They unmistakably imply a wonderful direction and a providential administrator, "an agent of agents, a generator of generators, a first of firsts and a cause of causes."[22] In another place al-Kindi says:

> The majestic structure of this universe, its regularity, the harmonious interaction of its parts, the admirable way some parts submit themselves to the guidance of other parts, the perfect arrangement so that the best is always preserved and the worst is always destroyed, is the best indication of the existence of a most intelligent adminsitration, and consequently of a most intelligent administrator.[23]

In his treatise *On the Proximate Efficient Cause...........*, after explaining how the physical phenomena are due to sidereal causes, al-Kindi alludes to the order of nature and its perfection. He attributes the existence of such regularity, order and harmony in nature to the wise administration of Him whose perfection and all-wise accomplishments should be evident enough to all those who see with the clear eye of the mind.[24]

The teleological argument seems to have special fascination for the Philosopher of the Arabs. It underlines for him the design of the universe, its beauty, and the coordination of the laws of its nature which accentuates the dependence of the cosmos on God and minimizes its self - sufficiency.[25]

D—God: The Divine Predicates

A historian of Arab-Muslim philosophy has said that the problem of the divine predicates has played the same role in the Near East as the problem of universals in the West.[26] He is right. The starting point of Islamic theology was God's unity. It was on this point that the controversies of the different schools of theology centered.

The Qur'an defines God as the only One. "There is no God but Allah" is the first article of the Muslim creed. He is the Exalted, the Self-sufficing, the Creator, for nothing exists save Him and that which He has created. However, the Qur'an's emphasis on the unity of God does not form a systematic doctrine of the nature of the Creator. It was left to the theologians to put the issue of the essence of the One to discussion. In history, this problem is referred to as the problem of the attributes.

Among the theologians there were seventy-two sects who professed different opinions regarding the attributes of God. However, they are all variations of three main schools : the Anthropomorphists,[27] the Mu'tazilites, and the Ash'arites. The first group maintained that the attributes of God are similar to those of man. God has a body like that of man and even a throne upon which He sits. The majority of the Mu'tazilite, upheld the theory that the attributes of God are identical with His essence. They reject any positive attributes on the ground that they would do away with God's unity. God, for example, is powerful not by a power different from Himself but by a power which is of His own essence. Others among the Mu'tazilites, such as Abn Hashim, predicated for the attributes a state between existence and non-existence *(ahwal)*; according to this theory, the attributes cannot be known independently of God. The third group did not admit that the attributes are identical with the essence of God; the One possesses such attributes as immateriality, eternity, science, power, and will. But these attributes although different from the essence of God are not similar in any sense to those possessed by men. Hence, we can not assume that they destroy God's unity.

Considering the amicable disposition of al-Kindi; towards the Mu'tazilites and his affinity to their point of view, it should not surprise us to find him formulating his thesis regarding God's attributes along the same lines of thought as those pursued by the "liberal thinkers" of Islam.

Al-Kindi devotes a whole chapter of his *On First Philosophy* to a thorough defence of the essential identity of God and His attributes. He starts his discussion by considering some of the terms that are susceptible to comparison such as great, small, long, short, etc. And he comes to the conclusion that these terms can never represent absolute concepts but must always refer to relative ones, involving comparisons within the same genus.

Al-Kindi then makes a distinction between absolute unity and metaphorical unity. The former applies only to God, whereas the latter describes sensible objects, which always possess certain qualities and attributes and hence multiplicity. In the case of God, *one* cannot refer to a number, because this is a quantitative concept and quantities have attributes inseparably attached to them. To say that God is one in this sense would be to imply that the One has an equal one and also that He is unequal to some other similar one. In any case *one* as a number refers to a material, divisible quantity, and this God is not.[28] Equality and inequality are attributes of things that are material and comparable. Any comparison, therefore, between the One which is one by essence and the *one* which is a number leads to absurdity.

It may be pointed out in this regard that al-Kindi does not seem to have arrived at a clear conclusion. He is at his best in manipulating his favourite method of finding in words, the *one* in this case, a meaning which would fit in his theory. However,, the originality of al-Kindi is in making the concept *one* perform two functions : it was both a simple and indivisible unity and a unit of construction which served as a starting point for the pyramid of existence.

In another place, al-Kindi advances a different argument which was destined to wield a great influence on later philosophers and which Maimonides describes as a "correct method to prove the incorporeality and the unity of God."[29] The argument is as follows:

> If there were more than one God, they must be composite and multiple. Why? Because they must have one element in common : their being first agents, and one element to differentiate them from each other, their property. This imples that each would have more than one attribute, namely, the one in which they share the one by which they differ. This is tantamount to saying that they are composite. Now, the composite requires a composer, which implies that the Agent has an agent. The latter can be either one or manifold. If one, it is the only First Agent; if manifold, the agent of the manifold is multiple, hence, we will have an infinite regress of composers, which is impossible. The First Agent, therefore, is not manifold but one and unlide His creation.[30]

This same argument is made the basis of a lost

treatise entitled مقاله فى الرد على النصارى *(Refutation of the Christians)*, in which al-Kindi argues aganist the possibility of the Christian Trinity. His method is very interesting because he uses solely principles of logic and philosophy, disregarding all other dialectical and theological arguments usually used in Christian-Muslim polemics. He justifies the limiting of his arguments to a purely philosophical level on the ground that philosohical proofs, not being revealed, are acceptable to both Christians and Muslims.

The treatise contains three main arguments. In the first one he tries to demostrate that it is impossible to have three eternal persons having the same essence. By essence each one of the three persons of the Trinity is identical with the other, but at the same time each one possesses his own property, which differentiates Him from the others. The inference is that every one of the three persons is *composed* of an essence which is common to all of them and a property which is particular to each one. Now, whatever is composed is not eternal and it is maintained that the Father, the Son and the Holy Spirit are eternal, which implies that what is eternal is not eternal—an absurdity.

In the second argument, he shows that the Trinity does not correspond to any one of the five voices or Porphyrian *categories*. According to Porphyry, every being pertains to one of five categories : genus, species (form), differentia, property and accident. Under whatever category one considers the Trinity, the result will always be that God, the One, is composite and is, therefore, not eternal. The eternity of three different persons with one essence is unthinkable.

In the third argument al-Kindi tries to show the error of maintaining that three make one and one makes three. Unity is either numeric, generic or specific.[31] If numric, God must be made up of three single units and hence He cannot be the One. If specific (meaning that the three are individuals and that the One is a species), we know, he says, that species are attributed to several individuals, and consequently Gos is composed. The same applies to genus. In other words, al-Kindi maintains that the oneness of genus and species, in a Christian sense different from the Porphyrian meaning of the words, cannot be established. The Christians, no matter how hard they try to justify it, fall in the error of association *(shirk)*, that is, associating a companion with God and worshipping him.

Besides the unity of God, al-Kindi stresses His unlikeness *(mukhalafah)* to creation. He asserts that God can only be described by negation, and that His very essence in unknowable to us. We can only aspire to know what He is not, but never what He is.

> The truly One is not one of the intelligibles, not an element, not a genus, not a species, not a person, not a differentia, not a property, not a general accident, not a movement, not a soul, not a mind, not a whole, not a part, not a total, not a particular, not one in relation to another, but an absolute One unsusceptible to muliplicity. He is not composite, not manifold, not one who can be pigeonholed in any of the above-mentioned concepts, nor one to whose name can be attributed any of the above mentioned attributes..... The truly One is, therefore, incorporeal, formless, measureless, and unrelated. He cannot be described by any of the descriptions applicable to intelligibles. He is without genus, of differentia, or personality, or property, or general accident, or movement; He cannot be described by any attribute except unity. He is pure and absolute unity; I mean nothing else but unity; and every other unity/by aquivocation/except His is manifold..... The truly One is one by essence, never multiple, never divisible in any manner in respect to Himself, or in respect to others. He is not time or place, neither is He a body or a predicate, or a whole or a part, or a substance, or an accident.......[32]

But if God is not any of these categories, what is He? In what relation does He stand to the universe? The only attribute which al-Kindi affirms is His unity.[33] Outside of that, God is beyond all statements which describe either the sensible or the intelligible. Any affirmation or categorical attribute is of an object. Of God, the only attribute that can be given Him is that He is One, which attribute separates Him from all created beings, and places Him on a transcendental pedestal of being above and beyond the reach of our feeble faculties.[34]

Was this the complete conception of God as construed by al-Kindi? Does not such an ineffability entail unconcern on the part of God towards the universe? And does not this unconcern oppose directly the idea of Divine Providence upheld by Islam? This may be the case if one reads only the formal expositions of the idea of God made by al-Kindi. Al-Kindi does not construct an organized defence of Divine Providence as he does in the case of God's unity. However, it is my feeling shared as well by others that one can get a different view as one reads through his complete works. There are many references made to a divine concern for the world.[35] God appears to have not the Aristotelian or Plotinian characteristics, but rather the Philonian ones. It is true that al-Kandi describes God as an Unmoved Mover, an Uncaused Cause, which attributes are used by Aristotle and by the Peripatetics in general. Nonetheless he refers to Him on many an occasion as the Compassionate, the Generous, and the Providential. To al-Kindi God is the compassionately solicitous. His essential attributes *(sifat al-dhat)* do not conflict with His attributes of perfection *(sifat al-kamal)*.[36] They blend rather in a harmonious unity, a unity that is different, unknowable and essentially simple. Providence seems to permeate all the universe and to uphold it just as the soul upholds the body, embracing everything with the ever-open arms of a loving Father, although we cannot aspire to know His essence.

It is unfortunate that al-Kindi leaves us in the dark regarding his justifications of the immanence of Divine Provindence. He does not admit pantheism as did the Neoplatonists, nor does he subscribe to the ultra-orthodox theory of anthropomorphism; but neither does he explain how the Divine Providence works. One may be tempted to say that he approaches the Chirstian doctrine of the transcendence and immanence of God, but this surmise cannot be substaintiated.

E—The Organization of the Created World

Having discussed al-Kindi's conception of being, God and His attributes, we will pass now tó an examination of his conception of the created world, including his cosmological, astronomical and physical ideas.

The structure of the universe in al-Kinid's system is based on that of Aristotle and Ptolemy. Aristotle regarded the heavens as a series of concentric spheres arranged around the earth as a central body. There are eight celestial spheres and four terrestrial ones, including the earth itself. This entire system was contained within an outer sphere.[37] The eight celestial spheres, he describes, as crystalline and moving in circles. The greatest of these carries the fixed stars whereas each of the others carries a planet, and all of them eternally circle our earthly planet which stands immobile at the centre. The earth itself is the innermost terrestrial sphere, the others in order or density and of their distance from earth are water, air and fire.

The universe is limited in space in the sense that it is contained within the outer sphere. It is unlimited in time in the sense that it is subject neither to generation nor to destruction as a whole.

According to Aristotle matter is continuous : that is, Aristotle does not admit the Atomistic theory of the existence of a void. He believes that all earthly objects are made of the four simple elements: earth, air, fire and water, which in their trun, contain the four "qualites," dryness, moisture, heat and cold.

The stars and planets move with a uniform circular velocity in their spheres each of which is subject to the influence of those outside it. Circular movement, perfect since the circle is the perfect figure, represents the changeless, eternal order of the heavens. It is contrasted with rectlinear movement which prevails on our changing and imperfect earth.

The problem, raised by such a conception of the universe with two different physics, celestial and terrestrial, is how to explain the eternal and circular movement of the speheres. An eternal movement cannot be explained in the Aristotelian system except by an eternal and immobile mover. This mover is God, the Prime Mover. But Aristotle also says that aside from God, there are the "intelligences" which are likewise eternal and immobile movers. This introduction of the "intelligences" raises a difficulty. Does God act upon the "intelligences" which in their turn move the spheres, or does God act directly upon the spheres? In the latter case, what is the purpose of introducing the "intelligences"? The "intelligences" must really be subordinate to the Prime Mover, but their actual relation to God is left obscure, as is also their mode of operating on the spheres. Aristotle seems to have been forced to introduce them in order to resolve a problem he inherited from Eudoxus' system which he had adopted. Eudoxus had attributed a seprate system of spheres to every planet, but had not joined the different spheres together in any way. He had not required any such connection, since the only purpose of his model was to provide a geometrical schematization of the complex planetary movements. Aristotle, on the other hand, wanted to find the connection between all the sets of spheres, thus making a single uniform system of them all and presenting all the heavenly bodies, from the fixed stars to the moon to the centrally placed earth, as a single organic unit. In order to link each set of spheres with the one next to it. Arostotle was obliged to introduce more and more new spheres in those already in existence. He got fifty-five spheres in all.[38] According to the Stagirite, the motion of each of the planets may be broken down into a certain number of uniform rotations; each of these rotations is assigned a spherical orbit, an intelligence, and a soul. The last two are considered as the principles of the movement of each one of the spheres. The number of the "intelligences" and the "souls" is equal to the number of the spheres.

Besides this involved explanation of the principle of heavenly movement, Aristotle complicates his system by considering the stars not as geometrical points but as animated beings endowed with life.

Al-Kindi seems to have accepted the Aristotelian scheme as a whole as it was modified later on by Ptolemy who reduced the number of spheres and intelligences to nine of each. According to the Philosopher of the Arabs, the universe is made up of concentric spheres rotating around the immobile earth. Outside the universe there is neither void nor plenum. In the very centre of the universe lies the earth surrounded by the firmament beyond which are the spheres of the simple elements. From the earth outward, arranged in order of density, these spheres are water, air and fire. This arrangement is in accordance with the nature *(physis)* of each element. The nature of the earth and water is to move towards the centre of the earth whereas that of air and fire is to move away from it. Besides this, each element possesses two "qualites." Fire is hot and dry, air is hot and moist, water is cold and moist, earth is cold and dry.

Between the spheres of the elements, there is no interaction although the elements commingle at their respectice circumferences. The said spheres extend from the centre of the earth to the sphere of the moon, and that is why this part of the universe is called the sublunary world. Since all substances in this area are subject to the ineluctable law of coming-to-be and passing away, it is also refferred to as the world of generation and corruption.

All earthly objects are composite bodies which are destructible by virture of containing in themselves opposite qualities. However, like Empedocles, al-Kindi believes that the four simple elements, because of their indivisibility, are beyond the reach of the law of destruction. But unlike the Greek Philosopher, he believes that the ultimate fate of the elements is in the hands of God, who will make them last as He wills that they should last.

The elements are either in opposition to or in alliance with one another. For example, water is opposed to fire, but allied to earth. Each one of the elements is, moreover, in its turn composed of a pair of the "four qualities," heat and cold, dryness and moisture. These qualities, as do the elements, exhibit affinity and opposition. The very nature of the sublunary elements depends on this opposition that they exhibit, and rectilinear movement is nothing else but the manifestation of their natural propensities to move either away from their opposites or to move towards their likes.

All created things, says the Philosopher of the Arabs, are in motion (subject to change) and in time (subject to contigency). The motion of the sublunary substances is rectilinear, horizontal or vertical. The fact that some elements stand in direct opposition to or in affinity with each other, makes the objects they compose pass constantly from one into another and puts them in continuous change and motion.

Beyond and above the sublunary world, lies the world of the celestial spheres and heavenly bodies. Like the simple elements of al-Kindi, all heavenly bodies are beyond the reach of the law of destruction. They are not subject to qualitative change nor to the laws of generation and corruption. However, they are made like the rest of Creation out of nothing and they will last as long as the Almighty wills that they should last.

The "material" of which the heavenly bodies are composed is purer and finer than that of the sublunary ones. Like Aristotle, al-Kindi believes that there is a fifth element, simple and free from all opposites, of which all celestial bodies are compounded. This element is neither light nor heavy, nor is it moist or dry.[39] The negative description of its nature is meant, I believe, to point out its absolute unlikeness to the four sublunary elements. And although al-Kindi does not mention it by name, it is no doubt the same as the *aither* of Aristotle.

The celestial bodies move in a circle and their motion is only local; that is, they do not suffer change. In fact, circular motion is the only motion they will accomplish by virtue of the fact that circular motion represents the perfect, the simple and the changeless order to which the heavens belong. An object possessing an opposite and a like has to move either away from its opposite or towards its like, but an object free from opposition moves in a circle and does not suffer change.

Nowhere in the extant writings of al-Kindi do we find the number of celestial spheres mentioned, but we can safely surmise that al-Kindi follows the Ptolemaic system in this respect and not the Aristotelian. There is an outermost sphere beyond which there is no void nor plenum and there is the sphere of the moon which is contiguous with the sublunary world. Between the two lie the other seven spheres of the different planets.

According to al-Kindi, the heavenly bodies are not only different in nature and constitution from the sublunary objects, but they are also animate, endowed with reason and the power of discrimination. As regards the animality of the heavenly bodies, al-Kindi tries to prove it by the principle that the effect cannot be superior to the cause. According to him, the heavenly bodies are the proximate afficient cause of generation and corrruption. Consequently, how can they endow other beings with life unless they themselves have life? To say that they are lifeless would amount to saying that the cause is inferior to the effect, which is absurd.

As to the rationality of the heavenly bodies, al-Kindi proves it by pointing out that they seek virtue. In this universe, one who seeks virtue must be rational, for reason is the instrument of discrimination between what is virtuous and what is not. However, having proved that the heavenly bodies are rational, al-Kindi furthermore affirms that the heavenly bodies are endowed with two senses:[40] hearing and sight. And if one asks why the heavenly bodies posses only these two faculties and not others, the philosopher answers that there is a divine purpose behind this fact. God created nothing in vain— there is nothing superfluous in this universe. Now, the heavenly bodies are always in actuality (being) and therefore not subject to growth. Hence, they will need only those faculties by which virtue (well-being) is acquired, namely, sight and hearing. They are thus differentiated from man, who, being subject to growth, needs all the faculties that are necessary for both rationalization and growth.

Having established the difference in nature between the heavenly bodies and their earthly counterparts, al-Kindi proceeds to discuss the relations between the two. His treatise *On the Proximate Efficient Cause* is devoted to a discussion of this relation. He admits the principle formulated by Aristotle, which was also accpeted by the Chaldeans and the Stoics, namely, that all the changes that take place in the sublunary world are caused by the motion of the heavenly bodies.

This very important principle converted ancient physics to a branch of astrology. It is by the motion of the heavenly bodies that the things in the world which we inhabit come to be or pass away. It is the observation of the stars which permits us to prognosticate the fecundity of the plants, the growth and death of animals, the happy and unhappy events; it is this same observation which permits the doctor to foresee a crisis and to intervence at the opportune moment. Al-Kindi follows this same line of thought, and there is no evidence that he was original in this as has been claimed.[41]

In the above-mentioned treatise, al-Kindi shows at the very beginning how the orderly and organized working of nature points to an all-pervading and most wise Being who is responsible for the administration of the world. However, he mentions later on that the problem that interests him in this treatise is that of the efficient cause of generation and corruption. An efficient cause, according to him, can be either proximate or distant. Now, if God is the distant cause of all which is sensible and intelligible, what is the proximate efficient cause? By using a dialectical approach, al-Kindi proves that this cause cannot be one of the elements of which the sublunary objects are compounded, nor can it be inherent in them, but necessarily it has to be outside them and different from them. Like Aristotle, he finds this proximate efficient cause in the heavenly bodies. The evidence of this fact is clear, he maintains, once we observe the motion of the sun and its correspondent effects. According to him, a caloric energy emanates from the motion of the heavenly bodies and is transmitted to the sublunary objects, thus effecting in them a continuous change. The strength of this energy depends on the magnitude, velocity and distance of the motion in respect to the effected body. The velocity of the movement of a planet in its own circle is proportional to its distance from the outermost sphere which causes the motion of all spheres. Whenever a heavenly sphere is farther away from the earth, its effect is predominantly cold, and whenever it is nearer, its effect is predominantly hot. Hot and cold, according to al-Kindi, are the two active qualities, whereas moist and dry see the passive ones.

As a result of the heavenly motion, the sun, which

is considered by al-Kindi the greatest of the efficient causes, approaches and retires, and thus produces perpetual generation and corruption.[42] The approaches and retreats of the sun are so harmoniously organized that they demonstrate a unique and great universal order. The sun's position in the sky harmonizes perfectly with its distance from the earth. If the sun were to go into its retreat just a little farther away, everything on earth would freeze to death, every area would transform into an ice-bound space similar to the areas near the poles where no life or civilazation can flourish. Also if the sun in its approach came a little nearer to the earth, everything there would burn to ashes and the world would become equally devoid of life and civilization. It is the this harmonious keeping of certain varying distances that blesses us with the four seasons, the growth of plants, the development and deçay of animal life, and the exactly right amount of cold and heat, rain and drought. To think of a different arrangement is to think of one continuous season, and we know from experience that the perpetuation of either hot or cold will always result in the destruction of life and the spread of disease.

Also had it not been that the sun follows an annual movement along the ecliptic, we would not have the necessary resting time that enables us to subsist and overcome the exhausting worriness that afflicts us every day. The passage of the sun along the ecliptic and its movement from east to west, produced by the movement of the outermost sphere, provides us with the opportunity to sleep and rest at night, and to enjoy the revivifying sunshine in the morning.

To sum up, the perfectly harmonious position of the sun in respect to its distance from the earth, its annual movement along the ecliptic, and its approances and retreats from the earth, all work so harmoniously in a divinely preordained order as to cause the four seasons with the ensuing generation and corruption, and day and night.

In the system of al-Kindi, the sun is considered the most important heavenly body in causing generation and corruption. However, the moon is conceived as a great helper *('azim al-'awn)* of the sun in the causation of coming to be and passing away. The moon is made responsible for the formation of clouds and rain, and also for bringing about the most convenient temperature for each of the four seasons. It is by the proper alternation of warm and cold temperature that things integrate and disintegrate.

No mention is made of Posidonius' theory on the causes of tides in this treatise, but al-Kindi explains the influence of the sun and the moon in his treatise *On the Efficent Cause of the Tides* in a manner very reminiscent of Posidonius.[43] The sun and the moon warm the water and hence cause it to expand. It is this expansion that makes the water spring out of the centre of the earth, and depending on the yearly, monthly and daily movement of the sun and the moon, it also causes the ebb and flow of the sea water known as tides.

Apart from the sun and the moon, the rest of the heavenly bodies influence the sublunar world, each in accordance with the magnitude of its power, its distance from earth, and the selective receptivity of earthly matter.[44]

The problem of the relation between the heavenly bodies and the earthly bodies leads us to the consideration of al-Kindi's attitude towards astrology. Al-Kindi was a well-known astrologer of his time. He wrote several books on the subject. However, this should not detract from his prestige as a philosopher; astrology was then not different from astronomy, and as such astrology was considered as a branch of philosophy. The pseudo-science and the real science had the same origin. Astrology as well as astronomy were thought to be based on certain observations and the laws inferred from them. Al-Kindi was not a magician; he clearly distinguishes between the two and does not think, as the magicians do, that one can conjure up fate by charms or by other means. Like most of his contemporaries, he considered astrology a science; as such it was backed up by a long tradition and an enormous prestige among all classes of society.[45]

Astrology postulates that in the case of man the influence of the heavenly bodies is not limited to generation and corruption. It goes beyond that into the realm of man's destiny and his civilization. According to al-Kindi, human temperament is determined by the position, movement and phases of the heavenly bodies. Consequently, it is possible to foretell the future of any man, once we know the exact date of his birth and make the proper astrological calculations.

On a social scale, the heavenly bodies, likewise, influence national characteristics. The peoples who live south of the equator are black, their hair curly and coarse, their noses flat, their eyes bulging their lips heavy. In addition to being concupiscent, they are excitable. The peoples who live near the two poles possess characteristics and features diametrically opposed to those of the peoples of the equator. Their lips and eyes are fine and delicate, their hair straight. They are warmhearted, phlegmatic, and chaste. There is a third category of peoples : those who live in the temperate zones. They are keener than the other two categories and tend towards a contemplative life.[46] Likewise, by applying the laws of astrology and by a proper calculation, it is possible to foretell the future of nations. The method one has to use in this connection is a calculation based on the conjunctions of Saturn and Mars, the supposedly unlucky stars, in the sign of Cancer which occur every thirty years.

A contributive element to the theory of sympathy is the conception of man as a microcosm. Man contains in himself all the faculties that are found in the universe *(al-kull)*, that is, growth, animality and rationality. Besides, man is composed of the same elements of which the other bodies are composed and in him occur all the phenomena that occur in the sublunary world such as rain, winds, evacuation and quakes. It is not impossible, says al-Kindi, that the Almighty fashioned the universe as one animal within which are found the phenomena with which we are familiar, and perhaps He fashioned man as one in whom are found the same faculties, constitution and phenomena of the universe. Al-Kindi adds significantly that this is not against the teachings of Muhammad.[47]

There is one problem related to al-Kindi's scheme of the universe which is not clear. How does al-Kindi reconcile the determinism of astrology with his Mu'tazilite affinity? Astrology, as we know, is founded on a fatalistic concept of the cosmos : there is an immutable law regulating the movements of the heavenly bodies whose effects extend to all physical, social and moral phenomena.[48] The Mu'tazilites, on the other hand, maintain that at least in the moral order, man is the master of his own fate. He has a capacity *(istita'ah)* to determine his own actions, that is, he is morally free. Al-Kindi, we know, wrote a book on this very subject called *On Capacity* which unfortunately has not come down to us.

To clarify the attitude of al-Kindi, we should need to have access to his lost astrological writings. Under the present circumstances, all we can do is to glean those relevant phrases (they are not many, by the way) in which some kind of an attitude is apparent, such as his definition of the will in general *(iradah) :* the faculty by which, one *intends* to do one thing and not the other.[49] In another place al-Kindi defines the human will as a faculty which, when a thought occurs to it, is inclined *(tamil)* to action. Neither definition, however, leads inevitably to the idea of free choice, though such an interpretation might conceivably be forced upon them both. Such construction of al-Kindi's words would, however, be inconsistent with much of his thought as we know it and with a statement in which he declares that human wills are influenced by the heavenly bodies.[50]

The absence of effective choice, in the sense of electing and doing what one elects, is consonant with the attitude maintained by al-Kindi in different places regarding the unity of the universe and the concatenation of causes and effects. Every event that takes place in this universe is the effect of another *effect*, or approximate cause, upon which it depends for its own existence. But all causes and effects depend upon heavenly bodies and ultimately upon God, who so arranged the universe as to establish a permanent relation between every cause and effect. In a system like this there is no place for freedom of action. The determinism of al-Kindi sounds like Stoic fatalism criticised by the Sceptic Carneades and Plutarch, and rejected, before Islam, by Plotinus and, after Islam, by the Mu'tazilities.

Unless we get hold of new documents, we must have to assume that al-Kindi's system is deterministic and that it is extremely hard to reconcile it with his Mu'tazilite sympathies. Probably he upheld in his book *On Capacity* a non-fatalistic astral influence on human affairs and maintained that stars exercised merely an avoidable influence. This is only a conjucture which cannot, at the moment, he substantiated. However, if he had maintained such a doctrine he would have fallen into a logical inconsistency in his system.

F—The Philosophy of Nature

The works of al-Kindi on the practical aspects of the physical sciences far outnumbered those dealing with the philosophy of the sciences and with pure philosophy. However, among his extant writings the philosophical ones are more numerous that the practical, a fact which, in all probability, shows that people were far more interested in his philosophical ideas than in his scientific ones.

In spite of this preponderance of works on pure philosophy and on the philosophy of science found among the extant writings of al-Kindi, he did not leave us a manual on the philosophy of nature as did his successors in Arab-Muslim philosophy. We have, however, available several treatises dealing with different problems such as movement, matter, space, time and force which we will discuss in the following pages.

Physics and metaphysics are distinguished by their subject matter. Whereas physics investigates those objects that are subject to change, metaphysics investigates the immutable and eternal.[51] In other words, physical science deals with the particular, philosophy proper deals with the universal. Let us see why.

The Philosopher of the Arabs makes a distinction between objects that exist by nature and objects that exist by art. The former include the simple elements, plants and animals;[52] the latter include the compounds of simple elements. The distinction which he makes between the two is that the natural objects have in themselves the principle of movement and rest, while artificial objects move by virtue of the elements of which they are made. The movement of the artificial object is determined by the element that predominates in its composition. In the case of both types of objects, the kind of movement reveals the nature of the object.

The term *nature* is used in two different senses. In the first, it means the sum of physical or material objects. Anything that is material is natural, says al-Kindi;[53] and in the second sense, *nature* means the primary principle of movement and rest.[54] All simple elements exclusive of the celestial ones, exhibit a natural movement which has an end at which they come to rest. In this second sense nature closely resembles the Greek *physics*, a self-existent and immanent force in things which makes them move to reach their natural form or destination. However, as a Muslim, al-Kindi could not accept the self-existence of nature. Nature is created by God who determined the created universe and made it operate in a stable system.

Now, the definition of nature as the principle

created by God; which is the cause of movement and rest, makes physics, the study of nature, concerned with moving or changing things, as opposed to metaphysics which is concerned with immovable, or, eternal things.

To the problem of movement as such, al-Kindi devotes a great deal of attention.[55] He does this first, because his philosophy of nature is based on the Aristotelian physics which is in reality a physics of movement; second, because he resorts to the same principle of movement to refute the Aristotelian contention that the eternity of the world can be proved by establishing the eternity of movement.

Al-Kindi defines movement as a change, or an actualization of potentiality, and as such it occurs in the simple elements and their compounds i.e., if there is something whose essence is being changed, there is movement. But in accordance with al-Kindi's conception, celestial bodies do not change. Now, if movement implies change and we know that the celestial bodies do not change, in what sense are we to understand the term movement in respect to the aforementioned bodies. Al-Kindi uses movement in respect of celestial bodies in another sense. He admits the movement of the haeavenly bodies and denominates it *circular,* thereby equating it with immutability, whereas the movement defined as change and limited to natural objects, is called rectilinear.

Rectilinear movement is of two classes: a movement *from* the centre (of the earth) and a movement toward the centre (of the earth). By movement *toward* the centre, he means the movement of water and earth which is directed toward the centre of the earth, whereas by movement *from* the centre, he means the movement of air and fire which is directed away from the centre of the earth. The direction and speed of the movement is proportional to the weight of each element. The heaviest and the lightest move faster than the rest. Earth is the heaviest, therefore, it moves most rapidly toward the centre of the earth. Fire on the other hand, is the lightest and therefore it moves most rapidly away from the centre toward the outer sphere. Water is heavier than air but less heavy than earth; therefore it occupies a position intermediate between air and earth. Air occupies a position between fire and water.

Understood as change, movement will involve passing from one contrary to another, and it will imply an active agent and a passive one which al-Kindi finds in the four qualities of heat, cold, dryness and moisture. The active qualities are heat and cold and the passive ones are dryness and moisture. Heat is the quality that causes lightness while cold causes heaviness. Dryness causes rapid movement of both light and heavy objects towards their natural position while moisture causes their slow movement.

There are different types of change according to al-Kindi: generation, corruption, alternation, augmentation, diminution and locomotion. Generation and corruption are movements in respect to substance[56] as when a man (after death) turns into dust. Augementation and diminution are movements in respect to quantity, as when a body increases or decreases in size. Alternation is movement in respect to quality as when a bitter almond turns sweet. Locomotion is movement in respect to place.

However, although al-Kindi accepts the Aristotelian concept of movement as change, he does not share Aristotele's view that movement is eternal. Al-Kindi holds that movement, being inseperabaly related to the body that moves and to the time during which it moves, is, like both body and time, finite.

In his discussion of time, al-Kindi dismisses the doctrine that identifies time with movement. Time is not the same as movement although there is very intimate relationship betweem the two. He argues that movement belongs to the properties of things and hence differs in accordance with each species. Time is not a property and it is one and the same for all beings and does not differ as do the objects that move.

As to the nature of time, al-Kindi maintains that it is the *now* in our consciouness which links the past with the future. The present *now,* however, is nothing by itself—it passes away even before we think of it; consequently in itself it cannot be time. Time can be known in relation to a *before* and an *after,* and as such it is nothing but the number that measures the motion of a body. That is why there is no time without movement and no movement without a moving body.[57]

To turn to the problem of space, al-Kindi asks, does space exist? And if it exists, what is it? Is it a body, as Plato maintained? Or does it exist, but not as a body, as some other philosophers maintained? Space, answers al-Kindi following Aristotle, does exists as we know by the fact that when a body augments, decreases or merely moves in location, it moves within *something* which necessarily contains it and is bigger than itself. Also we know that space exists by observing certain phenomena such as the replacement of water by air. Whenever water comes into a place air goes out and vice versa; yet the place where both water and air were contained remains the same; it is not destroyed when it is abandoned by that which it formerly contained. One has to conclude from these observations and from other facts that space must exist.

But what is space? When we prove that space exists, we have not yet ascertained what it is—we must also discover its characteristics. It is a body, an empty receptacle; or is it a vaccum? It is neither, says al-Kindi. It is absurd to conceive of space as a material receptacle, that is a body. Such a conception imples that space is a receptacle and a received object *ad infinitum,* which is impossible. Besides, the recepatcle as an agent has to be different from the received object upon which it acts.

Now, coming to the problem of matter *per se* and

its relation to form we will to probe a little deeper than we have done before into the question of substance. Al-Kindi tells us in his *De Quinque Essentiis* that every thing that is substantial has to have matter, form, place movement and time; therefore, it is imperative to see the exact relation between substance and matter.

The most important characteristic of sunstance is self-subsistence; or to put it in another way, a substance is not found in a subject, but itself is the subject which does not suffer in essence when predicates are asserted of it. Other characteristics of substance are that it connot admit a contrary, it cannot be what it is and be something else at the same time ; and that it cannot be more complete than what it is. It is also prior in difinition: if one defines a substance one is also defining, at the same time, those accidental qualities which do not form a part of its essence, but enter in the formation of each particular substance.[58]

A list of what al-Kindi considers as substances will include genus, species (form), the differentia, the individual, the soul and finally matter. This means that substances can be found in different states. Sometimes they are material as in the case of an individual inanimate body or immaterial as in the case of the soul. And when a substance is a part of a body it can be its form or its matter.[59] Or if it is entirely separate, it can be the soul which moves it.

Like Aristotle, al-Kindi divides substance into primary and secondary types. And althogh secondary substance do not exist prior to primary substances, they are self-subsisting and are the object of true knowledge.

A primary substance is an individual. This may be natural like a tree or an animal, or artificial like a building. Whatever it is, an individual is a body made out of substance (*jawhar*, essence) which is its genus and a differentia which is its length, depth and breadth; or to put it differently, a body is composed simply of matter and form.[60]

A body, says al-Kindi, posseses five basic principles: a matter *(hyle)* out of which it is made, a form by which it is distinguished, a place in which it extends, a movement by which it is particularized, and a time which is the number of its movement.[61] However, the two most fundamental principles of every body are matter and form, which are not bodies but compose the bodies.

Secondary substances do not, like the first substance, exist concretely. But their relation to the first substances is so intimate that one has to call them substances. If we dignify a sensible object with the name of substance, how much more should we call that which gives the sensible object its name and definition a substance. And if the individual is the actualization of a secondary substance, this is its essence without which it cannot be what it is.

Secondary substances are of two types, the unifying *(al-jami')* and the differentiating *(al-mufarriq)*. When a unifying secondary substance is close to the primary substance of which it is predicated, it is called a species;[62] example, John is a *man*. When a unifying secondary substance is further removed from the primary substance of which it is predicate, it is called a genus; example, John is an *animal*.

The differentiating substance is that which distinguishes one species from others in the same genus. It is what al-Kindi calls *fasl*, or, differentia; example, man is retional.

Now, to come to the question of matter in itself: how does al-Kindi conceive of matter as a substance and what is its relation to form? A substance can be found in a state of potentiality and amorphous matter is that kind of substance. However, to know what matter is, one has to define it. A definition is a statement of the genus to which an object belongs and of the differentia which distinguish it from other members of the same genus. Matter, being a fundamental principle, and the base of all change, does not belong to a genus. There is no genus above it to which it can belong and therefore it cannot be known by definition. It can only be known by its properties. Matter is that which receives but is not received, that which retains but is not itself retained. If it is suppressed, what belongs to it is suppressed, but if what belongs to it is suppressed, it is not itself suppressed. It admits the contraties without changing in essence.[63]

Intimately related to matter is the other fundamental principle of form.[64] As in Aristotle, form and matter combine to make a body. Considered in a dynamic sense, matter and form are respectively, potentiality and actuality. Matter is potentiality in relation to the form which gives it determination, actuality. Al-Kindi, apart from considering form as the actualization of a potentiality, sees in form itself a potentiality *(quwwah, dyamis)*. However, this apparent contradiction in the use of the word in the sense of potentiality should not mislead us. Al-Kindi does not mean by it the actual reception of determination, but a positive force by which things are made out of matter. As an illustration of form as a potentiality al-Kindi offers the case of fire. Fire results from the combination of heat (form) and dryness (matter). Heat before converting into fire is potentiality latent in dryness and is reduced on combining with dryness. To put it differently, the form of fire or heat is latent in the matter of fire, or dryness, and as such it is a potentiality which on combining with dryness produces fire. Al-Kindi does not consider form from the point of view of its final structure but from the point of view of its dynamic capacity to develop into its final structure.[65]

NOTES

1. *Ta'rikh al-Hukama'*, p. 42.

2. Jaeger has proved that Aristotle maintained two definitions of first

philosophy. In the earlier one, when the philosopher was still to some extent under Platonic influence, he considered metaphysics as identical with the dialectial study of the various types of being, and especially with the study of the imperishable and eternal beings. In his later definiton, Aristotle considered first philosophy as the study of being *qua* being, without limiting it to any one particular species of being. See W. Jaeger, *Aristotle*,[2] trans. R. Robinson, Oxford, 1948, p. 194. Al-Kindi may well have taken as the basis of his definition the one established in Book *Lambda*, (XII) which is considered now by many textual critics as a separate treatise.

3. *Rasa'il*, I : 107-8.

4. *Ibid.*

5. *Ibid* : 266-7.

6. See also *Rasa'il* I : 214-5.

7. A. E. Taylor, *Aristotle*, Dover ed., New York 1955, pp. 56-7.

8. Aristotle, *Physics* 3. 204a, 206a; *Metaphysics* II, 1066b, 24.

9. *Rasa'il*, I : 162.

10. Cf. for example al-Farabi, *'Uyun al-Masa'il*, ed. Dietrici, p. 58. Also Ibn Sina, Risalat al-Hudud in *Tis' Rasa'il*, Cairo, 1908, p. 101.

11. Abu Hayyan al-Tawhidi, *al-Imta' wa'l-Mu'anasah*, ed. A. Amin and A. al-Zein, Cairo, 1939, part III, p. 133. Cf. R. Walzer, "New Studies on al-Kindi", in *Oriens*, X/1952, p. 217.

12. Sa'id al-Andalusi, *op. cit.*, p. 52 criticises al-Kindi unjustly for his rejection of the eternity of the world and for using rhetorical and sophistical arguments.

13. The Theologians defined accidents as the notions superadded to the notion of substance and which accompany the body of necessity; Cf. al-Juwayni, *Kitab al-Irshad*, ed. M. Y. Musa and A.A. 'Abd al-Hamid, Cairo, 1950.

14. Maimonides expounds the theories of the Theologians on the problem of creation in time and criticises their method as being based on dialectical principles rather than on apodictic reasoning.

Maimonides, *The Guide for the Perplexed*, tr. by M. Friedlaender, 2nd revised edition, London, 1951, p. 133ff.

15. See on the difference in meaning between the notion of creation among the Theologians and the Philosophers the treatise of Ibn Khammar, "La Notion de *muhdath* dans le Kalam et dans là Philosophie" in *Donum Natalicium H. S. Nyberg oblatum*, Uppsala, 1954, pp. 88-93. This treatise was later published in original Arabic by A. Badawi, *Neoplatonici a apud Arabes*, Cairo, 1955, pp. 243-7.

16. J. Philopponus, *De aeternitate mundi contra Proclum*, ed. Hugo Rabe, Leipzig, Tubner, 1899, pp. 8, 117, 20. John says that not everything created in time is necessarily subject to change, nor does everything that is created need matter in order to be created; God can create it out of nothing.

17. See the note on the theory of Philopponus in the English translation of Averroes, *The Incoherence of the Incoherence*, tr. Simon Van den Bergh, London, 1954, II : 8-9, in which Van den Bergh compares the theories of the Theologians, that of Philopponus, and the first antinomy of Kant. See also Basil Tatakis *La Philosophie Byzantine*, deuxieme fascicule supplementaire of Emile Brehier, *Historie de la Philosophie*, Paris, 1949, pp. 41-3. Also R. Walzer, "New Studies on al-Kindi", pp. 218-24 where we have a detailed study of the possible dependence of al-Kindi on Philopponus.

18. For a discussion of the arguments for the existence of God in Muslim theology, the reader is reffered to A.J.Wensinck, "Les preuves de I'existence de Dieu dans la theologie musulmane," *in mededeelingen der Konic. Akadamie van Wetenshappen*, Deel 81, Serie A. No. 2, Amesterdam, 1936 Also M. Fakhry, "The Classical Islamic Arguments for the Existence of God," *The Muslim World*, XLVII, No. 2 (April, 1957), pp. 133-45. However, al-Kindi is probably the first Muslim thinker to use the argument *a novitate mundi* in the form presented above.

19. M. Fakhry, *op. cit.*, p. 139.

20. *Rasa'il*, I : 143-67, 201-7. See also the execellent discussion of Abu Ridah in his Introduction, pp. 77-9.

21. *Rasa'il*, I : 174. We find this argument in Cicero *On the Nature of the Gods*, ii, 7. The fact that the analogy is Stoic does not imply that al-Kindi admitted the pantheistic viewpoint of "one divine and immanent spirit." He was an indomitable upholder of the

transcendence and ineffability of God. His acceptance of the analogy was of a methodological nature and does not refer to his attitude regarding God.

22. *Rasa'il,* I : 214-5; 230-1; 257-8.

23. *Ibid.,* 215.

24. *Ibid.,* 236-7.

25. Al-Farabi and Avicenna laid special emphasis on the argument from contigency; Averroes shows a predilection for the teleological argument as can be easily inferred from his refutation of the Theologians and of the Suff arguments in his book *al-Kashf 'an Manahij al-Adillah,* Cairo n. d., p. 45. The teleological argument has a basis in the Qur'an.

26. I, Madkour, *La Place d' al-Farabi dans l'ecole philosophique musulmane,* Paris, 1934, p. 47.

27. The *Mushabbihah,* or comparers. They compare God's attributes with those of man. Al-Shahrastani, *al-Milal Wa'l-Nihal,* ed. A.F. Muhammad, 3 vols., Cairo, 1948, I : 145-58.

28. *Rasa'il,* I : 146-57.

29. Maimonides, *op. cit.,* p. 153.

30. *Rasa'il,* I : 207.

31. Al-Kindi mentions here as his source Aristotle's *Topics (al-Jadal),* probably p. 121.

32. *Rasa'il,* I : 160. This description of the ineffability of God is very reminiscent of Jahm ibn Safwan, a Mu'tazilite who maintained that "in Him is neither upper nor lower, no parts or divisions, neither right not left. He is neither heavy nor light. Whenever you think that He is something which you know, then He is different from it." See A. S. Tritton, *Muslim Theology,* London, 1947, p. 63.

33. Al-Kindi mentions eternity as a positive attribute, but this can be reduced to a negative one.

34. Al-Kindi's pre-occupation with the problem of the unity of God is reflected in other works which, unfortunately, have not reached us.

'Abd al-Latif al-Baghdadi, *La relation de l' Egypt (Kitab Akhbar Misr)*, translated into French by M. Silvestre de Sacy, p. 463, reports that he wrote a book refuting al-Kindi's ideas on the attributes that appeared in his treatise *On Unity (Risalat al-Tawhid)*, now no longer extant. 'Abd al-Latif who lived in the twelfth century, criticises al-Kindi's conception of the absolute unity and ineffability of God. Also the anonymous author of a thirteenth century Latin work entitled *Tractatus de erroribus philosophorum* says that al-Kindi maintained that all perfections predicated of God do not indicate anything positive in Him *(Voluit enim quod perfections de Deo dictate nihil dicunt positive de Deo)*. See B. Horeau, *De la philosophie scholastique*, Paris, 1850, I : 346.

35. *Rasa'il*, I : 105, 162, 183, 193, 201, 207, 244 etc. Abu Ridah in his scholarly introduction to the *Rasa'il* tried to show that al-Kindi attributed to God positive as well as negative attributes. He mentions as positive the unity of God, the essential attributes and the attributes of action. As negative, he mentions the negation of multiplicity and the unlikeness to created objects. See *Rasa'il*, the introduction, p. 80 (6).

36. The essential attributes refer to those qualities which are always positively attributed to God such as power and glory, whereas the attributes of perfection refer to such qualities as compassion and grace. Abu Ridah maintains that all attributes like the Powerful, the Compassionate, etc. show an inclination congruent with the orthodox belief in Divine Providence. However, al-Kindi does not make an effort to prove that his idea of Providence is not contradictory with his idea of ineffability. Whenever he refers to Providence, he does so in a laudatory manner, following a very common tradition when one is referring to God.

37. A sphere as used in this context refers in reality to a spherical system as will be seen further on.

38. S. Sambursky, *The Physical World of the Greeks*, tr. Merton Dagut, New York, 1956, p. 61. See also W. D. Ross, *Aristotle*, 5th ed., London, 1956, pp. 97-8.

39. Cf. *Rasa'il*, II : 45.

40. This statement is contrary to Aristotle's view on the simplicity of heavenly bodies as expressed in *De Caelo*, 268b 12-270b, Bk. I : pp. 2-3.

41. *Rasa'il,* I : 213.

42. It is the alternating approach and retreat of the sun that causes the ascent and descent of water, air and fire. This process brings the elements together and causes them to interact, with the result that the substances themselves are transformed. The heat which the sun and the other planets produce is engendered as the air is chafed by their movements. It is the nature of movement to ignite even wood, stone and iron. See on this point Aristotle's *De Caelo,* 289a 20-25.

43. P. Duhem, *Le systeme du monde,* new impression, Paris, 1954, II : 285 says : "Posidonius avait amene la theorie des marees a un point qu'elle ne depassera guere avant le XVI esiecle." In fact, al-Kindi's explanation of the causes are based on those of Posidonius.

44. Cf. *Rasa'il,* I : 322-5.

45. Aristotle's emphasis on the importance of the sphere of the fixed stars and the planets' control of earthly affairs lent his prestige to "scientific" astrology. Besides astrology had its longest tradition in Iraq where al-Kindi passed all his life.

46. *Rasa'il,* I : 226. This idea also is of an Aristotelian origin. See *Problemata,* 909a, translated by E. G. Forester, Oxford, 1927. Ptolemy elaborates it in his *Tetrabiblos,* II : 2.

47. Al-Kindi's conception of the universe as a living organism is no doubt of a Stoic origin. See Cicero, *On the Nature of the Gods,* Bk. II : 7-8.

48. Fr. Cumont, *The Oriental Religious in Roman Paganism,* New York: Dover, 1956, p. 179.

49. *Rasa'il,* I : 168.

50. *Ibid.,* 236.

51. *Ibid.,* 40.

52. Although al-Kindi does not state explicitly that animals and plants exist by nature, one is justified in supposing that he included them among natural objects on the ground of his Aristotelian affinities in respect to the interpretation of the universe. Furthermore, this surmise is corroborated by al-Kinid's definition of *nature* in his

treatise *On the Definition of Things* : "Nature is the principle of movement and rest and it is the first of the faculties of the soul." This could easily imply that the principle of movement in animate objects is intiated by the soul. In this case he must have included animals and plants among objects that exist by nature. And apart from this al-Kindi gives animals and plants as an example of a natural individual. See *Rasa'il,* I : 165.

53. *Rasa'il,* I : III.

54. *Ibid.,* al-Kindi uses the term *tabi'ah,* nature and *tab',* specific nature interchangeably.

55. *Ibid.,* I : 117-9; 216-7; II : 22-6;40-6.

56. Al-Kindi must have depended on the earlier of two Aristotelian conceptions of movement in respect to substance. In *Physics* iii, 200b 32 the Stagirite uses movement as synonymous with change and as including generation and corruption. In *Physics* v. 225b 10, he restricts movement so as to exclude change in respect to substance, i.e. generation and corruption. Ross, *op. cit.,* p. 83.

57. *Rasa'il,* II : 34.

58. *Ibid.,* I : 166.

59. *Ibid.,* II : 10.

60. *Ibid.,* I : 120.

61. *Ibid.,* II : 14.

62. Al-Kindi uses the term *"surah* (form)" for speices. The word as it is used by him in this context must be a direct translation of the Porphyrian voice *eidos* which in Greek has also the double meaning of form and species. The Stoics used it too in the sense of species.

63. *Rasa'il,* II : 18.

64. In the Aristotelian sense.

65. Al-Kindi uses the word *"quwwah"* in two different senses : as the susceptibility latent in dryness, and as the force by which two bodies are struck to produce fire. Carra de Vaux, in his book on *Avicenna,* Paris, 1900, p. 85, points out that the above example of

fire used by al-Kindi demonstrates that the Philosopher of the Arabs did not grasp Aristotle's conception of matter and form correctly. Carra de Vaux could not possibly have been aware of this double use of the term *"quwwah"* as used by al-Kindi since most of his extant writings were not available then.

4

ANTHROPOLOGY

A—The Soul and its Nature

The writings of al-Kindi on the soul are neither numerous nor comprehensive. Besides his treatise *On the Intellect,* they include the five treatises listed in *al-Fihrist*[1] of which only two have reached us, and a note entitled *A Discourse by al-Kindi on the Soul, Abridged and Concise.* This note deals in an almost incomprehensible manner with the relation of the soul to the body, and endeavours to demonstrate the compatibility between the ideas of Plato and those of Aristotle regarding this relation. These few treatises are of supreme importance and of great interest because of the light they shed on the origins of Arab-Muslim psychology and particularly on the idea of natural prophecy.

In the first and more important treatise, *On the Soul, Abridged from the Book of Aristotle and Plato and from the Other Philosopher,* al-Kindi answers the letter of a friend who had asked to "summarize for him some discourse on the soul and to indicate the purpose thereof aimed at by the philosophers *[sic],* and to summarize, besides, the book of Aristotle *On the Soul*" (*Rasa'il,* I : 272-3). However, Aristotle seems to play a minor role in this treatise in spite of what the title may indicate. Al-Kindi did not know *On the Soul* at first hand as he seems to have only known parts, at least, of the *Metaphysics* and other writings of Aristotle.

The trend of the treatise is Neo-Pythgorean and Platonic. This is proven by the definition, functions and capacities of the soul as given by al-Kindi. And if we are to take this treatise, as I am inclined to do, as representative of al-Kindi's opinion and not merely as an exposition of the ideas of the ancient philosophers, we have to accept the fact that al-Kindi here so much drifted away from Aristotle in regard to psychology as he had never done before. The Philosopher of the Arabs, however, tried to reconcile Plato and Aristotle in his other short treatise, *A Discourse on the Soul,* but in spite of this effort the tone of his whole writings on the nature of the soul is Platonic.

As to the nature of the soul, al-Kindi opposes any materialistic conception. Most of the orthodox Muslims as well as the materialists such as were *al-Dahriyah*[2] believed the soul to be composed of a very fine and subtle material invisible to the naked eye. It is not clear, however, whether he had in mind those two groups when in his treatise *That There Exist Substances Without Bodies* he refuted the materialistic ideas, or whether he was aiming at the Epicureans and the Stoics who held that all substances, including the soul, are made out of matter.

According to al-Kindi, the soul is "simple, and of a perfect and noble nature. Its essence derives from the essence of the Creator, just as sunshine is derived from the sun. It has been explained *[sic]* that the soul is separate from the body and different from it, and that its essence is divine and spiritual in view of the excellence of its nature and its aversion to the passion and irascibility that blight the body".[3]

Now, if the soul is of a divine nature this implies that man can reach a state of excellence, nobility and bliss in this world as well as in the other by purifying his soul from all material contaminations. Just as a "polished" mirror reflects the shapes of all things, similarly a "polished" *(saqilah)* soul, that is, a purified soul, is capable of reflecting the hidden mysteries of the universe. According to Plato, by abandoning the body and returning into its own world, the world of divinity, it acquires a capacity for knowledge and divination, similar to that of the Almighty. The future becomes for it an open book, and it loses all sense of time:

> When the soul attains the utmost degree of purity, it beholds in dreams a world of marvels, and it will be able to converse with those souls that have already separated from their bodies. It gains God's light and mercy, and it will partake of an eternal bliss superior to all other kinds of pleasures derived from food, drink, cohabitation, hearing, sight, smell and touch. These are sensual and defiled plearures that end in pain, but its pleasures are divine, spiritual and heavenly that lead to the utmost nobility.[4]

The soul, then, is simple, and when separated from the body in sleep, is able to foreknow. Furthermore, it is always vigilant, never asleep; and it is immortal. During sleep, it only relaxes its control over the senses but does not lose consciousness. As to its immortality, its presence in this world is of a transitory nature. This earth is only a bridge to the nobler heavenly world where the souls make their permanent abode in proximity to their Creator, and where they see Him intellectually but not sensibly.

Al-Kindi seems not to believe in the eternal punishment of the soul but in its final salvation. Not all souls, however, end immediately in the heavenly world, he says.[5] Some of them separate from their bodies yet retain certain impurities which prevent them, for a time, from reaching that wonderful world. They have to reside in the spheres of the Moon and then of Mercury until they are completely purified from all material impurites. Then, passing the uppermost sphere, they ascend to the intelligible world. This residence in the "purgatory" of the spheres of the planets seems to sufficient to save all souls. I say *all souls* because al-Kindi, unlike the orthodox Muslims who believed that ultimately only Muslim souls will be saved, maintained that salvation is a kind of purification ending in gnosis.

Now, to describe this earth in terms of a "bridge" for the soul, leads us to the consideration whether or not al-Kindi believed in the pre-existence of the soul. It is very hard to prove anything concerning this point; all we can do is to point out a few clues. First, al-Kindi, by characterizing the earth as a bridge, would seem to presuppose that the soul, originally a dweller in eternity, passes transitorily over the "bridge" of the earth in order to re-enter enternity. Another clue consists of a lost treatise by al-Kindi entitled *On the Reminiscences of the Soul in the Intelligible World before its Descent to the Sensible world.* If we are to take this title as indicative of its contents, this evidence would strengthen the view that al-Kindi believed in the pre-existence of the soul. However, the term "bridge" may have been merely a rhetorical simile without philosophical significance; and, we cannot be sure of the contents of the lost treatise. Therefore, until we possess stronger evidence, it would be risky to affirm that al-Kindi departed from the accepted Islamic view of the creation of the soul and its immortality.

As to the relation of the soul to the body, al-Kindi maintains that it is accidental. He emphasizes the soul's separateness from the body and its substantiality, but introduces a novel idea in the sense that the action of the soul on the body constitutes the form of the body.

In his treatise *On the Definition of Things,* al-Kindi gives three different definitions of the soul, two Aristotlian and one Pythagorean, but does not voice any personal opinions. Meanwhile, in his short treatise entitled *A Discourse on the Soul,* he tries to reconcile Plato and Aristotle in a manner which anticipates the method of the Arab-Muslim Philosophers. Still more important is his anticipation of Avicenna in the theory that the soul is the intelligible form of a living being (its species), or to put it differently, the soul is what makes a particular living being a member of a living species. The term *form* sounds Aristotelian but it is not so; an intelligible form is a self-subsisting substance united to the body through its action. The idea that the soul (though not its actions) can exist separate from its body is brought in to reconcile the two points of view, the Aristotelian and the Platonic.

The union between soul and body is not to be understood as similar to the union that occurs between elements in transmutation and transformation; rather it is a union of action and passion. The soul acts on the body it is the form of the living human being in the sense that it acts on the body in its particularizing capacity but not as one with it in substantiality. It inhabits the body, but is not essentially one with it. In fact, it is always striving to free itself from all material ties and from the rigid limits of this obscure world which keep it away from the light of the intelligible world. It is immortal *(la tadthur)* and does not die with the body.

As to how the soul acts on the body, it must be pointed out that al-Kindi equates the soul to the intellectual faculty in man, or to his reason. And he affirms that the human mind is a denizen of two worlds. The soul as a separate substance belongs to the intelligible world but its field of action while in this world is the human body. In his treatise *A Discourse on the Soul,* al-Kindi says, "Both (Plato and Aristotle) prove somewhere in their writings that the soul performs its actions on the bodies that suffer generation and corruption through the agency of *(bitawassut min al-falak)* the heavenly bodies"[6] and he hastens to explain that this means that the action of the soul on the body is not like the action of one corporeal body on another, but like the actions of the planets on a corporeal body. According to al-Kindi, Aristotle maintains that the soul "is a simple substance manifesting its actions in the bodies"[7] while Plato maintains that the soul is "united to a body"; he interprets the expression *united to a body* to mean a celestial body *(jirm)* by means of which the actions of the human soul are manifested in the corporeal body *(jism)*. But al-Kindi does not explain to us the exact relationship between the celestial body, which could be the Active Intellect, and the soul. Does the soul realize itself by its own efforts? Is the soul's realization of itself a union with the Active Intellect? The answer to this question in intimately related to al-Kindi's conception of the Acquired Intellect, and this conception is not clear in the extant writings of the Philosopher of the Arabs. It leads to two different and opposite interpretations. However, one interpretation is more probable and that is that he refuses to accept Alexander's opinion which identifies the Acquired Intellect with the Active Intellect, as we shall see later.

B—The Faculties of the Soul

Al-Kindi following Plato, divides the soul into three parts : the intellectual *(al-quwwah al-'aqliyah* القوة العقلية *)*, the passionate *(al-ghadabiyah* الغضبية *)*. and the concupiscent *(al-shahwaniyah* الشهوانية *)*; and like Plato in the *Phaedrus*,[8] he compares the intellectual part to a charioteer and the other two to the two horses that draw the chariot. The two latter parts, he maintains, cannot be one with the intellect. In accordance with the law of contradiction, that which drives cannot be the same as that which is driven.

The division of the soul into three parts is not meant to be an exhaustive classification of all the soul's functions. Al-Kindi mentions three types of faculties: sensation *(al-hiss)*; the middle faculties, which include retention *(al-hifz)*, passion and irascibility, nutrition and growth, as well as the Imaginative Faculty; and the Intellectual Faculty, which is the most important of all.

Sensation is the faculty which perceives the images of sensible objects in their material grab. Its organs are the five external senses, or the "secondary" instruments as al-Kindi calls the eye, the ear, the nose, the tongue and the skin. By secondary, he means less dependable organs whose clarity and strength of perception are determined by their material constitution. Now, since these organs do not remain constantly in a uniform state of health, the images they capture are not always of the same quality. The clarity of images impressed on matter is necessarily determined by the matter on which they, the images, are impressed. All sensibles, hence are determined by the organs in whose bosom they are received and impressed.

Sensation perceives only the particulars, such as the colour, the form, the taste, the voice, the smell of individual objects. And this faculty cannot compose new concepts and images; its actions are limited to sense-perception of the individual bodies. But in spite of his Platonic definition of the soul, al-Kindi sees the function of the faculties with Aristotelian eyes. Not oblivious of the Aristotlian conception of the soul as a unity, he affirms that "the sensitive faculty is nothing else but the soul; it is not in the soul as an organ in the body, but it and the soul are the same thing"

Among the middle faculties, al-Kindi assigns to retention (of memory) the task of storing the forms imparted by the Imaginative Faculty. Recollection does not seem to be one of its functions as is the case with the system of Avicenna.

The passionate faculty is that "which when it moves in man makes him commit great sins".[9] It is identified with anger and compared to a dog. The concupiscent faculty, on the other hand, is defined with sensual desires and compared to a pig.

Al-Kindi mentions also among the middle faculties those of nutrition and growth which in the system of Avicenna are considered as parts of the vegetative soul, but are left unexplained by him.

The most important of the middle faculties is what al-Kindi calls the Imaginative Faculty *(al-musawwitah=formativa)* and identifies with the Greek *phantasia.*[10] Its main function is to make us perceive the sensible individual forms separated from all matter, after the object which first excited this faculty is withdrawn. This means that such function of the Imaginative Faculty is limited to the grasping and representing of particular objects garbed in their sensible qualities; when the Imaginative Faculty has to deal with universal forms, it cannot grasp them in themselves as does the Intellect, but has to express their truth in symbolic or figurative imagery.

It is clear from what has been said that the Imaginative Faculty is different from sensation in several respects. In the first place the sensitive faculty makes us perceive the sensibles in their matter, whereas the Imaginative makes us perceive them separated from matter after the object which excited it is withdrawn. In the second place the sensitive faculty uses secondary instruments in order to perceive, whereas the Imaginative uses a primary instrument, the brain. The third difference between sense and imagination is implied in the second one. Since what is ties to matter cannot be as pure and definite as what is separated from it, the sensible forms perceived by the senses cannct be as pure and definite as the forms grasped by imagination, especially when the senses use instruments much more susceptible to infirmity than the instrument used by the Imaginative. And finally the function of the sense is limited to a passive role of receiving the forms, whereas the Imaginative Faculty, unencumbered by any material attachments, can and does create and compose new forms, such as a flying man, or a winged horse.

The Imaginative Faculty, it must be understood, cannot always perform this function of composing new forms because in waking life it is engaged as an intermediary between the senses and the intellect. And although this faculty functions both in ordinary waking life and in sleep, it is at its best in sleep. Whenever it is disengaged from the senses, as in sleep, its performance gains in strength as well as in clarity. However, this last statement is true only in the case of the ordinary man, for there are certain individuals who are not subject to this law, individuals who are apt to see the forms of things abstracted from matter even when their senses are engaged in material things. These are the *"Elite (al-khawass)* in intelligence, reason and discrimination". Al-Kindi does not clarify the term *elite;* it could, however, mean the philosophers or the prophets, or even both of them.

One of the most important functions of this faculty relates to visions *(sl-ru'ya)*. Al-Kindi was, as far as we know, the first thinker in Islam to introduce into the contemporary thought the theory of vision as a natural and not as a supernatural and animistic phenomenon. According to him, vision, defined from the point of view of the agent, is "the soul's use of cogitation *(fikr)*[11] to the exclusion of the senses". But defined from the point of view of the results, a vision is "the Imaginative Faculty's impression in the soul of the form of any of those things that have forms". The interesting point in this definition is the identification of Imaginative Faculty with cogitation. This is not original with al-Kindi, but, most probably, to him goes the honour of introducing it into Muslim thought with all the implications it carries in regard to the theory of prophecy.

In antiquity the central problem of the theory of visions was not whether or not visions represent the truth, but why there are differences in the clarity and veracity of the various Kinds of visions. Whereas it was taken for granted, almost universally, that visions are symbols of truth, there was no agreement on the sources and causes of visions. Al-Kindi asks himself, in his treatise *On Sleep and Vision,* the following four questions: Why do we sometimes foresee things directly? Why are things to come represented sometimes in our visions by means of symbols? Why do these symbols at times represent their opposites? And finally, why do we sometimes have visions that have no connection, symbolic or otherwise, with any future happenings?

As to the causes of true visions, al-Kindi upholds that the soul knows by nature and is the seat of all intelligibles and sensibles. Now, if a person becomes prepared for the perfect reception of the forms by purifying himself from all those accidents that harass the reception, the soul can foresee the exact occurrence of things; or it can see the symbols of what will occur, if it is less perfectly purified. The purification of the soul is what makes the Imaginative Faculty more receptive; it does not have to serve the senses but only the intellect.

This capacity of the soul to foretell the future is illustrated in the treatise *On the Soul*[12] by a story presumably told by Aristotle of a Greek king who became disquieted, and who for several days lingered between life and death. When he came to, he instructed the people in the occult sciences. He informed them of the souls, forms, and angels he had seen. And as a proof of his true experience, he told a group of his close relatives the age of each one of them. His estimate proved accurate in every case. He also predicted that within a year an abyss would be opened in the land of *al-aws* (probably Greece), and a flood would occur in some other place within two years. All happened exactly as he had predicted.

When the Imaginative Faculty is less prepared for reception, the soul represents future events in symbolic forms. The soul uses the Imaginative Faculty to impress and to store the realities it sees in the invisible world. But the Imaginative Faculty is not of the same strength in all men; some have stronger and purer faculties. The strong ones receive and register the intelligible forms as they are in their original purity, whereas the poor ones, either because they are weaker by nature or because they are not so pure, distort these forms into symbols which we must interpret in order to understand them. For example, a man may dream that he is flying, yet the true meaning of such a dream can be a journey he will undertake, or when one dreams of the sudden death of a friend, the friend may live longer than expected.

In al-Kindi's conception of visions there are, therefore, three categories : the direct visions of the very pure souls and strong Imaginative Faculties which are received always corresponding to the truth and not needing interpretation; the two other categories are what we may call symbolic visions. The first of the two is the vision nearer to the truth and symbolized by events similar but not corresponding to the truth. The other is farther away from the truth and symbolized by events opposite to the truth. These two categories of visions, i.e. symbolic visions, are compared by al-Kindi to opinions (*zann* = doxa). An opinion is not always false; neither it is always true. It corresponds to the truth whenever it leans towards something truthful or it corresponds to a falsehood whenever it leans towards something untrue. When a symbolic vision falls nearer to the truth, it must be interpreted allegorically, but when it falls away from the truth, we have to look for its opposite in order to find out what it means. There is no explanation, however, as how to distinguish between a symbolic vision that is leaning towards the truth and the one that is not. Nonetheless, both visions indicate the coming of an event, or a fact and the difference between the two lies in the manner the event, or the fact, is represented in our dreams. This should answer the third question.

As to the fourth question, why do we see things that do not indicate any future event, al-Kindi says that persons weakest in imagination do not really dream but hallucinate. What they see bears no semblance to the truth nor to its opposite; their dreams are merely and simply a natural phenomenon without any significance.

One gathers from all this that the Imaginative Faculty is on the border-line between sense and intellect, that it makes us perceive the individual forms after the object which first excited it has withdrawn; that it stores these forms in the retentive faculty and can compose out of them new images; that, although its perception of the forms is purer than that of the senses, it cannot grasp the intelligibles in themselves; it can represent them, however, with a sensible image, and finally that it is used by the soul in connection with visions and dreams.

Coming to the question of prophecy, according to al-Kindi, the *"elite"* which could include the prophet as well as the philosopher, are distinguished from the others by a strong Imaginative Faculty, which enables them to foresee things in their true realities. The principle used by al-Kindi is that the Imaginative Faculty represents in a sensible image the universal truths grasped by the philosopher or the prophet. This type of knowledge is rather intellectual and depends on the purity of the soul. Hence there is no difference between the philosopher and the prophet in this respect, for both can, through the use of their Imaginative Faculties, come to know the same truths with the same certainty.

Al-Kindi, however, makes a clear distinction between the way by which the philosopher comes to know and the way by which the prophet comes to know. The philosopher seeks knowledge by delving into mathematics and logic; he has to work hard to reach certainty, whereas the prophet is inspired by God. "God inspires him (the prophet) and enlightens his soul without resorting to the use of any first principles." But apart from this, the prophet expresses himself much more concisely and clearly. His knowledge, being direct, is the clearest and most dependable. It is true that the prophet and the philosopher may know the same truth but the pronouncements of the prophets are more dependable because of their divine inspiration.

We can add a final note and say that al-Kindi's theory of prophecy is not really well developed. The contribution of the Philosopher of the Arabs to this field lies in his establishment of the relation between the Imaginative Faculty and visions, which relation became the basis of the more developed and elaborate theories of al-Farabi and Avicenna.[13]

C—Mind

To overcome the difficulties of presenting a satisfactory reconstruction of al-Kindi's theory on the mind, one has to cope with the problem of the scarcity of material, the lack of clarity or articulation, and the modern misinterpretations of his ideas.

Al-Kindi left us only one treatise *On the Intellect*,[14] neither long enough nor clear enough to render our task easy. The recent discovery of the original Arabic text, however, enables us to re-assess with more exactitude the nature of his theory and its place in Arab-Muslim philosophy.

Mind is defined by al-Kindi as a "simple essence cognizant of things in their true realities."[15] There are four intellects,[16] the first of which is separate and seems to be construed in the image of Aristotle's active intellect. It exists outside the human soul; it is divine and always in actuality. And although al-Kindi, like al-Farabi and Ibn Sina, believed that the celestial spheres possess intellects, there seems to be no indication that our philosopher ever thought of the First Intellect as the intellect of the moon, better known as the "Donator of Forms", as maintained by the above-mentioned philosophers.

The secondary intellects, three in number, refer to the human intellect, and are similar, in more than one respect, to the passive intellect of Aristotle. They are not separate from the soul as the First Intellect is. Their trinity corresponds to the three states in the soul's pursuance of abstract knowledge and its conveyance.

The second intellect--called by al-Kindi "Intellect in

Potentiality"-- is the state of pure potentiality in the soul. It is the mere disposition to receive sense impressions as well as intelligent forms. In other words, it is the human mind before having received any sensible or intelligible forms.

The third intellect is the Acquired Intellect.[17] It is the human mind after having passed from potentiality into actuality, that is, after having united with the intelligible forms and becoming one with them. As in Aristotle, the intelligent and the intelligible become one and the same thing.[18] But what does it mean to have united with the intelligibles, or to have become an acquired intellect? Where do the intelligibles come from? What is the exact relation of Acquired Intellect to the First Intellect and to the Intellect in Potentiality?

Most probably, al-Kindi uses the word "acquired" to indicate the fact that the intellect is acquired by the soul from outside, i.e. from the First Intellect which causes the Intellect in Potentiality to pass into actuality by uniting with the intelligibles. However, there seems to be a less probable meaning of the term "acquired"; namely that the intellect is an acquisition *(qunyah)* already gotten and can be used at will. The intellect does not come into actuality until after it comes into possession of the universals which make it what it is.

But in spite of its positive character--being in actuality--this intellect does not exhibit any dynamic traits. Al-Kindi compares it to a writer's art of writing, that is to the developed ability of a writer, but not to the process of writing at a precise moment. As we shall see later, the difference between the Acquired and the Demonstrative Intellects shows clearly this static trait of the Acquired Intellect and the dynamic trait of the Demonstrative.

Now, as to the relation of the Acquired Intellect to the First Intellect, we have said above that the Acquired is a state of actuality, meaning that it has united with the intelligible forms. But it is hard to determine the exact nature of the union because the way in which al-Kindi expresses his ideas in regard to this relation does not permit us to determine wherefrom do the intelligibles originate. The linguistic complications of all the references to this problem in al-Kindi's writings make it extremely difficult to determine a precisely meaningful standpoint. One has to search among various references for a ray of hope. One such ray is the clear distinction made by al-Kindi in the sense that the union between intelligent and intelligible is in respect of the soul only and not in respect of the First Intellect which remains always and in all cases separate.[19]

There are two texts where al-Kindi talks of the Acquired Intellect. In the first one he says: "The Universals when found in the soul in actuality, after having been in potentiality, are the Acquired Intellect of the soul, an intellect which it (the soul) possessed in potentiality. They (the universals) are the intellect in actuality which made the soul to pass from potentiality into actuality."[20]

The identification of the Acquired Intellect with the universals smells of Neoplatonism. However, the nature of the Acquired Intellect as it appears in this text remains ambiguous. We do not know whether the intellect is a different aspect of the universals or a perfection of the soul. The fact that al-Kindi mentions the potentiality of the Acquired Intellect lends some weight to the latter alternative.

In the second text, al-Kindi refers to the Acquired Intellect as the "form which is not material nor of the nature of imagination (the soul possessed it in potentiality) and is given to the soul by the First Intellect which is the species of the things that are always in actuality".[21] When the soul unites with the above form, it becomes one with it; the intelligent and the intelligible are the same thing. At this point al-Kindi adds significantly that the union of the intelligent and the intelligible concerns only the soul and not the First Intellect. It is soul itself which has realized itself and was converted into actuality. This conclusion, I believe, should surprise nobody because of its consistency with the philosophy of al-Kindi which repudiates emanation as a solution.

Now, if the Acquired Intellect is the perfection of the soul--and not the First Intellect united with the human soul--how are we to understand the reference that the Acquired Intellect causes the soul to pass from potentiality into actuality.[22] Such an action is reserved usually for the separate First Intellect. We are in an empty desert with no clear text from al-Kindi to lead us out of the difficulty. However, al-Kindi *seems* to have followed Aristotle in considering the First Intellect as "a sort of positive state like light; for in a sense light makes potential colours into actual colours".[23] The First Intellect changes the Intellect into potentiality from its state of acquisition in potentiality to a real acquisition in actuality when the universals are united with it. And just as the rays of the sun which illumine a dark place turn darkness into light without the sun suffering any change, so do the universals turn the state of readiness into a state of perfection without the First Intellect suffering any change. The universals cause the potentiality to pass into actuality by virtue of their being an instrument of the First Intellect and by virtue of their being one with it. Touched by the magic light of the First Intellect, the universals shine into actuality.

Actualization or knowledge accrues through ascendant stages from the sensible to the imaginative, from the imaginative to the intellectual. The first stage is sense perception. The senses are employed by the soul to receive the sensible forms (sense impressions) emitted by the various individuals of external objects. On being received by the soul, they are not received as a vase receives water, or a piece of wax an impression; the sense perceived and the soul become one and the same thing.

The second stage is the imaginative which al-Kindi

calls phantasy, and whose function consists in preserving the forms separated from matter whether they come from the phenomenal or the intellectual world. Now, when the forms are received and are "ready", i.e. abstracted from matter, the soul gets in touch with the First Intellect and is acted upon. The intelligible forms which are potential in it, are then converted into actuality.

Finally, the universals are registered in the Imaginative Faculty in a material garb, this being the only garb with which man can dress up his concepts and ideas.

As to the fourth intellect, or the last of the secondary intellects, this is described by al-Kindi as that which "upon being brought by the soul is made present to others in actuality". This is to say that the fourth of the intellects is a manifestation of the soul when it is in active contact with the First Intellect. One has to see in this another faculty of the mind and not simply another function of the Acquired Intellect. The Acquired Intellect refers to an *effect* of the union of the intelligible form with the human intellect. The Demonstrative Intellect,[24] on the other hand, refers to a *process*, the process of bringing out the intelligibles into open action. To use the analogy of writing, the third intellect would be equal to the positive ability which one acquires by learning how to write. The fourth would be equal to the process of writings when one is actually writing.

This quadripartite division of the mind is interesting and problematic at the same time. What is the source of such a division; was it Alexander of Aphrodisiac, *Peri Nou*, or was it some other commentator of Aristotle, or was it Aristotle himself? It is very hard to know. Up till now, those who attribute the origin to Alexander are many; they maintain that the functions of the four intellects of al-Kindi are, more or less, the same functions which Alexander assigns to his three intellects. There are, however, many proofs against such an attribution. Al-Kindi himself never mentions Alexander but Aristotle and Plato as a source. After comparing the only Arabic translation extant of *Peri Nou* with al-Kindi's treatise, I found no parallels in either to warrant immediate dependence on Alexander's work. Furthermore, the terms used by al-Kindi and the Alexandrian translator to denominate the intellects are completely different, the only exception being the Acquired Intellect. Besides, al-Kindi does not believe in the identity of the First Intellect and the Acquired Intellect whereas Alexander does.[25]

As a final word on this subject, we can say that al-Kindi, although he did not probe deep into the noetic problem, set a model for later Muslim philosophers by introducing a fourth intellect and establishing the bases for the theory of abstraction.

NOTES

1. See Appendix I, Nos. 193-5, 197-9.

2. Those who maintained the eternity of the world and that it is self-moving without the need for a first mover. They believed also that time has no beginning or end. They were rightly considered followers of the Democritan system. Cf. al-Ya'qubi, *Ta'rikh,* Bulaq, 1263/1847, p. 235, also al-Ghazali, *Deliverance from Error,* tr. by W. Montgomery Watt, London, 1953, p. 30.

3. *Rasa'il,* I : 273.

4. *Ibid.,* 277.

5. This is a Hermetic idea found in *Poimandres,* I : 25-6. *Corpus Hermeticum,* Tome I, text established by A. D. Nock, and translated into French by A. J. Festugiere, Paris, 1945.

6. *Rasa'il,* I : 281.

7. *Loc. cit.*

8. Plato, *Phaedrus,* 253.

9. *Rasa'il,* I : 273-4.

10. The function of the Imaginative Faculty is much more similar to Aristotle's *phantasia, De Anima,* iii. 3. 429a1, than to the elaborate functions of the same faculty as construed later by al-Farabi and Avicenna.

11. It is difficult to ascertain the source of the identification between cogitation the Imaginative Faculty. We know, however, that John of Damascus mentioned that the "cogitative faculty *(almufakkirah)* is also that which in dreams tells us future events, which alone the Pythagoreans, following the Hebrews, declare to be true divination". One also can trace this identification further back to Aristotle's calculative imagination, *De Anima,* iii 10, 433b 29, in which he associates cogitation with imagination. Yet it is only in John of Damascus that we find this association extended so as to include dreams. Avicenna indentified this faculty cogitation in his early writings on the soul, but later on he made a definite and clear distinction between the two. Now, in view of the fact that cogitation was connected first by John of Damascus and later by al-Kindi with dreams, this association of imagination, dreams and prophecy could have given rise to those speculations on the connections between imagination and prophecy which we find in late Arab-Muslims philosophy.

12. *Rasa'il,* I : 279. Professor R. Walzer suggests that this fragment was taken from an Aristotelian work *Eudemos,* no longer extant. See R. Walzer, "Un frammento nuovo di Aristotle", *Studi Italiani di Filologia Classica* (New Series), XIV (1937), 125-37. However, the theory of the purity of the soul as the means to foreknowledge can be traced all through history from Pythagoras to Cardano. Plato in his *Republic,* x, 614; Cicero, *De Divinatione,* I, 30; and the *Corpus Hermeticum,* xiii, 1-11 maintain such a theory. Most probably al-Kindi adopted it from the Harranians who upheld similar ideas and were followers of Hermes.

13. As to position of the prophet in society and his role as a law-giver it is not discussed in the extant writings of al-Kindi. We know that al-Kindi wrote a treatise entitled *On the Affirmation of Prophecy, al-Fihrist,* p. 362, but its contents are not available to us either directly or otherwise so that we may be able to form an opinion on this very important problem in Muslim thought. See also F. Rahman, *Prophecy in Islam,* London, 1958, pp. 37-8.

14. See Appendix II.

15. *Rasa'il,* I : 165.

16. This quadripartite division is attributed by al-Kindi to Aristotle.

17. *Al-'aql al-mustafad;* and in the Latin translation of John *Intellectus adeptus.*

18. Aristotle, *De Anima,* 43a 3-4, 431b 17.

19. *Rasa'il* I : 356.

20. *Ibid.,* I : 155.

21. *Ibid.,* I : 356.

22. There seems to be some doubt as to the antecedent of the "species of things". Abu Ridah maintains that the antecedent is the Acquired Intellect. Although it is possible in Arabic to have such a construction, it is by overtaxing a mere possibility that one can assume the antecedent to be the Acquired Intellect.

23. W. D. Ross, *op. cit.,* p. 150.

24. Our use of the term "Demonstrative" is based on the authority of both the Latin translations of *On the Intellect* (see Appendix I, No. 22). The Arabic manuscript which Abu Ridah and al-Ahwani edited separately reads *al-thani,* i.e. the second, written in this form الثانى Such a reading, which is most probably an error of the copyist, is not acceptable because al-Kindi uses *al-thani* to denominate the human intellect in a general sense, and because al-Kindi calls this same intellect "demonstrative" الظاهر at the end of the treatise. Dr. A. Badawi in the introduction to his edition and new translation of Aristotle's *De Anima,* Cairo, 1954, p. 6, intro., refers to this problem and suggests the plausible reading of البيانى.

25. Those who maintain that Alexander talked about three intellects and that al-Kindi drew upon Alexander's *Peri Nou* are: G. Thery, O. P. in his *Author de Decret de 1210 : II. Alexndre d'Aphrodise,* apercu sur l'influence de sa noetique. *Bibliotheque Thomiste* VII, Le Soulchoir, Kain, 1927; and E. Gilson in his article "Les Sources Greco-Arabes de l'Augustinisme Avicennisant" in *Archives d'Historie Doctrinale et Litteraire du Moyen Age,* IV (1929), pp. 5-27. There are those who believe that Alexander has maintained four intellects

and not only three as it is commonly accepted. Hence, al-Kindi's and al-Farabi's quadripartite division could, very possibly, have come from Alexander. Cf. F. Rahman, *Avicenna's Psychology*, Oxford, 1952, p. 89. On the other hand, Prof. Abu Ridah of Egypt believes that the third intellect of al-Kindi is identical with Aristotle's *intellectus habitus* and the Demonstrative Intellect of al-Kindi is a different aspect of the function of Aristotle's *intellectus habitus*. Aristotle and not Alexander must be the source of al-Kindi's division. Abu Ridah was challenged later by J. Finnegan, S. J., in an article entitled "al-Farabi et le *Peri Nou* d'Alexandre d'Aphrodise" in *Melanges Louis Massignon*, II, Damascus, 1957. Although Rev. Finnegan accepts Abu Ridah's removal of Alexander as a source, he doubts that Aristotle could be that source.

5

ETHICS

A—Al-Kindi's Ethical Theory

Muslim ethics[1] is two-dimensional. It is based first on the Qur'an and Traditions in which we find, as in Christianity, a belief in the Day of Judgement and that virtuous deeds weigh heavily on that Day. The ethical code is regarded as divine commands revealed to the human race through a series of prophets of which Muhammad is the last. Any deviation from these divine commands is punishable by the strictest measures. The second dimension is built upon the assumption that the human person, in front of the Law, has an irreducible value derived from God, the creator and the holder of the balance of justice.

Hence we find side by side in the Muslim ethical literature a cumbersome legalism hindering, in my opinion, the fullest realization of the human personality, and a humanism founded on the interiorization of the concept of freedom, or on the emancipation of the mind. Many a Muslim who felt that the strict observance of law was not always conducive to a high or noble morality sought in Wisdom[2], the realization of his personality. The moral principles he cherished were either inspired by the remote experiences of his environment or derived from the Greek ethical literature.

Greek ethical thought must have passed to the Arabs both orally[3] and in a written form through translation. By the time of al-Kindi, the ethical works that had been already translated did not amount to a large number. Nevertheless, the indelible mark of the Greek influence on al-Kindi's ethical thought is seen throughout his few extant writings on the subject. This naturally determined for him his main problem, namely, to reconcile, within a logical framework, the Greek tradition with the Islamic.

Out of twelve treatises[4] written by al-Kindi on the general topic of politics, only two complete ones have reached us. With the few fragments in *al-Muntakhab* including some anecdotes, maxims and selected paragraphs, mainly from his lost ethical works, they constitute our only source of information.

A striking characteristic of the materials that we have is the apparent departure from the current ethical theme which occupied the Muslims of al-Kindi's time. They all seem to have been based on late Hellenistic popular literature and do not fit easily within the framework of the hitherto known genra of Arabic literature. This should not mean that al-Kindi was not aware of the very important problem of freewill versus determinism which was hotly debated at the time by the Mu'tazilities on one side and orthodox Muslims on the other. He wrote a book *On that Actions of Creator are all Just* which we presume must have contained ideas along the Mu'tazilite line of thinking : upholding the theory that God can do only what is best *(al-aslah).* Furthermore his Greek-oriented method is not incompatible with his ethical position as a Mu'tazilite. In fact it strengthens his position since the Mu'tazilites start from the Greek principle that reason is sound.

Among Arab-Muslim philosophers, Wisdom is divided into two main branches : a theoretical one and a practical one.[5] The first aims at certainty in the knowledge of those things whose existence does not depend on man; the second aims at the formulation of sound opinions, concerning those actions that convince man to do the good. Having to do with actions, ethics belongs therefore to the second branch. The position of the first of the philosophers is no exception to this rule.

In his treatise *De Quinque Essentiis,* he also divides philosophy in two branches : theoretical *('ilm)* and practical *('amal);* he further justifies the division on the basis of the dichotomy in the soul's nature into intellectual and sensible souls. Practical philosophy corresponds to the sensible soul and is divided into several sciences which al-Kindi did not think it was then opportune to enumerate in a treatise dedicated to the theoretical sciences.[6] There is no reason, however, not to presume that the practical sciences include ethics : the study of man's actions as an individual, as a member of a family and as a member of society. There are those who include the Muslim Divine Law and Prophecy as a fourth science, but as far as al-Kindi is concerned, we cannot safely presume that he ever considered the science of Law and Prophecy as a branch of political science. If he ever did, he would have been the first Muslim to do so.

Al-Kindi, as we have seen,[7] considers that the final aim of philosophy lies in its relation to morality. The philosopher's aim is both to know the truth and to act accordingly. This means that wisdom, the highest aspiration of man, combines in itself speculation and action without necessarily implying the identification of knowledge and virtue as in Socrates. Al-Kindi rather approaches the Stoic ideal of *Sophia* with one big difference : that virtue and speculation are not to be sought for their own sake but as a means to the happiness one finds in knowing God. Hence the purpose of the ethical science is to know in order to acquire virtue and avoid evil. Knowledge is not only necessary to discriminate between Good and Evil but also to help preserve the purity of the soul which is the only means to conjoin[8] the light of the Creator and thus attain real happiness. Philosophy is, in a sense, the emulation of the Creator who is wise and just; therefore by imitating Him, we bring ourselves nearer to Him.[9]

Of special interest is al-Kindi's theory of the natural inclination of man to do the good. Al-Kindi thinks that by virtue of the mind's divine nature, man has a propensity to do the good. Evil is not appropriate to his nature. "What is just is true to man's nature, what is evil is only an accident."[10] Evil results from the triumph of passion over reason. In the conflict that ensues from the residence of the soul in the human body, knowledge helps keep under control the onslaughts of our senses. Hence virtue results from doing what is only natural to man : keeping the passions under control in order to let man's nature run its proper course. Consequently virtue and vice are voluntary actions. The good is a choice between being ourselves or being similar to animals. It is also a choice of values. The Platonic dichotomy of the universe into an intellectual and a phenomenal world is adapted by al-Kindi; and thus he is led to value the intellectual world and the spiritual possessions as the only true and lasting things worthy of any consideration. Our residence in this phenomenal world is transitory;[11] it is a journey towards the eternal one. The most miserable man, he says, is he who prefers for himself the material above the spiritual,[12] for the material, apart from its ephemeral nature, obstructs our passage to the spiritual world. Man should "not disregard any means to protect himself against all human vices, and he should seek to rise to the highest ends of human virtue......., that is, to the knowledge by means of which we protect ourselves against spiritual and bodily diseases, and acquire the human virtues in whose very essence goodness is grounded."

However, when al-Kindi comes to define virtue he sounds less otherworldly. Human virtues seem to preoccupy him greatly but without overshadowing the importance and value of the divine virtues. The way to worldly happiness, he says, is to reduce to a minimum all external possessions, which cause only sorrow, and the way to otherworldly happiness is to know God and to perform those actions which we know bring us nearer to Him.[14]

Now, if al-Kindi's main principles of ethics are

Platonic and Islamic, the constituent elements of virtue are Aristotelian. He defines virtue as a "praiseworthy human disposition,"[15] and he adopts the four cardinal virtues of Plato : wisdom, courage, continence, and justice. The first three are virtues of the soul, meaning that they are harmonious actions within the soul itself. The fourth is an "activity of the soul outside the body," which, it may be presumed, means an activity within the body social, because justice refers to man's harmonious actions within the realm of social relations. Moreover, when al-Kindi refers to the harmonious activities of all the elements in the soul and in relation to each other he uses the term equilibrium *(i'tidal),* and not justice *('adl).*

To al-Kindi the term *'adl* also signifies the golden mean. It is the happy balance between the two extremes of excess and deficiency. The very essence of the soul's true actions is moderation *(i'tidal)* which is derived from the golden mean *('ald).*[16] "The golden mean is found in all things, and it is the essence of true nature *(al-tab' al-haqqi),* because accidents are deviations from the true mean, between the extremes of excess and deficiency. The mean of the discriminating faculty is neither to fall short of the very useful truth, not to lean towards falsehood, i.e., the evils of cunning, trickery, etc. The mean of the irascible faculty is neither to eat less than is necessary to keep one alive, nor to overeat as to make a man sick and his soul unable to perform its noble duties.[17] The mean of the passionate soul is not lack in courage, that is, not to slight bodily injuries or to minimize the importance of protecting ourselves against misfortune, nor is it to overstep our limits and grab what is not ours, or to fall a victim to anger, stupidty and wrath.[18] What is natural to ourselves, therefore, is wisdom, justice, continence and courage. Their opposites, although found in us, are accidents and do not belong to us by nature.[19]

Moreover, al-Kindi mades use of another Aristotelian idea, namely, that the objects of our love and hate depend on habit and frequent use. How can we, then develop the habit of doing what is virtuous? The answer of al-Kindi is linked to a great extent with what he adopted from the Hellenistic tradition.

B—Al-Kindi and the Hellenistic Ethical Tradition

We have seen above on several occasions how al-Kindi's work is influenced by late Hellenistic thought. However, in the case of his ethics, this influence is most evident. For although al-Kindi changed the end of virtue so as to conform to the Islamic point of view, the form of his ethical writings, and to a great extent the content, remained Hellenistic. We possess a certain number of maxims, a treatise, and a collection of Socratic analects which demonstrate unequivocally this truth.

Maxims are very common in popular and classical Arabic literature and are frequently employed by Orientals as a general rule. However, the collection of maxims which al-Kindi left us is not the kind of witty sayings that characterize Arabic popular maxims. They are rather counsels exhorting man to self-improvement and to the ennoblement of his soul. They are humanistic in nature for they underline the soundness of man's just actions. Here are some of them : He who takes justice for a law is well defended. He who conducts himself truthfully, nothing does he miss. Honesty is an armour of protection. Treason of friends is the worst kind of bankruptcy.

On the Means to Drive Away Sorrow is the only complete ethical work of al-Kindi that has reached us. Its theme is centered no sorrow, its nature, causes and the means to prevent its coming or overstaying.

In the first part which is a general exposition, with a certain degree of theorizing, al-Kindi deals with the causes of sorrow. This is a psychological pain, he says, resulting from the loss of what is dear to one's heart.

It is common to all human beings since we all seek and desire the things that are by nature subject to generation and corruption.

Sorrow is also caused by desiring what is difficult to obtain, and by strongly anticipating the things we would like to own, and by a sense of affliction, should we lose them.

To avoid sorrow, one should look upwards at the intelligible world and should confine one's desires and objects of love to those things that really matter, the things that are indestructible and always accompany us. We should also maintain a certain spiritual equilibrium by limiting the objects of our desire to what is possible to obtain, and by reducing our sense of anticipation for the things we desire and of affliction for the things that we lose.

Man should know that sorrow is either the result of our own actions, or of certain forces that are beyond our control. If it is within our power, we have to refrain from such actions as result in sorrow. Should we give vent to our passions, we will lose our freedom and make fools of ourselves. Now, if on the other hand, sorrow results from actions that are beyond our control, by realizing that what is subject to generation and corruption does not last for ever we can shorten its duration. Furthermore, one should never feel miserable when it is possible for one to be content.

Al-Kindi then goes on, in the second part, to give a series of practical advice. The best advice to avoid sorrow, he counsels, is to remember our past sorrows with which we have been consoled, and the sorrows of others with which they have been consoled. He illustrates this principle by referring to an apocryphal anecdote taken from the Hellenistic legends of Alexander the Great. Anticipating his death, Alexander tried to console his mother by making her dramatically realize the evident rule that man cannot change the laws of nature.

He wrote her saying: "Oh, mother of Alexander....... should you ever hear of your son's death, try not to forget that he has not adopted for himself the manner of the idle kings. Therefore, you his mother, should also refrain from adopting these manners for yourself. Upon hearing of his death, see to it that a big new city is built, and that people from Africa, Europe and Asia are invited to its inauguration. And ask your guests to celebrate the occasion by eating, drinking and getting merry. But, when you send out the invitation, make it clear that only those people who have not suffered any disgrace are welcome, because a funeral cannot be celebrated merrily unless the people who take part in such a celebration have not experienced sorrow."[20]

Upon hearing the news of his death, the mother gave orders to put into effect her son's last wishes. On the specified date for the inauguration, to her surprise and dismay, nobody showed up. Then she said, "How come that people have not responded to our invitation?" And she was answered, "You have invited only those who have not suffered any disgrace, and since they do not exist, how could they possibly have showed up for the celebration." She then said, "Oh Alexander! how similar is your end to your beginning, you wanted, in a most kind way, to console me out of my disgrace in losing you, by having me find out that I am not the first unhappy woman, not that I am singled out for disgrace."

The second practical advice is correlated to the principle that true riches are not material by nature. What constitute true riches is the spiritual wealth whose loss should really make us feel most unhappy. Material wealth is a common property in our custody loaned to us by the Almighty, who is able to retrieve it at any time. Being in the nature of a loan, man should never feel sorry to turn this wealth over its lawful owner. In fact, material possessions are the cause of man's suffering, and a wiseman should never invite suffering to corrode his own soul. Socrates is cited as an example and he is made to say that he never gets sorry because he never owned anything whose loss he could fear. Consequently he who is really wise tries to avoid sorrow by possessing little or no material objects. Al-Kindi refers to another anecdote to illustrate this second principle. Nero and not Alexander is the hero this time.

Nero was offered a most beautiful canopy. A philosopher who was present at the time advised him to turn down the offer. He counselled saying : "If you should ever lose this canopy, you will never be able to replace it. Great will be your sorrow, for your poverty in front of the impossible will be laid bare." But the advice of the philosopher went unheeded. Nero went picnicking one day and he ordered that the canopy be shipped to him. The boat carrying the highly cherished load sank, and the emperor hopelessly tried to replace his lost canopy. Unable to find a similar one, he died of his great sorrow.

The struggle to overcome sorrow, therefore, is an internal struggle over external possessions. Human life is compared by al-Kindi to a journey in a small boat full of passengers. Among them are some, who like to load all kinds of perishables, others prefer to travel light with no material possessions or with very little of them. The space on the ship assigned to each passenger is limited and those who fill it up with extras will naturally suffer from the narrowness of the space for relaxtion.

To the two principle causes of sorrow : loss of externals and failure to attain what we highly cherish, al-Kindi adds a third principle, the fear of death. However, he explains that death is only a fulfilment of our human nature, and therefore one should never fear what is only natural since this is the result of causes beyond our control.

It is interesting to note how al-Kindi adopted the Cynic ideals of despising the externals and of educating the soul but tempered them down to practicable measures. For he is unlike them in regard to material possessions, he only thinks 'the less the better'.

The third work of al-Kindi where we find the Hellenistic tradition most apparent is his collection of Socratic analects known as *The Maxims of Socrates.*[21] Moreover, al-Kindi is the first Muslim to be inspired by the personality of Socrates. His many works on the different aspects of the Socratic teaching and personality show unmistakably his administration of the Greek philosopher. Being both victims of persecution for the sake of the truth, this could have attracted al-Kindi to the personality of Socrates, and it explains why he devoted a whole work to the subject of his death. The theme of Socrates' death was of special interest among certain philosophical circles. We know that the Brethren of Purity *(Ikhwan al-Safa)* compared the death of Socrates to that of Jusus and the martyrs of Karbala.[22]

There is some reason to believe that al-Kindi tried to imitate Socrates by living up to the Socratic teachings as he knew them. The several anecdotes in *al-Muntakhab* show al-Kindi a man who, like Socrates, does not seek his fortune in the courts of the kings or the houses of the rich. However, the Socrates known to the Arabs is not exactly the historic Socrates, and not even the Socrates of the early Platonic dialogues. Abu Bakr Muhammad al-Razi, whose death occurred some fifty years later to al-Kindi, tells of two different Socratic traditions current in his time.[23] One upheld by certain critics of al-Razi probably the Theologians, describes Socrates as an ascetic, averse to society and even to the conservation of the human race. The other, upheld by al-Razi himself, makes of Socrates the ideal of moderation, a man who would take up arms to defend his country, who seeks the company of others, and who is a father to several children. The difference in the two traditions is explained by al-Razi by assigning each tradition to a different phase in the life of the Greek philosopher. However it is not difficult to find out the source of the two opposing portraits of the personality of Socrates. During the Hellenistic period a fusion of the portrait of Diogenes the Cynic with that of Socrates took place,[24] which seems to have been uncritically received by the Arabs as it had been relayed to them. The Theologians, therefore, held to the Cynic aspect of this portrait while al-Razi held to the more authentic portrait derived from the *Apology, Phaedo,* and *Crito.* The other Arab authors were even less critical than al-Razi, because they kept the two opposing traditions massed together without even suspecting any contradiction.[25]

However, the general picture one gets from the different Arab authors is essentially synthesized by al-Shahrastani, "Socrates studied wisdom with Pythogoras and Archelaus, but his interest in philosophy was limited to theology and ethics. He practised asceticism, self-discipline and the cultivation of morality. He spurned all mundane pleasures and took to the wilderness of a mountain to live by himself. Because he warned the leaders of his time against idol-worship, they excited the commoners against him and made the king order his death. He was put in prison and administered the hemlock, as it is commonly known." Sa'id adds that Socrates held debates with the king and that he left us "useful counsels, noble maxims and famous dicta. Apart from certain doctrines on divine attributes, similar to those of Pythagoras and Empedocles, his eschatology is weak and distant from pure philosophy, because it deviates radically from the confirmed doctrines."[26]

The portrait of Socrates that we get from al-Kindi's work is that of a great moralizer. The Diogenic anecdotes which portray Socrates as an ascetic are there. His living in a cask, and his famous answer to Alexander (?), "get away from my sun" are there too. But all the anecdotes we have mentioned seem to have been accepted by al-Kindi by virtue of their moralizing spirit, and not as representative of the ascetic tendencies of Socrates. What is more important is that Socrates appears as the champion of the ideal of moderation and of the spiritual values of man. He is a man who refuses to write down his living thoughts because he would not confide them to dead material. He is portrayed as a monotheist opposed to idol-worship, he counsels against external possessions; but upholds the superiority of the spiritual. Spiritual values are the essence of life. All external possessions are ephemeral, whereas the spiritual are everlasting and accompany their owners at all times and under any circumstances. Here we find ourselves confronted with the theme which al-Kindi uses to build his theory on the cause of sorrow and the means to drive it away.

Wisdom is considered of the greatest value and a secure means to real happiness. Death should not frighten us, for the bitterness of death does not result from death itself but from the fear of it. Finally, justice is considered as the greatest of all virtues; what is just is good and what is not is evil. Justice, in other words, is the criterion of good and evil.

The similarity of some of these principles with those used by al-Kindi in the previous work is striking, although not surprising. It should mean that the other ethical works related to Socrates attributed to al-Kindi follow the same trend of thought with regard to spiritual possessions, justice and moderation as the highest virtues.

Moreover these maxims which al-Kindi attributes to Socrates are of great importance in another sense, namely of being, most probably, the oldest collection in Arabic of a series of similar collections found scattered in different Arabic works. Al-Kindi could very easily have served, rather than Hunayn b. Ishaq, as the source for the later Arab authors who wrote about Socrates or collected his maxims.[27]

C—The Place of al-Kindi in Muslim and Western Thought

One of the most interesting document on al-Kindi's place in Muslim thought is the biographical note in *al-Muntakhab,* which not only throws new light on his method and work but also places him in perspective with earlier workers in this field. It says, "Abu Yusuf Ya'qub ibn Isahq al-Kindi was the first to distinguish himself among the Muslims in philosophy and all its branches, and in the exact sciences and every thing connected with them, as well as by his familiarity with the sciences of the Arabs and his execellence in humanities like grammar and poetry, astrology, medicine, various arts and sciences : virtues which are seldom united in a single individual. The list of his books exceeds one quire of paper (24 sheets) folded. He was the tutor to Ahmad b. Muhammad al-Mu'tasim and composed many of his works for him, and addressed to him most of his epistles *(rasa'il)* as well as answers to his queries. He is the first among the Muslims to introduce this form of writing which was later followed by the succeeding (generations of scholars) among the Muslims. During the days of al-Ma'mun those who acquired name and fame before him were mostly Christians who had adopted in their works the old style of writing."

"Due to the fame of his books and treatises and their being widely in circulation as well as being easily accessible at all places, I do not (intend to) exhaust (all) the (salient) points in his writings but would extract from them at random only a few sayings as are indispensable for embellishing this work."[28]

Now, if al-Kindi was the first to distinguish himself among the Muslims in philosophy, in what exactly does this distinction consist? The chief contribution of al-Kindi to Arab-Muslim philosophy lies in his acceptance of Aristotle as great an authority on truth as the religious Law itself. His endevours to naturalize philosophy to the Muslims and his defence of it as a discipline worthy of the utmost consideration gives him a special place as a torch bearer lighting the way for the succeeding generations of Muslim thinkers. He supplanted the half-hearted flirtations of his contemporaries with philosophy with a clearcut and definite acceptance of philosophy as an authoriative means to attaining the truth. By his translations or corrections of translations, by his commentaries and by his own original works, he put on the march the philosophical movement in Islam which culminated in names like Avicenna and Averroes.

Al-Kindi is responsible for introducing the problems of metaphysics, psychology and ethics into Arab-Muslim thought. His approach based on Greek logic and scientific method was later accepted by such a religious authority as al-Ghazali. In other words, he bridged the gap that existed between the rationalism of some of the theologians, like the Mu'tazilities, and pure philosophy. He shares with them, although not always consistently, their attitude towards prophetic knowledge, the theory of Creation out of nothing by the Will of God, and the idea of the unity and justice of God. However, he differs from them in his use of mathematics and logic to prove his hypotheses, in his interest in cultivating the humanistic studies, and perhaps in his deterministic attitude which his adoption of the Aristotelian scheme of the universe and astrology leads to.

Against Aristotle, Plotinus and the Arab philosophers, al-Farabi, Avicenna and Averroes who maintain the eternal creation and emanation of the world, he holds in accordance with the religious view the theory of creation out of nothing, and the active presence of the Will of God. However, we find in his philosophy, in embryonic form, the several Farabian and Avicennian ideas such as the theory of natural prophecy, substantiality of the soul and the division of mind into four classes.

The influence of al-Kindi's "system" was not widely spread although his works were popular. Probably because as philosophy progressed people looked back to al-Farabi and Avicenna as more representative of this discipline. Their more elaborate works and their greater consistency put them in a position which the more conforming al-Kindi could not reach. This may explain to us, at least in part, why al-Kindi's books, so popular in the time of al-Sijistani, became rare and almost extinct after a while.

The opinions about al-Kindi and his philosophy are very diametrically opposed. His fame fluctuated between the two extremes of abhorrence and admiration. Like all innovators, al-Kindi and his philosophy knew both the hatred of the religious fanatics, and the admiration of the devout disciples. He was one of those characters whose thoughts and activities always invite either bitterest disdain or unbounded admiration. During his lifetime his scientific and philosophical activities gained him the enmity of many a commoner and theologian. His encounter with Abu Ma'shar is typical. Al-Qifti reported that a neighbour of his fell very ill, but that he would not call him in, because of al-Kindi's occupation with philosophy.[29] It seems that al-Kindi's admiration for the Greeks and his own philosophical activities won him only the hatred of the orthodox party, in spite of his conforming point of view, during his lifetime as well as in later decades and centuries. Abu Hayyan al-Tawhidi reports that al-Kindi was easily confounded, and that he could not answer many of the questions that were once put to him. "He is the laughing-stock of Sabeans who relate anecdotes about him which would cause the grief-stricken to laugh, the enemy to rejoice, and the friends to sadden. All this was inherited from the 'blessings' of the Greeks and the 'benefits' of philosophy and logic."[30]

Sa'id condemned him for neglecting analysis,[31] and al-Qifti repeated the condemnation two centuries later. However, their condemnations were not caused by his occupation with philosophy, but rather by his apparent failure to utilize Aristotelian logic. Averroes criticized his mathematical method in medicine describing it as illogical and unscientific. 'Abd al-Latif al-Baghdadi, a twelfth century doctor, wrote a treatise on God and His divine attributes, whose only purpose, he says, was to refute the doctrines of al-Kindi.[32]

On the other hand, al-Kindi found favour with the caliphs, and he had many students who appreciated his learning and defended him and what he stood for, such as Abu'l-Tayyib al-Sarakhsi.[33] Al-Mas'udi, in his famous work *Muruj al-Dhabab,* very often quotes him and his student al-Sarakhsi as his authorities on many a scientific subject. Ibn Juljul says that no other thinker in the time of al-Kindi could penetrate into the meaning of Aristotle as he could, and that his commentaries have removed all difficulties and obscurities in understanding the great philosopher.[34] Ibn Nubatah describes him as a jewel for the reign and palace of al-Mu'tasim.[35] Ibn Abi 'Usaybi'ah defends him against the attack of Sa'id and attributes the latter's harsh judgment to prejudice and to Sa'id's purpose to discourage the study of al-Kindi.[36]

As to the influence of al-Kindi in Europe during the Middle Ages, several of his works were translated into Latin and a few into Hebrew.[37]

In an anonymous work by a seventh/thirteenth century author entitled *Tractatus de erroribus philosophorum,* it is said about al-Kindi that he was inclined towards astrology, and was an adept in Alexandrian mysticism. However, the views for which he is unwisely attacked is his doctrine of the ineffability of God, and the fact that he did not admit for Him any positive attributes.

Roger Bacon (1114-1294) praises al-Kindi's knowledge of optics, and Geronimo Cardano (d. 1576) considers him one of the twelve subtlest minds in the history of the world.[38] Albert the Great must have known al-Kindi's treatise *On the Intellect,* and he mentions the Philosopher of the Arabs by name.[39]

Nowadays, the problem of the importance of al-Kindi centers on what place in Arab-Muslim philosophy should he occupy, as also on his originality. He is still not included in the curricula of philosophical studies of most of the Arab countries. Professor Ibrahim Madkur, one of the leading historians of Arab-Muslim philosophy, considers al-Kindi only as a "paver of the way" for al-Farabi and Ibn Sina. For him al-Farabi is the real founder of Muslim philosophy, and al-Kindi is more of a scientist in the actual meaning of the word. 'Ali 'Abd al-Raziq, another leader and pioneer in the same field, shares this opinion and believes that the greatest contribution of al-Kindi was that he introduced new problems and subjects in Arab-Muslim thought.[40] Dr. Fu'ad al-Ahawani, expresses a similar opinion in his introduction to his edition of al-Kindi's treatise *On First Philosophy*.[41]

Professor Muhammad 'Abd al-Hadi Abu Ridah whose very diligent and scholarly edition of al-Kinid's treatise threw new light on the thought of the philosopher upholds a more radical view, namely, that al-Kindi was a consummate philosopher and, therefore he and not al-Farabi is the founder of Arab-Muslim philosophy.[42] The latter, Abu Ridah maintains, built on bases set by al-Kindi. Hence Arab-Muslim philosophy starts with al-Kindi and not with al-Farabi.

As for the originality of al-Kindi, Abu Ridah considers him a very original thinker. He does not seem to have studied al-Kindi's sources with care. F. Rosenthal considers the works of al-Kindi "not to exhibit originality in the highest sense but fulfil a very useful function and may possess that secondary kind of originality that consists in presenting known facts in another light."[43]

There is some truth in what Professor Rosenthal maintains. Al-Kindi, having a rich library at his disposal and access to the House of Wisdom, might have heavily borrowed from Greek and other works in order to epitomize and popularize their contents, an act not considered reprehensible in those days. This conclusion is corroborated by a quotation in *al-Muntakhab* which speaks of a discussion on philosophy at the palace of Abu Ja'far ibn Babuwayh, the King of Sijistan. When the discussion turned around the philosophers of Islam, the King said, "There is nobody among them who can take the place of a Socrates, a Plato or an Aristotle". He was asked, "What about al-Kindi?" He said, "Not even al-Kindi, because in spite of his prolificity and good reasoning, his style is bad and of little taste; and his life is but half-inspiring. He made many inroads on the wisdom of the philosophers." Yet, we cannot honestly maintain that al-Kindi was a mere popularizer of earlier works, he had his own views on the most basic problems of philosophy, such as the creation of the world in time, the final destruction of the universe, the immortality of the soul, which all fit together, to a certain extent into one frame of thought and give some coherence and organic unity to his philosophy.

It is true that he introduced the Aristotelian world view into Arab-Muslim thought, yet his attitude towards the problem of creation sets him apart from the rest of the philosophers. If he were not original in this respect, he was quite independent, and it is in this very fact that we have to look for the peculiarities of his "system" and for his originality.

As for his scientific works, unfortunately, no space can be dedicated to their study in this work. We may, however, say a few words about his scientific activities. In fact, some scholar should devote a whole work to the scientific writings of the great philosopher. It was not in vain that he was considered an engineer and an astronomer. Most of his writings deal with what we call nowadays, the exact sciences. He dealt with mathematics, geometry, spherics, astronomy, engineering, medicine, chemistry, meterology, and many other similar sciences.

Al-Kindi is the earliest Arab writer on music. His writings on this subject contain a notation for the determination of pitch.[44] He considered alchemy a false science.[45] He wrote on geometrical and physiological optics basing his works on Euclid, Heron and Ptolemy. His writings on aspects are based on that of Tideus.[46] In astronomy he depended mainly on Ptolemy or his commentat or Theon. In medicine, he tried to establish that the effectiveness of compounded medicine depends on the mathematical relation between the ingredients of the medicine.[47] His explanations of the blue colour of the sky is of great interest; he also exhibits some originality and independence of thought in this work.

NOTES

1. The best available work on this subject is D. M. Donaldson. *Studies in Muslim Ethics,* London. 1953.

2. See. for example, Abu'l-Hasan al-Mawardi (d. 450/1058). *Adab al-dunya wa'l-din,* ed. M. al-Saqqa, Cairo, 1955, p. 1: "Because man's heart gets bored with a single art, but finds his .rest in experiencing different arts."

3. Pierre Thillet, "Sagesse grecqae et philosophic Musulmane," *Les Mardi de Dar al-Salam,* Sommaire MCMLV (1958), p. 60.

4. See Appendix I, Nos. 200-11.

5. *Rasa'il,* II : 8, Al-Farabi, *Ihsa' al-'Ulum,* ed. Angel Gonzales Palenica, 2nd ed., Madrid, 1953, pp. 67-96; Ibn Sina, Fi taqsim al-'ulum al-'aqliyah in *Tis' Rasa'il,* pp. 105-6.

6. *Rasa'il,* II, 12.

7 See above, p. 20

8. *Rasa'il,* I : 278. Now in the light of a paragraph of al-Kindi's treatise, *A Discourse On the Soul, Abridged and Concise,* which has been preserved in *al-Muntakhab,* fol. 61a, we can correct the text of Abu Ridah which reads *tabaqat nur al-bari* (corresponded to the light of the Creator). The more correct reading would be *wasalat nur al-bari* (conjoined the light of the Creator).

9. *Rasa'il,* I : 274-5. "Plato compared man's irascible faculty to a pig, the passionate to a dog and the intellectual to a king. The man who permits his irascibility to take hold of him is like a pig. He is like a dog if he permits his passionate faculty to overpower him. But he who is mastered by reason and is prone to think, to discriminate, to know the realities of things, and to search in order to unravel the mysteries of science, is a virtuous man similar to God, because the things by which God, is described and which are attributed to Him are : wisdom, power, justice, goodness, beauty and righteousness, and man stands capacitated to emulate these attributes within his own limits."

10. *Al-Muntakhab,* fol. 63b.

11. *Rasa'il,* I : 280 "Don't you know, ye, ignorant man, that your residence in this world is just for a short time, and then you pass into the real world where you remain forever."

12. *Al-Muntakhab,* fol. 65a.

13. *Ibid.*

14. *Ibid.*

15. *Rasa'il,* I : 177.

16. *Ibid.* : 179.

17. The excess of the virtue of the irascible faculty is divided by al-Kindi into three classes to all of which greed is common. Greed for foods and drinks, greed for sexual intercourse, greed for material possessions; the deficiency is laziness Cf. *Rasa'il,* I : 178.

18. *Rasa'il* I : 178. The excess of courage is rashness and recklessness; the deficiency is cowardice.

19. *Al-Muntakhab,* fol. 63b.

20. This same saying is found in *The Maxims of Socrates,* discussed on page 133.

21. See Appendix I.

22. *Episties,* IV : 100, 120, 223, 309.

23. P. Kraus, "Raziana I=*al-Sirah al-Falsafiyah*", *Orientalia.* IV (1935), pp. 300-21.

24. This fusion goes back as far as Epictetus (ca. 55-ca. 135 A.C.) Cf. *Discourse* II : 13, 16; III : 21, 26; IV : 9, 11.

25. *Ta'rikh al-Hukama'*, pp. 197-206; *'Uyan*, I : 43-5; al-Shahrastani, *op. cit.*, pp. 291-2.

26. Sa'id, *op. cit.*, p. 23.

27. Most important is the collection attributed to Hunayn and preserved in *al-Muntakhab*. Al-Kindi's work includes the Diogenic anecdotes which are missing in Hunayn's. Al-Kindi's work, on the other hand, contains the anecdote about the opposition to idol worship, the weeping of his wife before his execution (Diogenses Laertius, XV, Loeb, ed., p. 70) and lay a great emphasis on maxims related to justice. Hunayn's work further contains the story of Socrates learning music late in life (Diogenes Laertius XV, p. 69); the classification of men into four categories, and the anecdote about Socrates living on only seventy *dirhams* of dried bread a day. The other early authors such as Ibn Juljul, *op. cit.*, pp. 30-l; Ibn Fatik, *Mukhtar al-Hikam wa Mahasin al-Kilam* used etxensivly by Ibn Abi 'Usaybi'ah seem to depend more on the collection of al-Kindi than on that of Hunayn Ibn Miskawayh in *al-Hikmah al-Khalidah* (ed. A. Badawi), Cairo, 1952, pp. 211-13, repeats almost *verbatim* the collection Hunayn. Whether Prophyry's *Philosophos Historia,* a work in four books and partly translated into Arabic in the time of Hunayn and al-Kindi, is the source of both Hunayn and al-Kindi cannot be determined, but it remains a good probability.

28. D. M. Dunlop, "Biographical Material from the *Siwan al-Hikmah,*" *JRAS* (1957), PP. 88-9.

29. *Ta'rikh al-Hukama,'* p. 374 ff.

30. Abu Hayyan al-Tawhidi, *op. cit.*, I : 127-8.

31. Sa'id *op. cit.*, p. 52.

32. S. Munk, *Melanges de Philosophie Juive et Arabe,* new impression, Paris, 1955, p. 340.

33. For a biography and a study of this student of al-Kindi who was

probably a member of the Brethren of Purity, see F. Rosenthal, *Ahmad ibn al-Tayyib al-Sarakshi,* American Oriental Series 26, New Haven, 1943.

34. Ibn Juljul, *op. cit.,* 73.

35. Ibn Nubatah, *op. cit.,* p. 140.

36. *'Uyun,* I : 208.

37. M. Steinschneider *Die Europaeische Ubersetzungen aus dem arabischen bis Mitte des 17. Jahrhunderts,* new impression, 1956, p. 32. See also Appendix I.

38. Cardane *De subtilitate,* 264b, Paris, 1550 lists al-Kindi among the "viri subtilitate praestantes". He shares the honour with such great names as those of al-Khawarazmi, Ptolemy, Euclid, and Aristotle.

39. A. Jourdain, *Recherches critiques sur l'ages et l'origine des traductions latines d'Aristotle,* Paris, 1883, pp. 320-21. Also A. Cortabarria. "Tabla General de las citas de Alkindi y al-Farabi ces las Obras de San Alberto Magno". *Estudios Filosoficos,* vol. 3 (1953-54). pp. 247-50.

40. 'Ali 'Abd al-Raziq, *Faylasuf al-'Arab wa'l-Mu'allim al-Thani,* Cairo, 1945.

41. *On First Philosophy,* Cairo, 1948, p. 45.

42. *Rasa'il,* Introduction, pp. Arbi

43. Rosenthal, *"al-Kindi and Ptolemy",* p. 456.

44. G. Sarton, *Introduction to the History of Science,* Baltimore, 1927, I : 559.

45. Ibn Nubatah, *op. cit.,* p. 140, informs us that al-Kindi wrote a treatise refuting the allegations of those who claim that silver and gold can be transmuted from other metals. Al-Kindi maintains that man is not capacitated to do nature's work. Furthermore, the people who indulge in alchemy are cheats and ignorant. Abu Bakr al-Razi refuted his refutation in a treatise mentioned in *Risalah li 'l-Biruni fi Fihrist Kutub Muhammad Zakariyya' al-Razi,* ed. P. Kraus, Paris, 1936, No. 171.

46. Roger Bacon, *Opus Magus*, ed. R. B. Burke, 2 vols., Philadelphia, 1928, II : 468. Al-Kindi, like Tideus, affirms that sight never determines the distance between itself and the object seen, nor the size of the object seen, nor the position and situation of it, unless the visual rays pass to the object seen and not upon it, and grasp its surface and contain in extremities. Cf. also pp. 486 and 489.

47. Sarton, *op. cit.*, I : 559.

APPENDIX I

THE WORKS OF AL-KINDI

THE wide and varied knowledge of al-Kindi can only be matched by his literary output. The first list of his works that has come down to us is that of Ibn al-Nadim (377/987) who describes al-Kindi's knowledge of Greek science and philosophy as unique. He mentions the names of two hundred and forty-two works and divides them according to their subject-matter into philosophy, logic, arithmetic, spherics, medicine, astrology, polemics, psychology, politics, meteorology, divination, and miscellaneous. Flugel has collected and classified the names of two hundred and sixty-five works.[1] The various historians of science and philosophy like al-Qifti and Ibn Abi 'Usaybi'ah, who are our main source of information on the life and works of al-Kindi, give more or less the same number of works, but there seems to be no agreement among them as to their correct titles, which makes it rather impossible for us to indentify certain works of al-Kindi. Probably al-Kindi had not given definite titles to all his works when he died. Also the epistolary form in which many of his treatise are written does not always require a title by the author, especially in a period when the rules of editing were not yet fixed. A very useful volume on the works of al-Kindi appeared in Baghdad in connection with the millinery celebrations of al-Kindi held in 1962 prepared by Professor Richard J. McCarthy, S. J., entitled *al-Tasanif al-Mansubah ila Faylasuf al-'Arab.*

Unfortunately, very little of his huge output has come down to us and whatever has reached us was not easily accessible until the very recent past. Thanks to the editing and publication of two volumes of his treatises by Professor Muhammad 'Abd al-Hadi Abu Ridah of Egypt, we have now some substantial works, and consequently can base our synthesis of his philosophy on original sources rather than on paraphrases and quotations in the works of others.

In the following pages I shall try to list all the works that are attributed to him using as my source the *Fihrist* of Ibn al-Nadim, and following his classification except in certain cases where it is evidently clear that the work belongs to a different classification.

The titles are given both in Arabic and in English (translierated) as they appear in *al-Fihrist*. The Latin titles are used whereever they are well established.

The scientific works of al-Kindi are by far the most numerous. In fact, there are many scholars who consider al-Kindi a mere scientist and not a philosopher. They point to the great number of works he wrote on scientific problems in support of their thesis. They also allude to encyclopaedists, like al-Bayhaqi, who referred to him as an engineer.[2] Undoubtedly, al-Kindi was genuinely interested in the exact sciences; none the less it is unfair, especially after the publication of his philosophical treatise, to depreciate his contributions and overlook his pioneering work in the field of Arab-Muslim philosophy.

Besides, it is only recently that we began to classify the exact sciences and philosophy as separate disciplines. In Arabic, the word *"hakim"* still connotes both a physician and a wiseman or philosopher.

As to the chronological order of his works, up to the present time, there has been no attempt to establish it. In fact, no such attempt was possible until his original writings became available. Although it is quite difficult to assign his books a strict chronological order, yet the task is not impossible. Al-Kindi lists a series of his writings which he considers necessary for the understanding of his work on The Great Art *(al-Sina'ah al-'Uzmah)*.[3]

They are:

1. *Kitab fi 'l-'lm't* (?). Probably *Risalah fi 'l-Mu'tayat* (On the Date) رسالة فى المعطيات based on Elucid's *Dedomena.*

2. "On the Sphere and the Solids and Immediate Primary Plain (Figures) the Knowledge of which is connected with that of the Sphere" *(R. fi 'l-Kurah wa ma ittasala 'ilmuhu bi 'Ilmiha min 'l-Mujassamat wa Awa'il Qaribah min al-Basitah).*

رسالة فى الكرة ومااتصل علمه بعلمها من المجسمات و اوائل قريبه من البسيطه

3. "On the Motions of the Sphere" *(K. fi Harakat al-Kurah).*

كتاب فى حركات الكرة

4. "On Place" *(K. fi'l-Masakin).*

كتاب فى المساكن

5. "On Optics" *(K. fi 'l-Manazir).*

كتاب فى المناظر

6. "Introduction to Arithmetic" *(K. al-Madkhal ila 'l-'Adad).*

كتاب المدخل الى العدد

7. "On the Use of Analogical Arithmetic" *(K. fi Isti'mal al-'Adab al-Qiyasi).*

كتاب فى استعمال العدد القياسى

8. "On the use of the Indian Numerals" *(K. fi Isti'mal al-'Adab al-Hindi).*

كتاب فى استعمال العدد الهندى

9. "On the Purposes of the Use of the Indian Numerals" *(Limmiyyat(?) Isti'mal al-'Adad al-Hindi).*

لميات استعمال العدد الهندى

10. "On Spheres" *(K. fi 'l-Ukar).*

كتاب فى الاكر

11. "On the 'Introduced' First Philosophy" *(K. fi 'l-Falsafah al-Ula al-Dakhilah).*

كتاب فى الفلسفة الاولى الداخل

Other works of al-Kindi contain cross-references, although their number is extremely limited. In his treatise "On the Number of Aristotle's Books" al-Kindi refers to his major treatise "On Harmony" (*cf. Rasa'il,* I : 378). "On the Composition of Melodies" *(Risalah fi Khabar Ta'lif al-Alhan)* (رسالة فى خبر تأليف الالحان) he quotes the same work as well as the "Numerical Discourses on Temporal Proportions" [cf. the edition of R. Lachmann and Mahmud al-Hifni, pp. XI (23), XIV (25), XIX (29) and XIX (30), Leipzig, 1931]. In his "On the Explanation of the Proximate Active Cause of Generation and Corruption" as well as in "On the Bowing of the Outermost Sphere and its Obedience to God," and in "Why the Ancients Ascribed the Five Geometrical Figures to the Elements," al-Kindi refers to his "On First Philosophy"—to which we can assign withour much difficulty the date between 833-42 A. C., the caliphate of al-Mu'tasim (cf. *Rasa'il,* I : 215, 219, 251; II : 62). And in "On the Cause of Snow...." he mentions his treatise 'On the Scarcity of Rain in Certain Regions" (cf. *Rasa'il,* II : 80).

These cross-references and the names of the addressees in his writings may be of some help in establishing a comparative chronology. Internal criteria might also be of use.[4]

I—Philosophy

1. "On First Philosophy" *(Kitab al-Kindi ila 'l-Mu'tasim bi'llah fi'l-Falsafah al-Ula).*

كتاب الكندى الى المعتصم بالله فى الفلسفة الاولى

Published in *Rasa'il,* I : 97-162; also published separately with some variants by Ahmad Fu'ad al-Ahwani, Cairo, 1948. A translation into English and commentary is being prepared by Richard Walzer of the University of Oxford. See Ritter-Plessner 23; *GALS,* I : 372; *Philosophie,* 7. This work is mentioned in *al-Fihrist* (p. 357), under the same title. The book, as the title indicates, was addressed to al-Mu'tasim. The pharse "first philosophy" is an adaptation of the Aristotelian term that describes the study of being *qua* being as the first science. It is the study, according to al-Kindi, of the immovable eternal substance, the first substance in the order of things which deserve nothing less than the first science.

The book probably has not reached us in its complete form. We have only four chapters, which deal respectively with the following problems : philosophy, its meaning and uses; being and its categories; the First Cause and the efficient cause; oneness in reality and metaphor. In the first chapter, we have a definition and a defence of philosophy against those theologians who pretend to maintain that there is an irreconcilable discrepancy between reason and revelation. The second chapter establishes the nature and scope of physics and metaphysics. The former is discribed as the science of that which undergoes change and movement, or the study of the particulars. The latter is considered as the science of the intelligible and the immovable, to the study of the universals. There follows in the same chapter a discussion on the finite and the infinite. Al-Kindi proves that there is nothing infinite except God. Time, space and movement are finite, one and all. The third chapter deals with the necessity of a First Cause, and the impossibility of its being material. The First Cause is one and simple, whereas material causes are composite no matter how we consider them. The last chapter is devoted to a discussion of the problem of Unity. Unity is attributed to things other than God equivocally. The true one does not belong to any genus as such, it is a "genus" by itself. It is eternal, it cannot be one in relation to any other than itself.

2. "On Introduced Philosophy and Logical and Abstruse Problems and Metaphysics" *(K. al-Falsafah' al-Dakhilah wa 'l-Masa'il al-Mantiqiyah wa'l-Mu'tasah wa ma Fawq al-Tabi'iyyat).*

كتاب الفلسفة الداخلة والمسائل المنطقيه والمعتاصه ومافوق الطبعيات

3. "That Philosophy Cannot be Attained except by the Science of Mathematics" *(K. fi annahu ta tunal al-Falsafah ila bi-'Ilm al-Riyadiyyat).*

كتاب فى انه لا تنال الفلسفة الا بعلم الرياضيات

4. "Exhortations to Study Philosophy"*(K.al-Haththʻala Taʻallum al-Falsafah).*

كتاب الحث على تعلم الفلسفة

5. "On the Number of Aristotle's Books and What is Required for the Study of Philosophy" *(R fi Kammiyat Kutub Aristu wa ma Yuhtaju ilay-hi fi Tahsil al-Falsafah).*

رسالة فى كمية كتب ارسطو وما يحتاج اليه فى تحصيل الفلسفة

Published in *Rasa'il,* I : 363-84. Also edited and translated by M. Guidi and R. Walzer, *Studi su al-Kindi. I: Uno Scritto introduttivo allo studio di Aristotile* (Attidella Reale Accademia Nazionale de Lincei, VI, facs. 5, Roma, 1940, pp. 375-419. See Ritter-Plessner, 16, *GAL,S* I : 373, Philosophie 1. Translated into English by Nicholas Rescher. "Al-Kindi's Sketch of Aristotle's Organon", *The New Scholasticism,* XXXVII, 1 (January, 1963).

A short introduction to Aristotle surveying the contents and importance of his main works. Al-Kindi divides the Aristotelian works into four classes : logical, physical, mathematical and metaphysical. He affirms that man has to have a complete mastery over all these classes of knowledge before he can lay claim to being educated, i.e., a real philosopher. The study of mathematics is considered essential. The rest of the treatise contains a discussion on mathematics and its value and a digression on what al-Kindi calls the prophetic science, which he compares with their counterpart the mundane sciences or philosophy. The work ends with an explanation of the purpose of each of the Aristotelian works and its importance in the formation of the true philosopher.[5]

6. "On the Purposes of Aristotle in his Categories" *(K. fi Qasd Aristatalis fi 'l-Maqulat).*

كتاب فى قصد ارسطاطاليس فى المقولات

7. "On the Nature of Science and its Classification" *(K. fi Ma'iyyat al-'Ilm wa Aqsamihi).*

كتاب في مائية العلم و اقسامه

8. "The Classification of the Human Sciences". *(K. Aqsam al-'Ilm al-Unsi).*

كتاب اقسام العلم الانسى

9. "His major Treatise on his Scientific Rule" *(K. Risalatuhu 'l-Kubra fi Miqyasihi 'l-Ilmi).*

كتاب رسالته الكبرىٰ فى مقياسه العلمى

10. "His Short Treatise on his Scientific Rule" *(K. Risalatuhu 'l-Sughra fi Miqyasihi 'l-'Ilmi).*

كتاب رسالته الصغرىٰ فى مقياسه العلمى

11. "On that the Actions of the Creator are all Just, and are Exempt from Injustice" *(Fi anna Af'al 'l-Bari kulluha 'Adl la Jawr fiha).*

فی ان افعال الباری کلها عدل لا جور فیها

12. "On the Nature of That Which Can Never Be Infinite and That Which Is Said To Be Infinite" *(R. fi Ma'iyyat ma la yumkin an yakuna la Nihayat lahu wa ma 'Iladhi yaqalu la Nihayat lahu).*

رسالة فی مائية مالا يمكن ان يكون لانهاية له و ما الذی يقال لانهاية له

Published in *Rasa'il*, I : 194-98. See Ritter-Plessener, 25. Al-Kindi basing his arguments on evident mathematical propositions, proves that an infinite body cannot actually exist. He also proves the same concerning motion and time. Infinity outside of God can only exist in potentiality but never in actuality.

13. "On the Explanation that the Body of the World cannot Possibly be Infinite, and that it is only so in Potentiality" *(K. fi 'l-Ibanah annahu la yumkin an yakuna Jirm 'l-'Alam bila Nihayah, wa anna dhalika innama huwa fi 'l-Quwa).*

كتاب فی الابانه انه لا یكن ان یكون جرم العالم بلانهاية و ان ذلك انما هو فی القوی

14. "On Action and Passion from the First (Book) of Physics" *(K. fi'l-Fa'ilah wa 'l-Munfa'ilah min 'l-Tab'iyat al-Ula).*

كتاب فی الفاعله و المنفعله من الطبعيات الاولی

15. "On the Dictions of Comprehensive ideas" *(K. fi'Ibarat al-Jawami' al-Fikriyah).*

كتاب فی عبارات الجوامع الفكرية

16. "On Certain Questions He was asked to Answer on the Usefulness of Mathematics" *(K. fi Masa'il su'ila 'anha fi Manfa'at al-Riyadiyat).*

كتاب فی مسائل سئل عنها فی منفعة الرياضيات

17. "On Discussing the Allegation that Natural Objects Do Only One Kind of Action by Natural Necessity"*(K. fi Bahth Qawl al-Mudda'i anna al-Ashya' al-Tab'iyyah taf'alu fi'lan Wahidan bi-Ijab al-Khulqah).*

كتاب فى بحث قول المدعى ان الاشياء الطبعية تفعل فعلا واحدا بايجاب الخلقة

18. "On the Primary Data of Sensible Objects" *(K. fi Awa'il al-Ashya' al-Mahsusah).*

كتاب فى اوائل الاشياء المحسوسة

19. "On the Apposition of the Arts" *(R. fi 'l-Taraffuq fi 'l-Sina'at).*

رسالة فى الترفق فى الصناعات

20. "On How to Petition Caliphs and Ministers" *(R. fi Rasm Riqa' ila 'l-Khulafa' wa 'l-Wuzara').*

رسالة فى رسم رقاع الى الخلفاء و الوزراء

21. "On the Division of the Law" *(R. fi Qismat al-Qanun).*

رسالة فى قسمة القانون

22. "De Intellectu" *(R. fi Ma'iyat al-'Aql).*

رسالة فى مائية العقل

Published in *Rasa'il,* I : 353-58. Also published by A. F. al-Ahwani, in his *Paraphrase de "De Anima"*, Cairo, 1950, pp. 178-81. This treatise was translated twice into Latin. First by Gerard of Cremona who translated it under the title *Verbum Jacob Al Kindi de Intentione Antiquorum in Ratione.* Next probably by Johannes Hispanesis under the title *Liber Alkindi de Intellectu et Intellecto.* Both Latin translations were published by A. Nagy, *Die Philosophischen Abhandlugen ......,* pp. 1-11. See Ritter Plessner, 14; *GAL,S* I : 373; Philosophie 2. Translated into English with commentaries by Richard J. McCarthy, S.J. and published in *Islamic Studies,*

Karachi, III/2 (June, 1964). pp. 119-49. J. Jolivet is preparing a new edition and translation into French.

A short treatise of considerable importance to the understanding of the origins of Arabic-Muslim theories on the intellect. Here we have a first record on the number of the intellects and their classifications, the relation between the intellect and sense-perception, a definition of the intellects as an incorporeal form. Al-Kindi's sources (or source) for this treatise have been a matter of controversy among various scholars, but it is now known that al-Kindi did not depend on Alexander of Aphrodisiac.

23. "On the True First Perfect Agent and On the Imperfect One Which is said To Be an Agent by Metaphor" *(R. fi 'l-Fa'il-Haqq al-Awwal al-Tamm wa 'l Fa'il al-Naqis alladhi huwa bi 'l-Majaz).*

رسالة فى الفاعل الحق الاول التام و الفاعل الناقص الذى هو بالمجاز

Published in *Rasa'il,* I : 182-84. See Ritter-Plessner, 26, *GAL,*S I : 373; Philosophie 10. Al-Kindi explains the difference between the action of God which he considers the true, perfect and eternal action and the action of creation, which should be called action only be metaphor, and which in reality is all passion.

24. "On Cause and Effect Written for al-Ma'mun". *(Rasa'il al-Ma'mum fi 'l-'Illah wa 'l-Ma'lul).*

رسالة الى المأمون فى العلة والمعلول

25. "The Book of the Apple" *(K. al-Tuffah).*

كتاب التفاح

Known also as *Liber de Pomo.* The authenticity of this book is doubtful. We know of three manuscripts. A transcript made by Amin Zahir Khayr Allah in the Orthodox Patriarchate of Damascus and published in *al-Muqtataf,* IV (1919), pp. 475-84; VI (1920), PP. 18-22,

105-10, 217-21 with a note on page 295. This edition is not dependable as the editor interpolated many words of his own in the original manuscript.

The second manuscript is an abridgement entitled *Mukhtasar Kitab al-Tuffahah* (A Summary of the Book of the Apple) in the Taymuriyah Collection of the Egyptian National Library,(Ethics, 1290). It goes back to the fourteenth or fifteenth century. The third is preserved in Koprulu Library, Istanbul, 1608, entitled *Risalah al-Ma'rufah bi 'l-Tuffahah li Aristatalis* (A Treatise Known As That Of The Apple by Aristotle). There is a Persian translation along with an English translation published by D.S. Margoliouth in *JRAS* (1892), 187ff. A Latin translation was published by Mathias van der Goes in Antwrep in 1487. There is also a Hebrew translation in MS., Leiden, Or. 4764, 5.[6]

The manuscripts do not agree on the identity of the Greek philosopher on whose death the argument in the work centres. The Damascus and the Cairo manuscripts have Socrates, the Istanbul manuscript has Aristotle. So does the reference to this work in the *Rasa'il Ikhwan al-Safa'* (Epistles of the Brethren of Purity), Cairo, 1928, IV : 100. There are two facts which indicate that it is more plausible to think that the central figure was Socrates rather than Aristotle. The book is fashioned fundamentally after the *Phaedo* of Plato, and the title *al-Tuffahah* (Apple) is a very late one given to the work by one of its unknown editors. If this last fact is considered in the light of the information supplied by al-Qifti, namely, that al-Kindi, wrote a work entitled *Risalah fi Khabar Mawt Suqrat* (A Treatise on the Death of Socrates) the title *al-Tuffahah* will not then weigh against the attribution of the work to al-Kindi, as against the opinion that Socrates is the central figure.

Among the modern authors, Brockelmann, *Geschichte der Arabischen Literatur*, Supplementband I. Leiden, 1937, p. 373, Philosophie 4, and Massignon, *Texts inedits.....*,

p. 178 attribute the work, not without reservation, to al-Kindi.

The book receives its present title from the fact that during his last conversation with his students, the dying Socrates (or Aristotle) holds in his hand an apple, whose smell revives him whenever he is about to faint.

As the life of the philosopher draws to an end, some of his disciples—Crito, Simmias, Zeno, Lysias, Diogenes, visit him. Finding him in a cheerful mood, they ask him about knowledge and immortality. The conversation centres on the ways and means of acquiring knowledge. "This world of ours is divided into knowledge and ignorance", he says. True knowledge, which is according to him true virtue at the same time, leads one's soul after death to the bliss of the intelligible world. The true philosopher is the one who can free his soul from all passions and desires for wealth and earthly goods. Virtue is not different from knowledge; the relation of virtue to knowledge or vice to ignorance is like that of water to ice, i.e., it is the same thing in a different form.

26. *De Quinque Essentiis (Fl -'l-Jawahir al-Khamsah).*

فى الجواهر الخمسة

The Arabic original of this treatise is lost, but luckily we have a Latin translation published by A. Nagy "Die philosophische Abhandlungen des Ja'qub ben Ishaq al-Kindi" in *Beitraege zur Geschichle der Philosophie des Mittelaters,* Bd. II, Heft 5, ed. C. Baeumer and H. F. Herting, Munster, 1897. Professor Abu Ridah made a translation of the same, published in *Rasa'il,* II : 8-35 Nagy considers rightly that this treatise was made up of excerpts from a work based on Aristotle's *Physike Akroasis* known in Arabic as *Sam' al-Kiyan* سمع الكيان [7] The five essences are matter, form, movement, place, and time. Every substance is composed of matter out of which it is carved, and form by which it is distinguished. It is found with all its extensions in a place. Movement cause it *to be.* Time measures the movement. The rest of the treatise is a definition of each one of the five essences based mainly on Aristotle.

27. "On the Explanation of the Active Proximate Cause of Generation and Corruption" *(Risalah fi 'l-Ibanah 'an al-'Illah al-Fa'ilah al-Qaribah li'l-Kawn wa 'l-Fasad).*

رسالة فى الا بانه عن العلة الفاعلة القربية للكون والفساد .

Published in *Rasa'il,* I : 214-37. See Ritter-Plessner, 20; *GAL,*S I : 273, Physik 10. This treatise deals mainly with the role which the sun and the moon play in causing generation and corruption. It is maintained that the harmonious position of the sun in respect of the earth and the sun's transit in the "inclined sphere" plus the movement of the outermost sphere are responsible for the changes that occur in the realm of the four elements. Al-Kindi adheres on the whole to the Aristotelian scheme of the universe, but shows great inclination towards Ptolemy on some points.

28. "On Conjuring up Spirits" *(R. fi Istihdar al-Arwah).*

رسالة فى استحضار الارواح

Not yet published. Manuscript in the Sbath Collection' Aleppo; see Paul Sbath, *Catalogue,* Cairo, 1928, 1, 48, 3, p. 40; *GAL* S I : 373; Philosophie 13. A summary of ancient ideas on the subject of conjuring up the spirits.

29. "On the Definition of Things and Their Descriptions" *(R. fi Hudud al-Ashya' wa Rusumiha).*

رسالة فى حدود الاشياء و رسومها.

Published in *Rasa'il,* I : 165-80. See Ritter-Plessner 24; *GAL,*S I : 373; Philosophie 8. Not mentioned in *al-Fihrist. 'Uyun,* I : 210, refers probably to the same work under the title *Masa'il Kathirah fi 'l-Mantiq wa Ghayrihi wa*

Hudud al-Falsafah مسائل كثيرة فى المنطق وغيره وحدود الفلسفة (A Thesaurus of Questions in Logic and Other Things and the Definitions of Philosophy). It is the first known glossary of its kind in Arabic. It contains some one hundred definitions of philosophical terms based principally on Greek nomenclature. It is the fore-runner of Ibn Sina's *Risalat al-Hudud* رسالة الحدود (A Treatise on Definitions).

30. "On the Uniqueness of God and the Finitude of the Body of the Universe" *(Risalah ila 'Ali ibn Jahm fi Wahdaniyat Allah wa Tanahi Jirm al-'Alam).*

رسالة الى على بن جهم فى وحدانية الله و تناهى جرم العالم

Published in *Rasa'il,* I : 201-07. See Ritter-Plessner 2, *GAL,* S I : 372, Theologic 4. This treatise is based mainly on the very arguments of *On First Philosophy,* and uses almost the same words as the latter. See the Introduction of Abu Ridah, *Rasa'il,* I : 114ff. Translated into English by Nicholas Rescher and H. Khatchadourian, "Al-Kindi's Epistle on the Finitude of the Universe", *ISIS,* vol. 56 (1965).

31. "A Philosophical Treatise on the Secrets of Spiritual (Bodies)"[8] *(al-Risalah al-Hikmiyah fi Asrar al-Ruhaniyah).*

الرسالة الحكمية فى اسرار الروحانية

Not yet published. Manuscript in the Sbath Collection. According to P. Sbath, *Catalouge,* I, 48, 2, p. 40, it is a criticism of certain ideas of the ancients (Greeks, and probably the Harranians) on astronomy and its nature. See *GAL,* S I : 373, Philosophie 12.

32. "Refutation of the Christians" *(Maqalah fi 'l-Radd 'ala-Nasara).*

مقالة فى الرد على النصارى

The original work of al-Kindi is lost. However, we

have a polemical reply by Yahya ibn 'Adi (893-974 A.C.) who seems to have reproduced verbatim the main arguments of al-Kindi against the doctrine of The Trinity. Ibn 'Adi's reply was first published in *La Revue de l'Orient Chretien*, S. 3, tome II, XXII (1920-22), p. 3ff. There is a manuscript of this work in the Vatican, Ar. 127. See De Boer, "al-Kindi wider die Trinitaet" in *Festschrift Theodor Noldeke* (Giessen, 1906), I : 279ff; G. Graf, *Geschichte der Christlischen Arabischen Literatur* (Citta del Vaticano, 1947), Bd. II : pp. 243-4, *GAL*, S I: 372, Theologic 1. Using Porphyrian logic al-Kindi tries to prove that The Trinity cannot fall under any of the categories of beings, and that any conception of a trinity has necessarily to be composite and hence not eternal.

33. "That There Exist Substances without Bodies" *(Risalah annahu Tujad Jawahir bila Ajsam)*.[9]

رسالة انه توجد جواهر بلا اجسام

Published in *Rasa'il*, I : 265-69, under the title *Risalah annahu Tujad Jawahir la Ajsam* (That There Exist Substances and Not Bodies). See Ritter-Plessner 15. The main point in this treatise is to prove that there exist certain substances, the soul being one of them, which have an immaterial existence. Miskaway (d. 1030 A. C.) has a similar treatise entitled "On Proving That There Exist Essences *(Suwar Ruhaniyah)* Without Matter" which takes up the same problem and comes to the same conclusion.[10] The use of different words *jawahir*=substances by al-Kindi and *suwar ruhaniyah*=spiritual forms, by Miskawayh shows us the changes that occurred in Arabic philosophical terminology and the subtler shades of meaning which the words acquired. It seems that al-Kindi was following Plato in affirming the existence of non-material beings that interact with material ones. He considered genera and species as substances and thus entered into the dispute between realism and nominalism. However, he did not elaborate because the problem does not seem to have pre-occupied him. The method he uses to prove his conclusion is mathematical and seems to fir in with the general framework of his method.

II—Logic

34. "A Summary of Porphyry's Eisagoge" *(Ikhtisar Kitab Isaghuji li-Farfuris).*

اختصار كتاب ايسا غوجى لفارفوريس

35. "An Exhaustive Introduction to Logic" *(Risalatuhu fi 'l-Madkhal al-Mantiqi bi Istifa' al-Qawl fihi).*

رسالة فى المدخل المنطقى باستيفاء القول فيه

36. "Liber Introductorius in Artem Logicae Demonstrationis". Probably *(Risalah bi-Ijaz wa Ikhtisar fi 'l-Burhan al-Mantiqi).*

رسالة بايجاز و اختصار فى البرهان المنطقى

This is another treatise published in Latin by Nagy in the *Philosophischen Abhandlugen....* and attributed to a certain 'Mahometh' (var. 'Machomet'), a disciple of al-Kindi. Nagy believes that the author of the work might be al-Farabi, and he tries to show that al-Farabi was a disciple of al-Kindi in the sense that he, i.e., al-Farabi, had studied the works of al-Kindi and was inspired by them. T. J. De Boer identified this treatise as a literal translation of the fourteenth *Risalah* on the *Analytica Posteriori* in the first book of *Rasa'il Ikhwan al-Safa'* (Epistles of the Brethern of Purity).[11] De Boer maintains that Ahmad al-Sarakhsi, a well-known disciple of al-Kindi, might have been the author since we know that he wrote on such a theme, and the Latin translators could have mistaken Ahmad for 'Mahometh.'[12] Not an uncommon error even today.

The principal ideas in this work correspond to the ideas maintained by al-Kindi in his other writings; if he is not the author, and we maintain with DeBoer that al-Sarakhsi might have been the author or compiler of this work, the philosopher must have been the author of the notes on which the treatise was based. In general, al-Sarakhsi followed in the foot-steps of his master, especially in philosophy, rather faithfully.[13]

37. "On the Ten Categories" *(R. fi 'l-Maqulat al-'Ashr).*

رسالة فى المقولات العشر

38. "On Explaining Ptolemy's Commentary at the Beginning of Almagest Regarding What Aristotle Said in His Analytics" *(R. fi 'l-Ibanah 'an Qawl Batlimayus fi Awwal Kitabihi al-Majisti 'an Qawl Aristatalis fi Analutiqa).*

رسالة فى الابانة عن قول بطليموس فى اول كتابه المجسطى عن قول ارسطاطاليس فى انالوطيقا.

39. "How to Guard Against Sophistical Devices" *(R. fi 'l-Ihtiras min Khida' al-Sufista'iyyah).*

رسالة فى الاحتراس من خداع السوفسطائية.

40. "On the Five Voices" *(R. fi 'l-Aswat al-Khamsah).*

رسالة فى الاصوات الخمسة

41. "On the Construction of an Instrument that Extracts Genreal [Notions]" *(R. fi 'Amawl Alah Mukhrijat al-Jawami).*

رسالة فى عمل آلة مخرجة الجوامع

III—Arithmetic

42. "An Introduction to Arithmetic" *(R. fi 'l-Madkhal ila 'l-Aritmatiqi).*

رسالة فى المدخل الى الارتماطيقى

43. "On the Use of Indian Ṇumerals" *(R. fi Isti'mal al-Hisab al-Hindi).*

رسالة فى استعمال الحساب الهندى

44. "On Explanation of the Numbers Mentioned by Plato in his Politics" *(R. fi 'l-Ibanah 'an al-A'dad allati dhakaraha Aflatun fi 'l-Siyasah).*

رسالة فى الابانه عن الاعداد التى ذكرها افلاطون فى السياسة

45. "On the Harmony of Numbers" *(R. fi Ta'lif al-A'dad).*

رسالة فى تأليف الاعداد

46. "On Unity from the Point of View of Numbers" *(R. fi 'l-Tawhid min Jihat al-A'dad).*

رسالة فى التوحيد من جهة الاعداد

47. "On Elucidating the Implied Numbers" *(R. fi Istikhraj al-A'dad al-Mudmarah).*

رسالة فى استخراج الاعداد المضمرة

Manuscript in Aya Sofia No. 4830. See *GAL,* S I : 374; Mathematik 3. Both *al-Fihirist,* p. 359 and *Ta'rikh al-Hukama',* pp. 369-70 mention a work among the mathematical works of al-Kindi entitled *Risalah fi Istikhraj al-Khabiy' wa 'l-Damir* . رسالة فى استخراج الخبيئ و الضمير (A Treatise on Elucidating What Is Hidden and Concealed in the Mind), which may refer to the same work.

48. "On Prediction [by the Flight of Birds] and Augury from the Point view of Numbers" *(R. fi 'l-Zajar wa 'l-Fa'l min Jihat al-'Adad).*

رسالة فى الزجر و الفال من جهة العدد

49. "On Lines and Multiplication With a Number of Barley-corns" *(R. fi 'l-Khutut wa 'l-Darb bi 'Adab al-Sha'ir).*

رسالة فى الخطوط و الضرب بعد الشعير

50. "On Relative Quantity" *(R. fi 'l-Kammiyat al-Mudafah).*

رسالة فى الكمية المضافة

51. "On Measuring of Proportions and Times" *(R. fi 'l-Khalq al-Nusbiyah wa 'l-Zamaniyah).*

كتاب فى الخلق النسبية و الزمانية

52. "On Numerical Devices and the Art of Their Colcealment" *(R. fi 'l-Hiyal al-'Adadiyah wa 'Ilm Idmariha).*

رسالة فى الحيل العددية و علم اضمارها

IV—Spherics

53. "On That the World and all that is Therein are Spherical in Shape" *(R. fi 'l-'Alam wa Kulluma fihi Kuri al-Shakl).*

رسالة في العالم وكلما فيه كرى الشكل

54. "That the [Simple] Elements and the Outermost Body are Spherical in Shape" *(R. ila Ahmad ibn al-Mu'tasim fi anna al-'Anasir wa 'l-Jirm al-Aqsa Kurriyat al-Shaki).*

رسالة الى احمد بن المعتصم فى ان العناصر والجرم الاقصى كرية الشكل

Translated into English by Nicholas Rescher and H. Khatchadourian. "Al-Kindi's Epistle on the Structure of the Cosmos", *ISIS,* vol. 56 (1965).

Published in *Rasa'il,* II: 47-53. See Ritter-Plessner 17; *GAL,* S I : 374; Mathematik 2.

Al-Kindi tries to prove that a polysided body cannot revolve around its centre, and since the body that revolves around its centre must be spherical, the outermost sphere, therefore, must be so. In a similar way he proves the sphericity of the earth.

55. "On That the Sphere is the Greatest of the Solid Figures, and the Circle the Greatest of All the Simple (Plain) Figures" *(R. fi anna al-Kurah A'zam al-Ashkal al-Jirmiyyah wa 'l-Da'irah A'zam min Jami' Ashkal al-Basitah).*

رسالة في ان الكرة اعظم الاشكال الجرمية و الدائرة اعظم من جميع

اشكال البسيطة

56. "On Spherics" *(R. fi 'l-Kuriyat).*

رسالة فى الكريات

57. "On the Construction of an Azimuth on a Sphere" *(R. fi 'Amal al-Samt 'ala Kurah).*

رسالة فى عمل السمت على كرة

Manuscript in Berlin, Or. Oct. 2294 (neu). See J. Kraemer, *op. cit.*, p. 506, foot-note.

58. "On that the Surface of the Water of the Sea is Spherical" *(R. fi anna Sath Ma' al-Bahr Kuri).*

رسالة فى ان سطح ماء البحر كرى

59. "On How to Level a Sphere" *(R. fi Tastih al-Kurah).*

رسالة فى تسطيح الكره

60. "On How to Make and Use a Six-Ring Armillary" *(R. fi 'Amal al-Halaq al-Sitta wa Isti'maliha),* رسالة فى عمل الحلق الستة و استعمالها . This could be the same as "On the Armillary Sphere" *(R. fi Dhat al-Halaq).*

رسالة فى ذات الحلق

Manuscript in Paris, 2544. See *GAL,* S I : 374; Astronomie 9. An explanation of the meaning and function of *Dhat al-Halaq* is given in the sixth book of Ptolemy's *Almagest.* The armillary sphere is an arrangement of concentric rings in the form of a skeleton sphere representing the relative positions of the ecliptic and other celestial circles.

V—Music

61. "On Harmony" *(R. al-Kubra fi 'l-Ta'lif)* الرسالة الكبرى فى التأليف Published by Z. Yusuf, Baghdad, 1962, in *Medical Treatises of al-Kindi.*

62. "On the Arrangement of the Tunes Indicating the Nature of the Heavenly Bodies and on the Similarity of Harmony" *(R. fi Tartib al-Nagham al-Dallah 'ala Taba'i' al-Ashkhas al-'Aliyah wa Tashabuh al-Ta'lif).*

رسالة فى ترتيب النغم الدالة على طبائع الاشخاص العالية و تشابه التاليف

63. "Introduction to the Art of Music" *(R. fi 'l-Madkhal ila Sina'at al-Musiqi).*

رسالة فى المدخل الى صناعة الموسيقى

64. "On the Harmony of Sounds" *(R. fi al-Iqa').*

رسالة فى الايقاع

65. "On the Art of the Composition of Melodies" *(R. fi Khabar Ta'lif al-Alhan).*

رسالة فى خبر تاليف الالحان

Published with an introduction and commentary by Lachmann and Mahmud al-Hifni, Leipzig, 1931. There is a manuscript in the British Museum (Br. Mu. Suppl. 823, 8). Published also by Z. Yusuf in *Musical Treatise of al-Kindi,* Baghdad, 1962.

Probably this is the same treatise as mentioned in *al-Fihrist,* p. 359 under the title *Risalah fi Khabar Sina'at al-Ta'lif* . رسالة فى خبر صناعة التأليف (A Treatise on the Art of Musical Composition).

66. "On the Art of Poetry" *(R. fi Sina'at al-Shi'r).*

رسالة فى صناعة الشعر.

67. "On the Parts of Knowledge in Music" *(R. fi Ajza' Khabariyyah fi 'l-Musiqa).*

رسالة فى اجزاء خبرية فى الموسيقى

Manuscript Berlin 5503. See *GAL,* S I : 374, Musik

1. Published with a commentary by M. al-Hifni, Z. Yusuf, Cairo, 1962. Also in Z. Yusuf, *Musical Treatises of al-Kindi*, Baghdad, 1962.

Al-Kindi is one of the earliest Muslim writers whose works on music have come down to us. He tries in this treatise to determine the pitch. See H. G. Farmer, "Clues for the Arabian Influence on European Musical Theory" *JRAS*, (1925), PP. 61-80.

68a. "A Short Treatise on the Composition of Tunes and the Making of 'Uds [Lutes] addressed to Ahmad ibn al-Mu'tasim" *(Mukhtasar al-Musiqa fi Ta'lif al-Nagham wa Sin'at al-'Ud allafahu li-Ahmad ibn al-Mu'tasim)*. مختصر الموسيقى فى تاليف النغم و صناعة العودالفه، Published by Z. Yusuf, Baghdad, 1962.

لاحمد ابن المعتصم

68b. "Book on String Instruments With One to Ten Chords" *(Kitab al-Musawwitat al-Watariyyah min Dhat al-Watar al-Wahid ila Dhat al-'Asharat Awtar)*, ed. by Z. Yusuf, Baghdad, 1962.

كتاب المصوتات الوترية من ذات الوتر الواحد الى ذات العشرة اوتار

VI—Astronomy

69. "On That the Astronomical Observation of the New Moon Cannot Be Determined with Absolute Exactness" *(R. fi anna Ru'yat al-Hilal la-Tudbatu bi 'l-Haqiaqh wa innama al-Qawl fi-ha bi'l Taqrib)*.

رسالة فى ان روئة الهلال لاتضبط بالحقيقة و انما القول فيها

بالتقريب.

70. "Answers to Questions on the States of the Planets" *(R. fi Masa'il su'ila 'anha min Ahwal al-Kawakib)*.

رسالة فى مسائل سئل عنها من احوال الكواكب

71. "Solutions of Physical Problems on Some Sidereal Qualities" *(R. fi Jawab Masa'il Tabi'iyyah fi*

Kayfiyyat Nujumiyyah).

رسالة فى جواب مسائل طبيعية فى كيفيات نجومية

72. "On Projection of the Rays" *(R. fi Matrah al-Shu'a).*

رسالة فى مطرح الشعاع

73. "On the Two Seasons (Summer and Winter)" *(R. fi 'l-Faslayn).*

رسالة فى الفصلين

74. "On That to Every Country is Attributed a Different Sign of the Zodiac and a Different Planet" *(R. fi ma Yunsabu ilayhi kull Balad min al-Buldan ila Burj min al-buruj wa Kawkab min al-Kawakib).*

رسالة فى ما ينسب اليه كل بلد من البلدان الى برج من البروج و كوكب من الكواكب.

75. "On Requests to Explain the Difference in the Forms of Nativity" *(R. fi ma su'ila 'anhu min Sharh ma 'Arada lahu 'l-Ikhtilaf fi Suwar al-Mawalid).*

رسالة فى ماسئل عنه من شرح ما عرض له الاختلاف فى صور المواليد

76. "On What is Reported Concerning the Longevity of the Ancients and its being Otherwise Nowadays" *(R. fi ma Hukiya min A'mar al-Nas fi 'l-Zaman al-Qadim wa Khilafuha fi Hadha 'l-Zaman).*

رسالة فى ما حكى من اعمار الناس فى الزمان القديم وخلافها فى هذا الزمن .

77. "On the Correct Way to Construct a Horoscope Model, a Hilaj, and a Katkhuda" *(R. fi Tashih 'Amal Numudarat al-Mawalid wa 'l-Hilaj wa Katkhuda).*

رسالة فى تصحيح عمل نمودرات المواليد و الهيلاج و كتخدا

78. "On the Explanation of the Cause of the

Retrograde Motion of the Planets" *(R. fi Idah 'Illah Ruju' al-Kawakib).*

رسالة فى ايضاح علة رجوع الكواكب

79. "On the Explanation of the Difference Among the Heavenly Bodies" *(R. fi al—Ibanah 'an al-Ikhtilaf fi Ashkhas al-'Aliyah).*

رسالة فى الابانه عن الاختلاف فى الاشخاص العالية

80. "On What is Seen of the Rapidity of the Motion of the Planets in the Horizon and its Slowness as the Planets Go Higher" *(R. fi Sur'at ma Yura' min Harakat al-Kawakib idha Kanat fi 'l-Ufuq wa Ibta'i ha Kullama 'Alat).*

رسالة فى سرعة ما يرى من حركات الكواكب اذا كانت فى الافق و ابطائها كلما علت

81. "On (Stellar) Rays" *(Fi 'l-Shu'a'at).*

فى الشعاعات

Found only in a Latin translation. See Steinschneider, *Die Europaeischen Ubersetzugen*, part two, p. 32; *GAL,S* I : 374, Astronomie 10. Both Brockelmann and Steinschneider suggest that this treatise may be the same as appeared in another Latin translation under the titles *Theoricae artis magicae* (also *Magicarum artium theorica*), and *Effectu projectuquae radiorum.*

Al-Kindi conceives of force as an entity propagated by rays and describes his theory of rays in this original work. His point of departure is the radiation of light from stars, which carries also astrological forces. Each star transmits its peculiar force through space. The idea of parallelism between the transmission of light and the transfer of forces is in opposition to Aristotle's differentiation between these two.[14]

82. "On the Difference Between the Motion (of the Sun) and the Operation of the Rays" *(R. fi Fasl ma Bayn*

al-Sayr wa 'Amal al-Shu'a').

رسالة فى فصل ما بين السير و عمل الشعاع

83. "On the Causes of Sidereal Positions" *(R. fi 'Ilal al-Awda' al-Nujumiyyah).*

رسالة فى علل الاوضاع النجومية

84. "On [the Causes of Force Attributed to] the Heavenly Bodies Called Luck and Bad Luck" *(R. fi 'Ilal al-Quwwah al-Mansubah ila'l-Ashkhas al-'Aliyah al-Musammat Sa 'adah wa Nahasah).*

رسالة فى علل القوة المنسوبة الى الاشخاص العالية المسماة سعادة و نحاسة

85. "On the Causes of Those Attributes of the Heavenly Bodies That Indicate Rain" *(R. fi 'Ilal al-Quwwah al-Mansubah ila 'l-Ashkhas al-'Aliyah al-Dallah 'ala al-Matar).*

رسالة فى علل القوة المنسوبة الى الاشخاص العالية الدالة على المطر

We have only a Hebrew translation of this treatise. See M. Steinchneider, *Die Hebraeischen Ubersetzungen und die Juden als Dolmetscher,*[2] Photoreprint, Graz, 1956, vol. II, p. 565.

This treatise is an answer to a question on the causes of the actions of the heavenly bodies which lead to indications of rain. It is maintained that we can understand this only if we study all branches of philosophy, which, in this case, include mathematics, physics and metaphysics. The treatise also contains an interesting piece on the twenty-eight mansions *(Nakshtras)* of the moon *(Mnazil al-Qamar)* منازل القمر [15] See M. Steinschneider, "Uber die Mondstationen (naxatra) und das Buch Arcandam", *ZDMG* (1864), pp. 157-60, 181-85; *GAL,* S I : 374; Varia 4.

86. "On the Causes of Atmospheric Phenomena"

(R. fi 'Ilal Ahdath al-Jaww).

رسالة فى علل احداث الجو

87. "On the Cause of the Scarcity of Rain in Certain Regions" *(R. fi 'l-'Illah allati laha takunu Ba'd al-Mawadi' la takad tumtar).*

رسالة فى العلة التى لها تكون بعض المواضع لاتكاد تمطر

Published in *Rasa'il*, II : 70-5. See Ritter-Plessner 9.

Al-Kindi explains the causes of the production of rain by the condensation and precipitation of vapour in those regions which are far from the sun's azimuth. The vapour is carried to those regions where it can condense and be precipitated as rain. There are regions which lack natural containers such as high mountains where the clouds fail to condense. Egypt is such a country. Egypt does not have high mountains in the north; vapour usually passes from the south to the north and, not finding any obstacle to make it stop, travels away. The vapour carried by the southern winds from Ethiopia are diverted by the chains of mountains in northern Sudan.

88. "An Epistle to Dharnab, his Disciple, on the Mysteries of the Stars and the Teaching of the Principles of Their Actions" *(R. ila Dharnab Tilmidhuh fi Asrar al-Nujum wa Ta'lim Mabadi' al-A'mal).*

رسالة الى ذرنب تلميذه فى اسرار النجوم و تعليم مبادئ الاعمال

89. "On the Cause of the Halo Around the Sun, the Moon, the Stars and other Luminaries" *(R. fi 'l-'Illah allati tura min al-Halat li 'l-Shams wa 'l-Qamar wa 'l-Adwa' al-Nayyirah).*

رسالة فى العلة التى ترى من الهالات للشمس و القمر و الاضواء النيرة

90. "An Apology for his Death before the Completion of his Natural Years which are One Hundred and Twenty" *(R. fi I'tidharihi fi Mawtihi duna Kamalihi li sinn al-Tabi'ah allati hiya Mi'at wa 'Ishrun Sanah).*

رسالة فى اعتذاره فى موته دون كماله لسن الطبيعة التى هى مائة و عشرون سنة

91. "Discourse on the Moonless Nights in a [Lunar] Month" *[Kalam fi 'l-Jamarat (al-Jamharah)].*

كلام فى الجمارات (الجمحرة)

92. "On Stars" *(R. fi 'l-Nujum).*

رسالة فى النجوم

VII—Geometry

93. "On the Objectives of Euclid's Book" *(R. fi Aghrad Kitab Uqlidis).*

رسالة فى اغراض كتاب اقليدس

94. "On the Improvement of Euclid's Book" *(R. fi Islah Kitab Uqlidis).*

رسالة فى اصلاح كتاب اقليدس

95. "De Aspectibus" *(R. fi Ikhtilaf al-Manazir).*

رسالة فى اختلاف المناظر

The Latin translation of this work by Gerard of Cremona was edited by A. A. Bjoernbo and commented upon by Seb. Vogl in "Die Optische Werke", *Abhandlungen zur Geschichte d. Math, und Wiss.*, Heft. XXVI, 3 (Leipzig und Berlin, 1912). This publication includes *De Aspectibus* under the title *Die Optik des Alkindi,* together with two other works by Tideus and Pseudo-Euclid. Al-Kindi's treatise, most probably, is *R. fi Ikhtilaf al-Manazir* رسالة في اختلاف المناظر (A Treatise On the Diversity of Aspects). The complete Latin title is *Liber Jacob Alkindi de causis diversitatum aspectus et dandis demonstrationibus geometricis super eas.* See G. Sarton, *Introduction to the History of Science,* Baltimore, 1927, I : 559f; *GAL,* S I: 347; Physik 11.

A treatise on geometrical and physiological optics largely based on Euclid, Heron of Alexandria and Ptolemy with some interesting observation made by al-Kindi.

96. "On the Reason why the Ancients Ascribed the Five Geometrical Figures to the Elements" *(R. fi al-Sabab alladhi lahu Nasabat al-Qudama' al-Ashkal al-Khamsah li 'l-Ustuqussat).*

رسالة فى السبب الذى له نسبت القدماء الاشكال الخمسة للاسطقسات

Published in *Rasa'il,* II: 54-63. See Ritter-Plessner 11; *GAL,* S I : 374; Mathematik 1. Translated into English by N. Rescher, "Al-Kindi's Treatise on the Platonic Solids", *Mediaeval and Renaissance Studies* (ed. R Hunt, R. Klibansky and L. Labowsky) London, The Warburgh Institute, 1966.

Al-Kindi explains the reasons (based probably on a late commentary of Plato's *Timaeus*) why the ancients ascribed the five geometrical figures : cube, pyramid, octahedron, duodecahedron, icosahedron to the four elements and the heavenly bodies, and he affirms that these forms proclaim symbolically the Unity of God.

97. "On the Approximate Calculation of Archemides' Theory on the Magnitude of a Diameter, Known from its Circumference" *(R. fi Taqrib Qawl Arshamidas fi Qadar Qutr al-Da'irah min Muhitiha).*

رسالة فى تقريب قول ارشميدس فى قدر قطر الدائرة من محيطها

98. "On the Construction of the Figure of the Middle Lines" (?) *(R. fi 'Amal Shakl al-Mutawassitayn).*

رسالة فى عمل شكل المتوسطين

99. "On the Approximate Computation of a Circle's Table of Chords" *(R. fi Taqrib Watar al-Da'irah).*

رسالة فى تقريب وتر الزائرة

100. "On the Approximate Calculation of the Chord

of (an Arc) of a Ninth of (a Circle)" *(R. fi Taqrib Watar al-Tasa'/Tus').*

رسالة فى تقريب وتر التسع

101. "On the (Calculation) of the Area of a Roofed Vestibule" *(R. fi Masahat Iwan).*

رسالة فى مساحة ايوار

102. "On the Division of the Triangle and the Square and Their (Chord?) Functions" *(R. fi Taqsim al-Muthallath wa'l-Murabba' wa 'Amalihuma).*

رسالة فى تقسيم المثلث والمربع وعملهما

103. "On How to Construct a Circle Equal to the Plane Surface of a Given (?) Cylinder" *(R. fi Kayfiyat 'Amal Da'irah Musawiyah lisath Ustuwanah Mafrudah).*

رسالة فى كيفية عمل دائرة مساويه لسطح اسطوانه مفروضه

104. "How to Find the Rising and Setting of Planets by Geometrical Methods" *(R. fi Shuruq al-Kawakib wa Ghurubiha bi'l-Handasah).*

رسالة في شروق الكواكب وغروبها بالهندسه

105. "On the Improvement of the Fourteenth and Fifteenth Chapters of Euclid's Book" *(R. fi Islah al-Maqalah al-Rabi'ah 'Ashar wa 'l-Khamisah 'Ashar min Kitab Uqlidis).*

رسالة فى اصلاح المقالة الرابعة عشر و الخامسة عشر من كتاب اقليدس

106. "On the [Inscription of a Triangle in a Circle] to Divide the Circle into Three Parts" *(R. fi Qismat al-Da'irah Thalathah Aqsam).*

رسالة فى قسمت الدائرة ثلاثة اقسام

107. "Geometrical Proofs for Astronomical Calculations" *(R. fi 'l-Barahin al-Masahiyah min al-Husbanat*

al-Falakiyah).

رسالة فى البراهين المساحية من الحسبانات الفلكية

108. "Liber Esculegii" *(Kitab al-Matali').*

كتاب المطالع

Found only in a Latin translation supposedly made by Gerard of Cremona. This treatise is merely a correction of a translation made by Qusta b Luqa (d. *ca.* 912 A. C.) of the book of Hypsikles (*fl.* second century) on the rising of the stars. *Al-Fihrist,* p. 361, which mentions the work, and does not name Ibn Luqa, lists the book under this title "His (al-Kindi's) Treatise on the Correction of the Statement of Isqlaws (Hypsikles) on the Rising of the Stars" كتاب رسالة فى تصحيح قول اسقلاوس فى المطالع See *GAL,* S I : 374; Astronomie 8. On Hypsikles, see G. Sarton, *op. cit.,* I : 182.

109. "On the Parallax of the Mirror" *(R. fi Ikhtilaf Manazir al-Mir'at).*

رسالة فى اختلاف مناظر المرأة

110. "On the Geometrical Construction of an Astrolabe" *(R. fi San'at al-Asturlab bi 'l-Handasah).*

رسالة فى صنعة الاسطرلاب بالهندسة

111. "On the Geometrical Calculation of the Celestial Meridian and the Azimuth of the *Qiblah*" *(R. fi Istikhraj bi 'l Handasah Khatt Nisf al-Nahar wa Samt al-Qiblah).*[16]

رسالة فى استخراج بالهندسة خط نصف النهار وسمت القبلة

112. "On the Geometrical Construction of a Marble Sundial" *(R. fi 'Amal al-Rakhamah bi 'l-Handasah).*

رسالة فى عمل الرخامة بالهندسة

113. "On That the (Method of) Construction of the (Lines of) the Hours on a Plate Erected on a Plane Surface Parallel to the Horizon is Better than Other (Methods)"

(R. fi 'Amal al-Sa'at 'ala Safihah Tunsabu 'ala al-Sath al-Muwazi li'Ufuq Khayrun min Ghayriha).

رسالة فى عمل الساعات على صفيحة تنصب على السطح الموازى للافق خير من غيرها

114. "On the Geometrical Calculation (of the Lines) of the Hours on an Hemisphere" *(R. fi Istikhraj al-Sa'at 'ala Nisf Kurah bi 'l-Handasah).*

رسالة فى استخراج الساعات على نصف كرة بالهندسة

115. "On Good Omens" *(R. fi 'l-Sawanih).*[17]

رسالة فى السوانح

116. "On Surveying Rivers etc." *(R. fi Masahat l-Anhar wa-Ghayriha).*

رسالة في مساحة الانهار و غيرها

117. "On Temporal Proportions" *(R. fi 'l-Nisab al-Zamaniyah).*

رسالة فى النسب الزمانية

118. "A Discourse on Numbers" *(Kalam fi 'l-A'dad).*

كلام فى الاعداد

119. "On the Mirrors That Burn" *(Fi 'l-Miraya allati Tahruq).*

فى المرايا التى تحرق

VIII—The Heavenly Spheres

120. "On the Impossibility of Finding the Area of the Outermost Sphere Governing the Rest of the Spheres" *(R. fi Imtina' Wujud Masahat al-Falak al-Aqsa al-Mudabbir li 'l-Aflak).*

رسالة فى امتناع وجود مساحة الفلك الاقصى المدبر للافلاك

121. "On the Exposition that the Nature of the

Heavens is Contrary to ṭhat of the Four Elements" *(R. fi 'l-Ibanah 'an inna Tabi'at al-Falak Makhalifah li-Tabai' al 'Anasir al-Arba'ah).*

رسالة فى الابانه عن ان طبيعة الفلك مخالفة لطبائع العناصر الاربعة

Published in *Rasa'il,* II : 40-6. See Ritter-Plessner 3; *GAL,* S I : 373; Physik 2. English translation by Niclolas Rescher and Haig Khatchadourian, "Al-Kindi's Treatise on the Distinctiveness of the Celestial Sphere," *Islamic Studies,* Karachi, iv/1 (1965), pp. 45-44.

Al-Kindi tries to prove that the nature of a thing is recognizable through the kind of its movement. Simple bodies have simple movements, whereas the movement of a composite body is made up of the movements of its component elements. The last part of the treatise is devoted to a discussion of the nature of the elements and the heavenly bodies.

122. "On the Heavenly Phenomena" *(R. fi Zahiriyat al-Falak).*

رسالة فى ظاهريات الفلك

123. "On the Ultimate World" *(R. fi 'l-'Alam al-Aqsa).*

رسالة فى العالم الاقصى

124. "On the Exposition about Bowing of the Outermost Body and its Obedience to God" *(R. fi 'l-Ibanah 'an Sujud al-Jirm al-Aqsa wa Ta'atihi li'llah).*

رسالة فى الابانه عن سجود الجوم الاقصى وطاعته لله

Published in *Rasa'il,* I : 244-61. See Ritter-Plessner 32; *GAL,* S I : 373; Theologie 3. Al-Kindi tries by means of allegorical interpretation to explain the meaning of the Qur'anic verse : The sun and the moon to a reckoning, and the stars and tress bow themselves : and He raised it up set the balance. الشمس و القمر بحسبان و النجم و الشجر يسجدان و السماء رفعها و وضع الميزان (LV : 5-6. Maulana Muhammad 'Ali's translation). Bowing *(sujud),* according to al-Kindi, is an equivocal term meaning in one case, the act of bending one's head in the process of worshipping. In the other, it means simply obeisance to God's will. The heavens obey by working in harmony with his will. The heavenly bodies can work harmoniously because they are endowed with rational faculties which make their obedience a voluntary and not merely a mecahnical one. Al-Kindi adheres too in this treatise to the Aristotelian scheme of the Universe as subsequently completed by the Neoplatonists.

125. "An Answer to the Manichaens on the Ten Problems Concerning the Heavenly Spheres" *(R. fi 'l-Radd 'ala al-Mananiyah fi 'l-'Ashr Masa'il fi Mawdu'at al-Falak).*

رسالة فى الرد على المنانية فى العشر مسائل فى موضوعات الفلك

126. "On Constellations" *(R. fi 'l-Suwar).*

رسالة فى الصور

127. "On Celestial Optics" *(R. fi 'l-Mazdzir al-Falakiyah).*

رسالة فى المناظر الفلكية

128. "On the Impossibility of Transformation in the Outermost Body" *(K. fi Imtina' al-Jirm al-Aqsa min 'l-Istihalah).*

كتاب فى امتناع الجرم الاقصى من الاستحالة

129. "On the Great Art" *(R. fi 'l-Sina'ah al-'Uzma ila ibn-ihi Ahmad ibn Ya'qub).*

رسالة فى الصناعة العظمى الى ابنه احمد من يعقوب

Manuscript Aya Sofia. See the recent study of this manuscript by Professor Fr. Rosenthal, "Al-Kindi and Ptolemy" in *Studi orientalistici iz onore de Georgio Levi Della Vida*, II : 436-56. Professor Fr. Rosenthal believes the work to be based on Theon of Alexandira's (*fl.* 365-95 A. C.) commentary on *Almagest* or on a later epitome of

it. He suggests that al-Kindi must have introduced some minor alterations and that this procedure was typical of the Philosopher of the Arabs.

130. "On the Finitude of the Body of the Universe" ***(R. 'ila Ahmad ibn Muhammad al-Khurasani fi Idah Tanahi Jirm al-'Alam).***

رسالة الى بن محمد الخراسانى فى ايضاح تناهى جرم العالم

Published in *Rasa'il*, I : 186-92. See Ritter-Plessner 8; *GAL*, S I : 373; Physik 6.

Using his mathematical method, al-Kindi tries to prove the finitude of the Universe in this short treatise.

131. "On the Cause of the Deep Blue Colour that can be seen in the Sky and is thought to be the Colour of the Sky" ***(R. fi 'illat al-Lawn al-Lazuwardi alladhi yura fi 'l-Jaww fi Jihat al-Sama' wa yuzannu annahu Lawn 'l-Sama').***

رسالة فى علة اللون اللازوردى الذى يرى فى الجو فى جهة السماء و يظن انه لون السماء

Published in *Rasa'il*, II : 101-108; also published with an English translation by Otto Spies in *Journal of the Bombay Branch of the Royal Asiatic Society*, XIII (1937), Arabic text, pp. 15-18. Translated into German by E. Wiedemann, *Festschrift fuer J. Elster und H. Geitel* (Braunschweig, 1915), p. 118 ff.

Al-Kindi maintains that colour is merely the absence or presence of light in a sunlit of a shaded place. He attributes the blue colour of the sky to the mixture of the darkness of the sky with the light of the atoms of dust, vapour, etc. in the air illuminated by the light of the sun. Colour, therefore, does not exist in itself, but is the result of our perception of the interplay of darkness and light. Al-Kindi's arguments and conclusions show some independence of thought from Aristotle.

132. "On that Element of the Four Elements That Has

Colour by Nature and Causes Colours in the Others" *(R. fi 'l-Jirm al-Hamil bi Tiba'ihi 'l-Lawn min al-'Anasir al-Arba'ah wa 'lladhi huwa 'Illat al-Lawn fi Ghayrihi).*

رسالة فى الجرم الحامل بطباعه اللون من العناصر الاربعة و الذى هو علة اللون فى غيره

Published in *Rasa'il,* II : 64-8. See Ritter-Plessner 5; *GAL,* S I : 373; Physik 4.

Al-Kindi maintians that the earth is the only element with colour and that the colours we see in the other elements are there due to their mixture with earth.

133. "On the Demonstration of [the Existence] of Moving [Heavenly] Bodies" *(K. fi al-Burhan 'ala al-Jirm al-Sa'ir).*

كتاب فى البرهان على الجرم السائر

134. "On the Primary Data" *(R. fi 'l-Mu'tayat).*

رسالة في المعطيات

135. "On the Composition of the Celestial Sphere," *(R. fi Tarkib al-Aflak).*

رسالة فى تركيب الافلاك

136. "On the Bodies Descending From High Above and Racing with Each Other" *(R. fi 'l-Ajram al-Habitah fi 'l-Uluww wa Sabaq Ba'duha Ba'dan).*

رسالة فى الاجرام الهابطة فى العلو و سابق بعضها بعضا

137. "On the Use of the Instrument called *al-Jami'ah* (Universal)" *(R. fi 'l-'Amal bi 'l-Alah al-Musammat al-Jami'ah).*

رسالة فى العمل بالالة المسماة الجامعة

138. "On the Manner of the Retrograde Motion of the

Planets" *(R. fi Kayfiyat Ruju' al-Kawakib al-Mutahayyirah).*

رسالة فى كيفية رجوع الكوكب المتحيرة

IX—Medicine

139. "On Hippocratic Medicine" *(R. fi 'l-Tibb al-Buqrati).*

رسالة فى الطب البقراطى

140. "On Fatal Foods and Medicines" *(R. fi 'l-Ghidha wa 'l-Dawa' al-Mihlik).*

رسالة فى الغذاء و الدواء المهلك

141. "On the Fumes that Purify the Air from Pestilence" *(R. fi 'l-Abkhirah, al-Muslihah li 'l-Jaww min 'l-Awba').*

رسالة فى الابخرد المصلحة للجومن الاوباء

142. "On the Medicines That Cure from Obnoxious Smells" *(R. fi 'l-Adwiyah al-Mush fiyah min al-Rawa'ih al-Mu'dhiyah).*

رسالة في الادوية المشفية من الروائح الموذية

143. "On the Purging Effects of Medicines and the Reactions of Bodily Humours" *(R. fi Kayfiyat Ishal al-Adwiyah wa Injidhab al-Akhlat).*

رسالة فى كيفية اسهال الادوية انجذاب الاخلاط

144. "On Hemoptesis" *(R. fi 'Illat Nafth al-Damm).*

رسالة في علة نفث الدم

145. "On Antidotes of Poisons" *(R. fi Ashfiyat al-Sumum).*

رسالة فى اشفية السموم

146. "On the Care of Healthy Persons" *(R. fi Tadbir*

al-Asihha).

رسالة فى تدبير الاصحاء

147. "On the Cause of Delirium in Acute Illnesses" *(R. fi 'Illah Baharin al-Amrad al-Haddah).*

رسالة فى علة بحارين الامراض الحادة

148. "On Elucidating the Nature of the Principal Organ in the Human Body (Brain?) and the Explanation of Intelligence" *(R. fi Tabyin al-'Udw al-Ra'isi min Jism al-Insan wa 'l-Ibanah 'an al-Albab).*

رسالة فى تبيين العضو الرئيسى من جسم الانسان و الابانة عن الالباب

149. "On the Quality of the Brain" *(R. fi Kayfiyat al-Dimagh).*

رسالة فى كيفية الدماغ

150. "On Leprosy and its Cures" *(R. fi 'Illat al-Judham wa Ashfiyatuhu).*

رسالة فى علة الجذام و اشفيته

151. "On Rabies" *(R. fi 'Adat al-Kalb al-Kalib).*

رسالة فى عضة الكلب الكالب

152. "On the Fits resulting from Phlegm and the Cause of Sudden Death" *(R. fi 'l-A'rad al-Hadithah min al-Balgham wa 'Illah Mawt al-Fuja'ah).*

رسالة فى الاعراض الحادثة من البلغم و علة موت الفجاءة

Al-Sijistani selected this treatise for his collection of al-kindi's writings preserved in his *al-Muntakhab.*

153. "On Stomachache and Gout" *(R. fi Waja' al-Mi'dah wa al-Niqris).*

رسالة فى وجع المعده و النقرس

154. "An Epistle to a Man On an Ailment in his Belly

and Hand" *(R. ila Rajul fi 'Illat Shakaha ilayhi fi Batnihi wa Yadihi).*

رسالة الى رجل فى علة شكاها اليه فى بطنه و يده

155. "On the Kinds of Fevers" *(R. fi Aqsam al-Hummaydi).*

رسالة فى اقسام الحميات

156. "On the Treatment of a Callous Spleen Against Melancholia" *(R. fi 'Ilaj al-Tihal al-Jasi min al-A'rad al-Sawdawiyah).*

رسالة فى علاج الطحال اجاسى من الاعراض السودواية

157. "On the Disintegration of Animal Bodies" *(R. fi Ajsad al-Hayawanat idha Fasudat).*

رسالة في اجساد الحيوانات اذا فسدت

158. "On the Usefulness of the Practice of Medicine" *(R. fi Qadar Manfa'at Sana'at al-Tibb).*

رسالة فى قدر منفعة صناعة الطب

159. "On the Adminstration of Foods" *(R. fi Tadbir al-At'imah).*

رسالة فى تدبير الاطعمة

160. "On the Preparation of Dishes with Elements Different from Them" *(R. fi San'at At'imah min Ghayr 'Anasiriha).*

رسالة فى صنعة اطعمة من غير عناصرها

161. "On Pharmacology" *(K. fi 'l-Qarabadhin).*

كتاب فى القراباذين

162. "On Life" *(R. fi 'l-Hay at).*

رسالة فى الحيات

163. "On Tested Medicines" *(R. fi'l-Adwiyah*

al-Mumtahanah).

رسالة فى الادوية الممتحنة

164. "On the Difference between Insanity Resulting from a Demonic Touch and That Resulting from the Deterioration of the Humours" *(R. fi'l-Farq Bayn al-Junun al-'Arid min mass al-Shayatin wa Bayn ma Yakun min Fasad al-Akhlat).*

رسالة فى الفرق بين الجنون العارض من مس الشياطين و بين ما يكون من فساد الاخلاط

165. "On Physiognomy" *(R. fi 'l-Firasah).*

رسالة فى الفراسة

166. "On Lisping" *(R. fi 'l-Luthghah).*

رسالة فى اللثغة

Manuscript in Aya Sofia. See Ritter-Plessner 30; *GAL,* S I : 374, Varia 6.

166. (a) "De Medicinarum Compositarum Grabidus Investigandis Libellus" *(R. fi Ma'rifat Quwa al-Adwiyah al-Murakkabah).*

رسالة فى معرفة قوى الادوية المركبه

This treatise on determining the strength of compound medicines was first published in Latin (Strassburg, 1531), manuscript in Munich, 838, fols. 27-37; See *GAL,* S I : 374; Medizin 1; Sarton, *op. cit.,* I : 560. See also Curt Lantzch, *Alkindi und seine Schrift de medicinarum compositarum grabidus* (Diss., Leipzig, 8pp., n.d.).

Al-Kindi applies mathematical principles to posology (that branch of medicine which deals with dosages of drugs.) He bases the efficacy of compound medicines upon geometrical progression. The efficacy is considered to correspond to the proportion of the sensible qualities:

warm, cold, dry and moist. If a compound medicine is to be warm in the first degree, it must possess double the equable mixture, if it is to be warm in the second degree, it must possess four times as much; and so on in the progression, two, four, sixteen, etc. The idea of harmony between the sensible qualities, is original with al-Kindi.[18]

X—Astrology

167. "On the Foreknowledge of Events by the Observation of the Heavenly Bodies" *(R. fi Taqdimat al-Ma'rifah bi 'l-Istidlal bi'l-Ashkhas al-'Aliyah).*

رسالة فى تقدمة المعرفة بالاستدلال بالاشخاص العالية

168. "An Introduction to Astrology" *(R. fi Madkhal al-Ahkam).*

رسالة فى مدخل الاحكام

169. "His First, Second and Third Treatise on Astrology" *(Risalatuhu 'l-Ula wa 'l-Thaniyah wa 'l-Thalithah ila Sina'at al-Ahkam).*

رسالة الاولي و الثانية و الثالثة الى صناعة الاحكام

170. "On the Signs of the Unlucky Stars (Saturn and Mars) when in Cancer" *(R. fi Dala'il al-Nahsaya fi Burj al-Sartan).*

رسالة فى دلائل النحسين فى برج السرطان

171. "On the Election of Days" *(R. fi Ikhtiyarat al-Ayyam).*

رسالة فى اختيار الايام

Abu Ridaḥ in the Introduction to the *Rasa'il,* I : *sin* (.ar..) reports that there is a manuscript of this treatise in the Leiden Museum in a collection of astrological, astronomical and mathematical treatises no. 199. The date of the collection goes back to 608/1214. Both *al-Fihrist,*

p. 362 and *'Uyun,* I : 212 mention a treatise *Risalah fi Qadar Manafi' al-Ikhtiyarat* . رسالة فى قدر منافع الاختيارات (A Treatise on the Benefits of the Election of Days), which may refer to the same.

The election of days is a most important branch of astrology in which astrologer is supposed to choose the most propitious day for action.

172. "On the Degree of Usefulness of Astrology, and who Deserves to be Called an Astrologer" *(R. fi Qadar Manfa'at Sina'at al-Ahkam wa man al-Rajul al-Musamma Munajjiman bi-Istihqaq).*

رسالة فى قدر منفعة صناعة الاحكام و من الرجل المسمىٰ منجما باستحقاق

173. "His Short Treatise on the Limits of Nativity (Horoscope)" *(Risalatuhu al-Mukhtasarah fi Hudud al-Mawalid).*

رسالة المختصرة فى حدود المواليد

174. "Conversions of the Years of (Nativity)" *(R. Tahawil al-Sinin).*

رسالة تحاويل السنين

Manuscript in Escorial; See Derenbourg and Reneaud, *Les Manuscrite Arabs de 1'Escrurial,* tome II, Fasc. 3, 918.

175. "On Judging from Eclipses" *(R. fi 'l-Qada' 'ala al-Kusuf).*

رسالة فى القضاء على الكسوف

Manuscript Aya Sofia; see Ritter-Plessner 27; *GAL,* S I : 374; Astronomie 1. Latin translation found in Leiden, 1716 as reported by M. Steinschneider, *Die Europaeischen Uebersetzungen aus dem Arabischen bis Mitte des 17. Jahrhunderts,* vol. CLI of the *Sitzungsberichte der Akademic der Wissenschaften,* Wien, 1906, part 2, p. 32 entitled

De Judiciis ex Eclipsus. There is another manuscript of this treatise in Escorial, I : 913, 4. The Latin translator of this treatise is Robert the Englishman (6th/12th century), according to Ch. H. Haskins : *Studies in the History of Mediaeval Science,* Harvard 1924, p. 121.

176. "On the Duration of the Rule of the Arabs" *(R. fi Mulk al-'Arab wa kammiyatihi).*

رسالة فى ملك العرب و كميته

Published by Otto Loth, "Al-Kindi als Astrolog" in *Morgenlandischen Forshugen,* (1875) p. 261-309.

Al-Kindi calculates and predicts a period of Arab domination to last six hundred and ninety-three years after the Hijrah. He was wrong only by *fifty* year.

The treatise contains an introduction explaining the purpose and the occasion for writing it. Al-Kindi then sets out his approach for calculating the duration of reigns. He applies complicated formulas to thirty-year cycles marked by the conjunction of the two unlucky stars (Saturn and Mars) in the sign of Cancer. The conjunction that occurred during the Hijrah years is always taken as the starting point of these cycles. Al-Kindi then proceeds to calculate the duration of the Arab domination by applying the rules he has established. In order to verify his results he makes a second calculation, using the *jummal* method (حساب جمل) for determining the numerical values of the Qur'anic monograms[19] (حروف مقطعات) after omitting the recurring letters of each of them. Both methods give him the same results. He later surveys these conjunctions up to the year 242 A. H., and tries to interpret them by determined events in history, forecasting the future of the reigns until the year 333 A.H. The treatise ends with some general aphorisms on the calcultion of the rise and fall of dynasties by the use of other formulas.

XI—The Polemic Writings

177. "A Refutation of Dualism" *(R. fi 'l-Radd ala*

al-Thanwiyah).

رسالة فى الرد على الثنوية

178. "A Refutation of the Arguments of the Heterodox" *(R. fi Naqd Masa'il al-Mulhidin).*

رسالة فى نقض مسائل الملحدين

179. "On the Affirmation of the Apostles (of God)" *(R. fi Tathbit al-Rusul).*

رسالة فى تثبيت الرسل [عليهم السلام]

180. "On the Perfect and True and First Agent and the second Agent so called by Metaphor" *(R. fi 'l-Fa'il al-Haqq al-Awwal al-Tamm wa'l-Fa'il al Thani bi'l-Majaz).*

رسالة فى الفاعل الحق الاول التام و الفاعل الثانى بالمجاز

181. "On Capacity" *(R. fi al-Istita'ah).*

رسالة فى الاستطاعة

182. "A Refutation of the Allegation that Falling Bodies Have Stops in the Air" *(R. fi 'l-Radd 'ala man Za'ama anna li'l-Ajram fi Huwiyyatiha fi 'l-Jaww Tawaqqufat).*

رسالة فى الرد على من زعم ان للاجرام فى هويتها فى الجو توقفات

183. "A Refutation of the Allegation that there is a Period of Rest between the Natural and the Accidental Motions" *(R. fi 'l-Raad 'ala man Za'ama anna Bayn al-Harakah al-Tabi'iyah wa 'l-'Ardiyah Sukun).*

رسالة فى الرد على من زعم ان بين الحركة الطبيعية و العرضية سكون

184. "On the Falsity of the Opinion that a Body at Creation is neither in a State of Motion nor in a State of Rest" *(R. fi anna al-Jism fi Awwal Ibda'ihi la Sakin wa la Mutaharrik Zannun Batil).*

رسالة فى ان الجسم فى اول ابداعه لا ساكن و لا متحرك ظن باطل

185. "On Unity with Expositions" *(R. al-Tawhid*

bi-Tafsirat).

رسالة التوحيد بتفسيرات

186. "A Refutation of Those Who Allege that there is an Atom" *(R. fi Butlan Qawl man Za'ama anna Juz'an la Yatajazza').*

رسالة فى بطلان قول من زعم ان جزء لا يتجزى

187. "On the Essences of the Bodies" *(R. fi Jawahir al-Ajsam).*

رسالة فى جواهر الاجسام

188. "On the Principals of Bodies" *(R. fi Awa'il al-Ajsam).*

رسالة فى اوائل الاجسام

189. "On the Differences among Religious Communities on the Subject of Unity, and their Agreement on the Existence of the Unity" *(R. fi Iftiraq al-Milal fi 'l-Tawhid wa annahum Mujmi'un 'ala al-Tawhid wa Kullun qad Khalafa Sahibahu).*

رسالة فى افتراق الملل فى التوحيد و انم مجمعون على التوحيد و كل قد خالف صاحبه

190. "On the Incarnated" *(R. fi 'l-Mutajassid).*

رسالة فى المتجسد

191. "On Apodixis" *(R. fi al-Burhan).*

رسالة فى البرحان

192. "A Dialogue with Ibn al-Rawandi on the Subject of Unity" *(Kalam ma' Ibn al-Rawandi fi 'l-Tawhid).*

كلام مع ابن الراوندى فى التوحيد

XII—Psychology

193. "On that the Soul Is a Simple Substance, Eternal, and Active on the Bodies" *(R. fi anna al-Nafs Jawhar Basit*

Ghayr Dathir Mu'aththir fi 'l-Ajsam).

رسالة فى ان النفس جوهر بسيط غير داثر مؤثر فى الاجسام

194. "On the Nature of Man and His Principal Organ" *(R. fi Ma'iyat al-Insan wa al-'Udw al-Ra'is minhu).*

رسالة فى مائية الانسان و العضو الرئيس منه

195. "On the Reminiscences of the Soul in the Intelligible World before Her Descent into the Sensible World" *(R. fi Ma'li'l-Nafs Dhikrulu wa hiya fi 'Alam al-'Aql qabl Kawniha fi 'Alam al-Hiss).*

رسالة فى ما للنفس ذكره و هى فى عالم العقل قبل كونها فى عالم الحس

196. "On the Unanimous Agreement of the Philosophers Regarding the Erotic Signs" *(R. fi Khabar Ijtima' al-Falasifah 'ala al-Rumuz al-'Ishqiyah).*

رسالة فى خبر اجتماع الفلاسفة على الرموز العشقية

197. "De Somno et Visione" *(R. fi Mahiyat al-Nawm wa'l Ru'ya').*

رسالة فى ماهية النوم و الروباء

Published in *Rasa'il,* I: 293-311. A Latin translation was made by Gerard of Cremona in Cordova between the years 1167 - 1187 A.C., and was published by Albino Nagy in *Die Philosophischen Abhandlungen.........,* pp. 12-27. See Ritter-Plessner 6, *GAL,* S I : 373; Psychologie 2, Al-Kindi maintains that sleep is the temporary cessation of all sensations. Visions are the forms which the Imaginative Faculty receives while the senses are dormant. Al-Kindi outlines the difference between the actions of the senses and those of the Imaginative Faculty. The veracity and purity of visions are attributed to strength and purity of the Imaginative Faculty.

198. "A Discourse by al-Kindi on the Soul, Abridged and Concise" *(Kalam li 'l-Kindi fi 'l-Nafs, Mukhtasar*

Wajiz).

كلام للكندى فى النفس، مختصر و جيز

Published in *Rasa'il*, I : 281-82; see Ritter-Plesser 19. Explains the meaning of the soul's union with the body. The soul is united with the body in respect of its actions on the body. Body and soul, however, are not united in the same sense as the elements are.

199. "On the Soul, Abridged from the Book of Aristotle and Plato and From the Other Philosophers" *(Al-Qawl fi 'l-Nafs, al-Mukhtasar min Kitab Aristu wa Aflatun wa Sa'ir al-Falasifah).*

القول فى النفس المختصر من كتاب ارسطو و افلاطون و سائر الفلاسفة

Published in *Rasa'il*, I : 272-80. Translated into Italian by G. Furlani, "Una risalah di al-Kindi sull'anima" in *Rivisita Trimestrale de Studi Filosofici ẹ Religiosi*, III (1922), pp. 50-63, from the British Museum MS., Ar. 8060.[20] See *GAL*, S I : 373; Psychologie. 1. This treatise is identical with *(R. fi 'l-Nafs wa Af'aliha ila Yuhanna ibn Masawayh)* رسالة فى النفس و افعالها الى يوحنا ابن ماسويه "An Epistle to Yuhanna ibn Masawayh on the Soul and its Actions".

A definition of the soul and its functions derived not from Aristotle but from Platonic and Neoplatonic sources.

XIII—Politics

200. "His Major Treatise on Government" *(Risalatuhu al-Kubra fi al-Riyasah).*

رسالة الكبرى فى الرياسة

201. "On the Promotion of the Means to Attaining Virtue" *(R. fi Tashil Subul al-Fada'il).*

رسالة فى تسهيل سبل الفضائل

202. "On the Means to Drive Away Sorrows" *(R. fi 'l-Hilah li Daf al-Ahzan).*

رسالة فى الحيلة لدفع الاحزان

Published with an Italian translation by H. Ritter and R. Walzer, *Studi su al-Kindi II, un scritto morale inedito di al-Kindi,* in *Atti della Reale Accademia Nazionale de Lincei,* Memorie della classe de scienze morali, storiche e fiologiche, Serie VI, VIII (1938-1939), pp. 3-64. Professor Walzer believes the work to be either a translation or an epitome of Themistius' book called *Peri apulias.* See *GAL,* S I : p. 373, Psychologie 3. (For the contents, see the chapter on ethics.)

203. "On the Government of the Commoners" *(R. fi Riyasat al-'Ammah).*

رسالة فى رياسة العامة

204. "On Ethics" *(R. fi 'l-Akhlaq).*

رسالة في الاخلاق

It is reported that this treatise exists together with other works of al-Kindi in a private library at Aleppo. Cf. R. Walzer, "Aspects of Miskawayh's *Tahdhib al-Akhlaq*" in *Studi Orientalistici in Onore di Giorgio Levi Della Vida,* II : 608.

205. "On the Advice on the Ways of Attaining Virtue" *(R. fi 'l-Tanbih 'ala subul al-Fada'il).*

رسالة فى التنبيه على سبل الفضائل

206. "On the Traditions regarding the Superiority of Socrates" *(R. fi Khabar Fadilat Suqrat).*

رسالة فى خبر فضيلة سقراط

207. "On the Obiter Dicta of Socrates" *(R. fi Alfaz Suqrati).*

رسالة فى الفاظ سقراط

There is a manuscript of this treatise in Koprulu 1608. The present author is preparing it for publication. It is a collection of analects and anecdotes about Socrates in which the Greek philosopher is presented as a monotheist and a champion of justice and spiritual life.

208. "On a Debate that Took Place between Socrates and Archigenes"[21] *(R. fi Muhawarah Jarat bayna Suqrat wa Arshijanis).*

رسالة فى محاوره جرت بين سقراط و ارشيجانس

209. "On the Story of the Death of Socrates" *(R. fi Khabar Mawt Suqrat).*

رسالة فى خبر موت سقراط

210. "On what Took Place between Socrates and the Harranians" *(R. fi ma jara bayna Suqrat wa 'l-Harraniyyin).*

رسالة فى ما جرى بين سقراط و الحرانيين

211. "On the Analects of Philosophers" *(R. fi Nawadir al-Falasifah).*

رسالة فى نوادر الفلاسفه

XIV—Meteorology

212. "On the Cause About Which it is said That Fire, Air, Water and Earth Are Elements binding together All Things Subject to Generation and Corruption" *(R. fi 'l-'Illah allati laha qila inna al-Narwa 'l-Hawa wa 'l-Ma' wa 'l-Ard 'Anasir Tajma' al-Ka'inat al-Fasidah).*

رسالة فى العلة التى لها قيل ان النار و الهواء و الماء و الارض
عناصر تجمع الكائنات الفاسده

The manuscript of this treatise is found among a collection of treatises by al-Suhrawardi, a microfilm copy of which is in the Library of the American University of Beirut. Al-Kindi here explains how the four elements are the bases of all material objects.

213. "On the Different Times During Which the Force of the Primary Four Qualities Manifests Itself Strongly" *(R. fi Ikhtilaf al-Azminah allati Tazharu fiha Quwa al-Kayfiyat al-Arba'ah al-'Ula).*

رسالة فى اختلاف الازمنه التى، تظهر فيها قوى الكيفيات الاربعة الاولى

214. "On the Cause of Difference in the Years" *(R. fi 'Illat Ikhtilaf Anwa' al-Sanah).*

رسائل فى علة اختلاف انواع السنة

215. "On the Nature of Time, Instance, and Eternity" *(R. fi Ma'iyat al-Zaman wa 'l-Hin wa 'l-Dahr).*

رسالة فى مائية الزمان و الحين و الدهر

216. "On the Reason Why the Upper Part of the Atmosphere Rermains Cool Whereas the Part Nearer to the Earth Remains Warm" *(R. fi 'l-'Illah allati Iaha Yabrudu 'ala al-Jaww wa Yaskhunu ma Qaruba min al-Ard).*

رسالة فى العلة التى لها يبرد على الجو و يسخن ما قرب من الأرض

Published in *Rasa'il,* II : 90-100. Al-Kindi answers three questions : two meteorological and the third mathmetical. The first question concerns the condensing of vapour in the air and the methods to measure the rise of vapour. The second concerns the possibility of determining, from observing the sky, the place where a cloud would turn into rain, and the third deals with the question : if numbers are infinite, does it mean that numbered objects are infinite too.

This treatise could be the same as the one entitled *An Answer to Three Questions* رسالة فى جواب ثلاث مسائل mentioned in *al-Fihrist* and described by Ritter-Plessner 7.

217. "On the Sign That Appears in the Sky and is called a Planet" *(R. fi 'l-Athar alladhi Yazharu fi 'l-Jaww*

wa Yusamma Kawkaban).

رسالة فى الاثر الذى يظهر فى الجو و يسمىٰ كوكبا

218. "On Comets" *(R. fi Kawkab al-Dhu'abah).*

رسالة فى كوكب الذ ء ابة

219. "On a Planet That Appeared in the Sky and was observed [by al-Kindi] For Several Days Until Its Disappearance" *(R. fi 'l-Kawkab alladhi Zahara wa Rasadahu Ayyaman Hatta Idmahallah).*

رسالة فى الكوكب الذى ظهر و رصده اياما حتىٰ اضمحل

220. "On the 'Old Lady's Cold"[22] *(R. fi 'l-Bard al-Musamma "Bard al-'Ajuz").*

رسالة فى البرد المسمى برد العجوز

221. "On the Cause of the Genesis of Fog" *(R. fi 'Illat Kawal-Dabab) n*

رسالة فى علة كون الضباب

Published in *Rasa'il*, II : 76-8. See Ritter-Plessner 10; *GAL*, S I : 373; Physik 8.

This Short treatise explains how the air inside the clouds forces some of the clouds to precipitate into fog. Fog is defined as precipitated clouds and nothing else.

222. "On the Observation of a Great Sign (Comet) During the Year Two Hundred and Twenty-Two (222) of the Hijrah" *(R. fi ma Rusida min al-Athar al-'Azim fi Sanat Ithnatayn wa 'Ishrin wa Mi'atayn li 'l-Hijra).*

رسالة فى ما رصد من الاثر العظيم فى سنة اثنتين و عشرن و
ماتين للهجرة

XV—Magnitudes

223. "On the Magnitude of the Distances between the

(Seven) Climes" *(R. fi Ab'ad Masafat al-Aqalim).*

رسالة فى ابعاد مسافات الاقاليم

224. "On Habitations as Seen From Various Parts of the Globe" *(R. fi Ikhtilaf Mawadi' al-Masakin min Kurat al-Ard).*

رسالة فى اختلاف مواضع المساكن من كرة الارض

A commentary written for his son Ahmad on Theodosios of Bithynia's (*fi.* first century A.C.) book on habitations.

225. "His Great Treatise on the Inhabited Quarter (Oecumene)" *(Risalatuhu 'l-Kubra fi 'l-Rub' al-Maskun).*

رسالته الكبرىٰ فى الربع المسكون

226. "On the Magnitudes of the (Heavenly) Bodies" *(R. fi Akhbar Ab'ad al-Ajram).*

رسالة فى اخبار ابعاد الاجرام

227. "On the Calculation of the Distance between the Centre of the Moon and the Earth" *(R. fi Istikhraj Bu'd Markaz al-Qamar min al-Ard).*

رسالة فى استخراج بعد مركز القمر من الارض

228. "On the Construction of an Instrument to Calculate the Magnitudes of the Distances between the (Heavenly) Bodies" *(R. fi Istikhraj Alah wa 'Amaliha Yustakhraj biha Ab'ad al-Ajram).*

رسالة فى استخراج آلة و عملها يستخرج بها ابعاد الاجرام

229. "On the Construction of an Instrument to Find the Magnitudes of Observed Objects" *(R. fi 'Amal Alah Yu'raf biha Bu'd al-Mu'ayanat).*

رسالة فى عمل آلة يعرف بها بعد المعاينات

230. "How to Calculate Distances between an Observer and the Tops of the Mountains and How to Calculate the

Heights of Mountains" *(R. fi Idah Wujidan Ab'ad ma bayn al-Nazir wa Markaz A'midat al-Jibal wa 'Uluww A'imdat al-Jibal).*

رسالة فى ايضاح و جدا ابعاد ما بين الناظر و مركز اعمدة الجبال
و (فى) علو اعمدة الجبال

Manuscript in Aya Sofia. See Ritter-Plessener 31. The same authors mention the existence of another manuscript of this treatise in Aya Sofia, No. 4833. See also *GAL,* S I : 374; Mathematik 4.

231. "On the Measurement of Distances between Stars by the Use of *Dhat al-Shu'batayn*"[23] *(R. fi Istikhraj al-Ab'ad bi Dhat al-Shu'batayn).*

رسالة فى استخراج الابعاد بذات الشعبتين

Translated into German by E. Wiedemann, "Uber eine astronomische Schrift von alKindi" in *Beitraege zur Geschichte der Naturwissenschaft,* vol. XXI of the *Sitzungberichte der physikalisch-medicinischen Societat* (Erlangen, 1910), pp. 294-302. There is an Arabic manuscript in Leiden reported by Abu Ridah in *Rasa'il,* I : *sin* (..arbi.) of the Introduction. See *GAL,* S I : 374; Astronomie 3.

XVI—Divination

232. "On the Secrets of Divination" *(R. fi Asrar Taqdimat al-Ma'rifah).*

رسالة فى اسرار تقدمة المعرفة

233. "On Divination by (Observing the Meteorological) Phenomena" *(R. fi Taqdimat al-Ma'rifah bi 'l-Ahdath).*

رسالة فى تقدمة المعرفة بالاحداث

234. "On Prediction" *(R. fi Taqdimat al-Khabar).*

رسالة فى تقدمة الخبر

235. "On Divination of (Great) Events" *(R. fi Taqdimat al-Akhbar).*

رسالة فى تقدمة الاخبار

XVII—Miscellaneous

236. "On the Classes of Precious Gems and Their Imitations" *(R. fi Anwa' al-Jawahir al-Thaminah wa 'l-Ashbah).*

رسالة فى انواع الجواهر الثمينه و الاشباه

237. "On the Qualifications of (Precious) Stones" *(R. fi Na't al-Hijarah).*

رسالة فى نعت الحجارة

238. "On How to Make Panes of Glass" *(R. fi Talwih al-Zujaj).*

رسالة فى تلويح الزجاج

239. "On That Which Gives a Colour When Dyed" *(R. fi Ma Yusbaghu fa-Yu'ti Lawnan).*

رسالة فى ما يصبغ فيعطى لونا

240. "On Swords" *(R. ila Ba'd Ikhwanihi fi 'l-Suyuf).*

رسالة الى بعض اخوانه فى السيوف

Published in Cairo by 'Abd al-Rahman Zaki, as *al-Suyuf wa Ajnasuha* السيوف و اجنسها (Swords and their Kinds) in the *Bulletin of the Faculty of Arts* (Cairo University), 1952, XIV/2, pp. 1-36. There is a manuscript of the same treatise in Aya Sofia, No. 4832. See Ritter-Plessner 12. A discussion of the main ideas of the treatise is found in an article of Hammer-Purgstall, "Sur les lames des Orientaux", *JA,* Serie V, 3 (1854), pp. 66-79.

This treatise deals with different kinds of swords, their uses and even their prices. It enumerates some twenty-five kinds of swords and shows that there were other good swords manufactured in the World of Islam besides those made in Damascus.

241. "On What is Placed On Iron and Swords to Prevent Them From Breaking and Getting Blunt" *(R. ila Ahmad ibn al-Mu'tasim fi Ma Yutrah 'ala al-Hadid wa 'l-Suyuf Hatta la Tathallam wa la Takill).*

رسالة الى احمد بن المعتصم فى ما يترح على الحديد و السيوف حتى لا تثلم و لا تكل

242. "On the Human (Domesticated) Bird" *(R. fi al-Ta'ir al-Unsi).*

رسالة فى الطائر الانسى

243. "On the Anointment of Pigeons" *(R. fi Tamrikh al-Hamam).*

رسالة فى تمريخ الحمام

244. "On Bees" *(R. fi 'l-Nahl).*

رسالة فى النحل

245. "On the Making of a Gurgurling Scent Bottle" *(R. fi 'Amal al-Qumqun al-Nabbah).*

رسالة فى عمل القمقم النباح

246. "On Perfume and its Kinds" *(R. fi 'l-Itr wa Anwa'ihi).*

رسالة فى العطر و انواعه

247. "On the Chemistry of Perfumes and Distillation" *(R. fi Kimiya' al-'Itr wa 'l-Tas'idat).*

رسالة فى كيمياء العطر و التصعيدات

Published and translated into German by Carl Garbers, *Buch uber die Chemie des Perfum und die Distillationen,* vol. XXX of *Abhandlugen fur die Kunde des Morgenlandes* (Leipzig, 1948).

A very intresting work for the historian of chemistry containing a collection of recipes and instructions on how to produce perfumes.

248. "On Logoriphic Names" *(R. fi al-Asma' al-Mu'ammat).*

رسالة فى الاسماء المعمات

Manuscript in Aya Sofia No. 4832. See Ritter-Plessner 29. *GAL,* S I : 374; Varia 2. This is probably the same treatise as that mentioned in *al-Fihrist* as *R. ila Ahmad ibn al-Mu'tasim fi Istikhraj al-Mu'amma*[24] رسالة الى احمد بن المعتصم فى استخراج المعما (On the Elucidation of Logogriphs).

249. "On Warning Against the Devices of the Alchemista" *(R. fi 'l-Tanbih 'ala al-Khida' al-Kimiya'in).*

رسالة فى التنبيه على الخداع الكيميائين

250. "On the Two Effects Felt in Water" *(R. fi 'l-Atharayn al-Mahsusayn bi 'l-Ma').*

رسالة فى الاثرين المحسوسين بالماء

251. "On the Active Cause of the Tides" *(R. fi 'l-'Illat 'l-Fa'ilah li'l-Madd wa 'l-Jazr).*

رسالة فى العلة الفاعلة للمدو الجزر

Published in *Rasa'il,* II : 110-33. Arabic manuscript in Oxford. See Cod. Bodl. Ar. 1377, 12. Translated into German and published in *Annalen der Physik,* DXVII (1922), pp. 374-87. Mentioned by al-Mas'udi in *al-Tanbih wa 'l-Ishraf, Leiden,* 1893, p. 51.

This rather long treatise deals with the different kinds of tides and springs of water, their formation and general laws that govern their actions. Al-Kindi also discusses the influence of the heavenly bodies on generation and destruction. The last part of the treatise deals with the high tides and the ebb-tides.

The contents of the treatise are not so important as the method which al-Kindi uses to derive his conclusions. He displays a keen observational power and anticipates the Baconian approach of experimentation.

252. "His Major Treatise on the Bodies Submerged in Water" *(Risalatuhu al-Kabirah fi 'l-Ajram al-Gha'isah fi 'l-Ma')*.

رسالة الكبيرة فى الا جرام الغائصة فى الماء

253."On Falling Bodies" *(R. fi 'l-Ajram al-Habitah)*.

رسالة فى الا جرام الهابطة

254. "On Voice in Three Parts" *(R. fi 'l-Lafz wa hiya Thalathat Ajza')*.

رسالة فى اللفظ وهى ثلاثة اجزاء

255. "On Insects and Reptiles" *(R. fi 'l-Hashrat)*.

رسالة فى الحشرات

256. "On the Effects of the Winds Inside the Earth, Which Produce Many Earthquakes and Sinkings of the Earth" *(R. fi 'Amal Huduth al-Riyah fi Batin al-Ard al-Muhdithah Kathir al-Zalazil wa'l-Khusuf)*.

رسالة فى عمل حدوث الرياح فى باطن الارض المحدثة كثير الزلازل و الخسوف

257. "Anwers to Fourteen Questions on Physics Problems" *(R. fi Jawab Arba' 'Asharat Mas'alah Tabi'iyyat)*.

رسالة فى جواب اربع عشرة مسئلة طبيعيات

258. "An Answer to Three Questions" *(R. fi Jawab Thalath Masa'il)* رسالة فى جواب ثلاث مسائل See No. 216.

259. "On the Story of the Reticent pseudo-Philosopher" *(R. fi Qissat al-Mutafalsif bi 'l-Sukut).*

رسالة فى قصة المتفلسف بالسكوت

260. "On the Cause of Snow, Hail, Leightning, Lightning-bolts, Thunder and Frost" *(R. fi 'Illat al-Thalj wa 'l-Barad wa 'l-Barq wa 'l-Sawa'iq wa 'l-Ra'id wa 'l-Zamharir).*

رسالة فى علة الثلج و البرد و البرق و الصواعق و الرعد و الزمهرير

Published in *Rasa'il,* II : 80-5. See Ritter-Plessner 13; *GAL,* S I : 373; Physik 9.

A short meteorological treatise on the causes and nature of the different phenomena mentioned in the title.

261. "On the Refutation of the Claim of Those Who Pretend to Transmute Metals into Gold and Silver" *(R. fi Butlan Da'wa al-Mudda'in Sin'at al-Dhahab wa 'l-Fiddah wa Khida'ihm).*

رسالة فى بطلان دعوى المدعبن صنعة الذهب و الفضة و خداعهم

262. "On Horses and Veterinary Medicine" *(K. fi al-Khayl wa 'l-Baytarah).*

كتاب فى الخيل و البيطيره

263. "On Fidelity" *(R. fi 'l-Wafa').*

رسالة فى الوفاء

264. "On the Explanation That the Cause of the Four Qualities is the Wisdom of the Creator and not the Difference Among the Heavenly Bodies" *(R. fi 'l-Ibanah anna al-Ikhtilaf alladhi fi 'l-Ashkhas al-Aliyah laysa 'Illat al-Kayfiyat al-Ulawa-lakin 'Illatu dhalika Hikmat al-Mubdi').*

رسالة فى الابانه ان الاختلاف الذى فى الاشخاص العالية ليس علة
الكيفيات الاولى و لكن علة ذلك حكمة المبدع

265. "On Psychology" *(R. fi 'Ilm al-Hawass).*

رسالة فى علم الحواس

266. "On Rhetorics" *(R. fi 'Ilm al-Balaghah).*

رسالة فى علم البلاغة

267. "On the Usefulness of Astrology" *(R. fi Qadar al-Manfa'ah bi Ahkam al-Nujum).*

رسالة فى قدر المنفعة بأحكام النجوم

268. "A Discourse on the First Creator" *(Kalam fi 'l-Mubdi' al Awwal).*

كلام فى المبدع الاول

269. "Scapulomancy" *(R. fi 'Ilm al-Katif).*

رسالة فى علم الكتف

Manuscript in Aya Sofia. See Plessner, *Islamica,* VI, p. 557. Also *GAL,* S I : 374; Varia 3.

270. "On Matrimony" *(Kitab al-Bah).*

كتاب الباه

Manuscript Aya Sofia. See Ritter-Plessner 28; *GAL,* S I : 374; Medezin 2.

A clinical study and explanation of the causes of maladies and dysfunction of the urethra, and how to treat them.

These are the books of al-Kindi either published or still in manuscript form of which we know. Most of the rest are probably lost for ever. Let us hope, however, that some day other manuscripts will be retrived and brought to light as the interest in the history of Arab-Muslim philosophy grows.

However, there are certain works attributed to al-Kindi which are not his. An example of such works is the one mentioned by Brockelmann, *GAL*, S I : 374; Psychologie 4, entitled *Risalah fi 'l-Firasah* ..رسالة في الفراسة.. *(A Treatise on Physiognomy)*. The manuscript as described by O. Rescher, *ZDMG*, LXVIII (1914), p. 53 mentions the names of Ibn 'Arabi and Muhammad ibn Zakariyah al-Razi which indecates that the author must be a later al-Kindi or a student of the Philosopher of the Arabs. We know that many students of his attributed to their famous teacher works which they themselves wrote, and sometimes they did the opposite.

NOTES

1. For a complete list of al-Kindi's works whose titles have come down to us, see Flugel, *op. cit.* For other less complete lists, see *al-Fihrist*, pp. 358-65. *Ta'rikh al-Hukama'*, pp. 368-76; *'Uyun al-Anba'*, I : 209-14; *al-Bayhaqi, op. cit.*, p. 47. See also H. Ritter and M. Plessner, "Schriften Ja'qub Ibn Ishaq al-KIndi in Stambuler Bibliotheken," *Archiv Orientalni*, IV (1932), pp. 363-72. hereafter referred to as Ritter-Plessner. I must apologize here for not being able to compare all extant manuscripts of al-Kindi to avoid possible repetition of titles.

2. al-Bayhaqi, *op. cit.*, p. 47.

3. F. Rosenthal, *al-Kindi and Ptolemy*, pp. 440-43.

4. These are the suggestions of Professor Resenthal as to how to proceed on assigning chronological order for al-Kindi's works as offered in the aforementioned article.

5. Of revealing importance is the absence of any mention of the paraphrase of Plotinus IV-VI *Enneads* famous as the *Theology of Aristotle*, and mentioned in *al-Fihrist*, p. 352 as being corrected in respect to its translation, by al-Kindi. This shows that the Arab-Muslim philosophers did not depend completely on books attributed to Aristotle as Duhem, for example, would like us to think. However, this does not prove conclusively that they knew Aristotle and the other Greek philosophers directly through translations of their books.

Jorg Kraemer, *"Das arabische Original des pseudo-Aristotelische Liber de Pomo"* in *Studi orientalistici in onore di Giorgio Levi Della Vida,* Rome 1956, I : 484-506. Kraemer is of the opinion that al-Kindi could have been the author of this work.

Al-Fihrist, p. 358; *'Uyun,* I : 214.

Spiritual bodies was the name given by the Harranians to the heavenly bodies.

Rasa'il, I : 166, 267. There is a similar work published by A. Badawi in his *Aristu 'ind al-'Arab,* ارسطو عند العرب Cairo, 1947, pp. 291-92. entitled *Fi Ithbat al-Suwar al-Raḥaniyah allaṭi la Hayula laha* ... في اثبات الصور الروحانية التى لا هبولى لها *(On Proving the Existence of Spiritual Forms without Matter)* attributed to Alexander of Aphrodisias. See B. Lewin, "Notes sur une texte de Proclus en traduction arabe" in *Orientalia Suecana,* IV (1955), pp. 101-108 who proves that this was wrongly attributed to Alexander and that it is taken really from Proclus, *Elements of Theology,* 15-7.

'Abd al 'Aziz 'Izzat, *Ibn Miskawayh,* Cairo, 1946, p. 130.

Ed. Khayr al-Din al-Zirikli, Cairo, 1928. pp. 343-62.

T. J. De Boer, "Zu Kindi und seiner Schule" in *Archiv fuer Geschichte der Philosophie,* Bd. VI, N. F. (Berlin, 1900), p. 175.

F. Rosenthal, *Ahmad ben al-Tayyib al-Sarakhsi* (Publications of the American Oriental Society, No. 26), New Haven, 1943, p. 18.

Aristotle *De Anima.* 418a 20; Max Jammer, *Concepts of Force,* Harvard, 1957, p. 57.

15. According to Arabic and medieval astronomers, a 'mansion' is one of the twenty-eight divisions of the heavens occupied by the moon on successive days.

16. The *Ka'bah* in Mecca toward which the Muslims turn their faces in prayer.

17. The passing of a bird or a gazelle on the right of a person was considered a good omen.

18. This theory of al-Kindi was the object of admiration in different periods of history. Cardano (d. 1576) considered al-Kindi one of

the greatest twelve minds in history for advancing this theory. Recently Leon Gauthier, *Antecedents Greco-arabe de la psychophysique*, Beirut, 1938, tries to establish that al-Kindi, ten centuries before Weber and Fechner, established the laws of psychophysics.

19. The Qur'anic monograms, or *al-Fawaith,* whose meaning has not been determined, are mysterious letters occurring at the beginning of twenty-nine *Surahs.*

20. The Italian translation follows very closely the Arabic text edited by Abu Ridah which is based on a manuscript in the Taymuriyah Collection 55 : fol. 65-76 in the Egyptian National Library, Cairo. However, the name of Pythagoras in the Abu Ridah edition is the correct rendering of *Afiscurus,* whereas Furlani's interpretation of this name as Epicurus is incorrect. Epicurus in Arabic would be *Afiqurus* or *Abiqurus* rather than *Afiscurus.* Furthermore, the context dealing with the theory of visions, has Neopythagorean elements, and therefore the Abu Ridah reading makes more sense. Furlani's misreading at this point led him to incorrect conclusions concerning al-Kindi's knowledge of Epicurus.

21. This is how the title appears in *al-Fihrist.* However, it is more plausible to believe that Aeschines, Socrates' disciple in meant here.

22. The cold during the week from the 7th to the 14th of February, is called the "Old Lady's" cold.

23. *Dhat al-Shu'batayn* (literally, that of the two branches) is an instrument used for astronomical and geodetic measurement.

24. *Al-Mu'amma* is a verse in which the meaning is intentionally concealed, called *ch'stan* in the Persian and *paheli* in the Urdu languages.

APPENDIX II

ON THE INTELLECT

I. May God enlighten you to perform what is useful and bestow upon you happiness both in this life and in the hereafter.

I have understood your request for a succint and informative account of the intellect according to the opinions maintained by those ancient Greeks who were held in high esteem.

Among these are Aristotle and his teacher Plato, the philosopher. Since, the substance of Plato's doctrine, is identical with what was held by his disciple Aristotle, my discourse, henceforth, will be limited to mere historical information.

II. Aristotle holds that there are four classes of intellect : The first is the intellect which is always in actuality, the second is the intellect in potentiality, belonging to the soul, the third is the intellect which, within the soul, has passed from potentiality into actuality, the fourth is the intellect we can "demonstrative".

And he (Aristotle) likens the mind to the senses, because of the senses' nearness to living things, and their being common to all of them. He maintains that there are two kinds of forms : the material form which falls under the sense-perception, and the immaterial form, which falls under the intellect, and this latter form is the species of things and what is above it (the genus).

The form which is in matter is what is in actuality sense-perceived. It would not have fallen under the senses, should it not in actuality be sense-perceived.

When acquired by the soul, a form is in the soul. It is acquired by the soul by virtue of its being in it in potentiality. And once joined[1] to the soul it passes to be in the soul in actuality. However, to be in the soul is not similar to being in a vase, nor is it similar to an impression engraved upon a body, because the soul is not a sensible body, nor is it divisible.[2] It (the form) is in the soul and it is one and the same thing with it. There should be no necessary difference between two things just because that which sustains is different from that which is sustained.

Likewise the sense-perceiving faculty is nothing else but the soul, nor is it in the soul as an organ in a body; it is the soul and it is the sense-perceiving (faculty). Similarly, the sensible form is not in the soul because of any (essential) difference *(ghayriyyah)* between itself and the soul. Therefore, the sensible in the soul is the sense-perceiving (faculty).

But the sensible of a primary matter is different from the sense-perceiving soul. Hence from the standpoint of matter the sensible is not sense-perceiving (faculty).

III. And in like manner, (Aristotle) represents the intellect. When the soul joins the intellect, I mean, with the forms which have neither matter nor imagination, it (the form) unites with the soul. I mean, it was present in it in act after not being present in it in act, but in potentiality. This form which has no matter nor imagination is the Acquired Intellect, acquired by the soul from the First Intellect, which is the species of things that are always in actuality.

Now, the reason why the First Intellect has become a giver and the soul a recipient is because the soul is intelligent in potentiality whereas the First Intellect is intelligent in actuality. No entity that receives its essence *(dhat)* from outside could have had that essence in actuality, but only in potentiality; all that which belongs to a thing in potentiality cannot by itself pass into actuality. Should a thing exist by itself, it would always be in actuality, for a thing's essence accompanies that thing so long as it is existent. Hence everything which is in potentiality passes into actuality by another agent which is always in actuality.[3] Accordingly the soul is intelligent in potentiality and on joining the First Intellect it passes to be intelligent in actuality.

Now, when the soul is united with the intelligible form, it and the intelligible form are not different from each other. Being indivisible, the soul does not differentiate itself (from the form). Whenever the intelligible form unites with the soul, the latter and the intellect are one and the same thing. It is at once intelligent and intelligible. Thus from the standpoint of the soul, the intelligent and the intelligible are one.

As for the intellect which is always in acutality and which caused the soul to pass from potentiality into actuality after it has been intelligent only in actuality, is not one with its intelligible.[4] Therefore, the intelligible in the soul and in the First Intellect are not the same thing from the Standpoint of the First Intellect. Yet from the standpoint of the soul the intelligent and the intelligible are one and the same thing. "And this intellect which in simplicity is similar to the soul is much more stronger in respect to the intelligent than are the senses in respect to the sensible".[5]

Therefore, the intellect is either cause and prior to all intelligibles or secondary and then it belongs to the soul in potentiality excepting when the soul is intelligent in actuality. The third is that which belongs to the soul in actuality; and is already acquired and existent in it. The solul uses it at will and makes it manifest to others.[6] This is comparable to a writer's art of writing which is ready and possible for him; it is his acquistion, well-grounded within himself. He can bring it forth and he can exercise it at will. The fourth of the intellects is that which appears from the soul when it brings it forth and makes it present to others in actuality.

The difference between the third and the fourth lies in that the third is an acquisition of the soul, whose principle of acquisition has already passed and the soul is free to bring it forth at will, whereas the fourth is, either first at the moment of its initial acquisition, or second at the moment of its appearance, whenever it is used by the soul. Hence the third is that which is a property of the soul, previously possessed and which can be brought forth whenever the soul so wishes. But the fourth is that which appears in the soul when it appears in actuality.

These are the opinions of the (Ancient Philosophers) concerning the intellect and this is all that I shall say about it. I believe what I have already said is enough to give you the information you have requested. Be content with it.

NOTES

1. *Bashcra* is to be translated in this context "to unite" or "to join", it connotes something more than mere contact. Cf. Ibn Manzur, *Lisan al-'Arab*, Beirut, 1955, IV : 61.

2. It is possible to read : *mutahayyizah* (circumscribed) instead of *mutajazi'ah* (divisible). In John's translation we find *"circumscripta"*.

3. We prefered here John's translation. The Abu Ridah edition reads: "Which is that entity in actuality", but John's translation reads: *"nisi per aliud quod est in effectu"*, i.e., but by another which is in actuality.

4. Probably, intelligent.

5. This paragraph follows John's translation and not the Abu Ridah edition.

6. In John's translation, *et facialt cum esse in alio a se*. It makes it present in something different from her.

APPENDIX III

SAYINGS OF AL_KINDI

From the Sayings of al-Kindi as recorded in the
Munatakhab Siwan al-Hikmah of al-Sijistani

ARABIC TEXT

عن الفاظ الكندى

الواردة فى منتخب صوان الحكمة

الوموز

ب- الأصل وهى مخطوطة المتحف البر يطانى رقم ٩٠٢٢ شرقية، ورقة ٦٠و ٦٥٠ ظ.

ك- مخطوطة كوبرولو، استنبول، رقم ٠٩٠٢ ورقة ٨٥ و-٩٢ظ.

<>- اضافة من عندنا أو بحسب ك-

()- فى الأصل و نقترح حذفه لأنه زائد من عندنا أو بالأستناد على ك-

ارقام الاقسام و الاقاويل من عندناوكذلك الفو اصل والنقط.

اورقة ٦٠و) أبو يوسف يعقوب بن اسحاق الكندى

١- هو أول من تخرج من المسلمين فى الفلسفة و سائر أجزائها وفى الرياضيات وما يتعلق بها سوى تبحره فى علوم العرب و براعته فى الآداب من النحو و الشعر و أحكام النجوم و الطب و ضروب من الصناعات و المعارف التى قل ما يجتمع معارفها فى انسانٍ واحدٍ. و فهرست كتبه يزيد على دست كاغذ (١) مثنى. وكان استاذ أحمد بن محمد المعتصمى وباسمه عمل أكثر كتبه و إليه كتب بجل (٢) رسائله وأجوبة مسائله، وهو أول من أحدث هذه الطريقة التى احتذاها بهده من جاء من الاسلامين، و إن كان قد تقدمه من ارتفع اسمه و حسنت حاله فى أبام المأمون من الذين كان جلهم تصارى و تصانيفهم يجرى (٣) الأمر فيها على الرسم القديم .

ولإ شتهار كتبه ورسائله وتداول الأيدى لها وسعة وجودها فى كل موضع لم استقص بطلب (٤) النكت و استخراجها منها على العاثرة فى أمثالها إلا اليسير الذى لم أجسد بداً من تزيين هذا الكتاب به.

(ورقه ٦٠ظ) ٢- فمن ذلك قوله إذا كانت العلة الاولى < أى الله > تعالى متصلاً بنا لفيضه عليناوكنا غير متصلين به إلا من جهة فيضه

(١) ب - كاغذ

(٢) ك - كل وقد تكون "مجمل

(٣) ب - بحرى

(٤) ب - تطلب

فقد يمكن فينا ملاحظته على قدر مايمكن المفاض عليه أن يلحظ (١) الفائض فيجب (٢) أن لاينسب قدر احاطته بنا إلى قدر ملاحظتنا له. لأنها أغزر (٣) و أوفر وأشد استغر اقاً لنا فاذا كان هذا هكذا فقد بعد عن الحق بعداً كثيراً من ظن أن العلة الاولى لا تعلم الجزئيات.

٣- وقال : أحسن الكلام ما كان صفو العقل من ناحية المعنى و عفو الطبع من جهة التأليف فيجتمع فيه صواب المراد و حلاوة الإبراد .

٤-وقال: النظر فى كتب (٤) الحكمة اعباد النفوس الناطقة.

٥- وقال : إن أفلاطون قاس الشهوة التى للإنسان بابخزير والقوة الغضبية بالكلب والقوة العقلية بالملك. قال: فمن غلبت عليه الشهوة فهو خنزير ومن غلبت الغضبية عليه فهو كلب ومن غلب عليه العقل فهو ملك، وإذا كان ملكاً كان قريب الشبه من الله لأن الأشياء التى

(١) ك . تلحظ

(٢) ب . فجب

(٣) ك . اعز

(٤) ب . الكتب ، غير واضحة . ك . كسب ، ويمكن "الكتب الحكمية "

يوصف بها البارى وتضاف (١) إليه هى الحكمة والقدرة والعدل و ابحيرو الجميل والذكر والكرم والإحسان و التفضل (٢) والانعام (٣).

٦- قال : والانسان لايكون ذافضل إلابأن تكون هذه الفضائل قنية له و حلى فيه و حاصلة لديه و غالبة عليه فقد بان من هذه الجملة أن عواقب الناس إلى هذه المصحوبة بين الكون و الفساد و المستصحبة إلى هناك أعنى على طريق الزاد (٤) و العتاد (٥) قال : وهذا التثليث قال بعض القائلين بالتناسخ : الأنفس ثلثة، نفس مالكة و نفس سالكة و نفس هالكة. قال < الكندى > : المالكة الناجية و السالكة الراجية و الهالكة لاحال لها (٦) فيذكر (٧).

٧- ثم قال : فأما فلاطون فإنه قال ان مسكن الأنفس العقلية إذا تجر دت كما قالت الفلاسفة القدماء خلف الفلك فى عالم الربوبية حيث نور البارى وليس كل نفس تفارق البدن تصير من ساعتها إلى ذلك المحل لأن فى الأنفس مايفارق (ورقه ٦١ و) البدن وفيها

(١) ك ـ يضاف

(٢) ك ـ الفضل

(٣) راجع رسائل ، ١ : ٢٧٤

(٤) ك ـ الراد

(٥) العناد فى المخطوطتين

(٦) ك ـ فيها

(٧) ب ـ مدكر

دنس و اشياء خسيسة (١) فمنها ما يصير ألى فلك عطارد فيقيم هناك مدة من الزمان فاذا تهذبت ونقيت ارتقت إلى فلك كوكب (كوكب) فيقيم مدة فإذا صارت إلى الفلك إلا على ونقيت غاية النقاء وزالت أدناس الحس و خبائثه (٢) منها ارتقت (٣) حينئذ إلى عالم العقل و جازت الظل و صارت فى أجل محل واشرقه وصارت حينئذ لاتخفى عليها خافية و واصلت نور البارى وصارت تفكر فى الأشياء قليلها وكثيرها كعلم الانسان باصبعه الواحدة و صارت الأشياءكلهالها(٤) مكشوفة بارزة ففوض البارى إليهامن سياسة العالم أشياء تلتذ بفعلهاوالتدبيرلها.

٨-وقال : لو أن رجلا افسد بيده أو اختياره أخس أعضائه لكان مذموما ومن العقل بعيداً. فكيف بمن أفسد أشرفها وهى التى تظهر منه القوى الحساسة والأفعال لبدنه أجمع اعنى الدماغ، فإن الحى يحد بأنه حساس السايسة، متحرك حركة إر ادية و الحس فى البدن انبثاثه من الدماغ وكذا جميع القوى النفسانية من الروية (٥) المولدة للإرادات و الفكر.

(١) ب ـ حسيه

(٢) خباريثه فى المخطوطتين

(٣) ك ـ ارنقت منها

(٤) ك ـ له

(٥) ب ـ الرديه .

٩- قال : ومستعملوا السكر مدخلوا الفساد على ادمغتهم (١) ومتى توالى السكر على بدنٍ مرض دماغه و اشته ضعفة و بعد عن القوة المظهرة للأفعال الارادية حتى بطل عنها فمن أعدم لنفسه ممن كان سبباً لتلف حياته ؟ والعجب أن يكون ذلك منهم وهم حرصاء (٢) على طول الحياة فإذا كانت ارادتهم نقص الحياة (٣) فكأنهم يريدون مالا يريدون.

١٠- وقال له رجل وكان جده أميراً على الكوفة، ما اشد توانيك فى طلب المعاش، فقال: لو عرفت المعاش لنسبتنى إلى شدة الحرص عليه. قال : مانراك تحضر مواضع الطلب من أبواب السلطان ومجامع التجار و مواضع الحرب (٢). فقال : نلك مواضع يغلبنى عليها أنت و نظراؤك على (٥) المطلوب فأما مواضع طلبتى فحيث أغلب عليه المنغلبين على مطلوبى. قال (ورقه ٦١ظ) و من يغلب (٦) المتغلبين؟ قال : من لا تصل (٨) أيدى المتغلبين إلى الاستيلاء عليه واستلابه

(١) ب ـ اذمغتهم

(٢) ب ـ صرعا

(٣) ب ـ الحيوة

(٤) ك ـ الحرث

(٥) غير واضحة فى ب

(٦) ك ـ تغلب

(٧) فى المخطوطة ـ ولا لصل ـ ولكن المعنى غير واضح بغير "من"

قنيته ويقدر خوله و اتباعه على استلاب المتغلبين قنيتهم، قال : فأين ابحول و الاتباع؟ لازاهم ولا يراهم غيرنا. قال: ماأكثر ماشاهدو كم تقنص واسرٍ وايثاقٍ وقتلٍ للناس والحيوان، وإنك لتتكلم الآن وانت فى ربقة أحدهم، فظهر (١) من السائل عند قوله "وأنت الآن فى ربقة أحدهم" غضبه. وقال : ماأشبه هذا القول بالهذيان. قال (٢) : فتبهم الكندى وقال: ليس بمستنكر أن يقع القول الصحيح عند من أشتد مرضه وغلب على عقله موقع الهذيان وأن يتناول الطبيب المشفق عليه الحريص على أنقاذه من مرضه بالشتم واللطم وغير ذلك من الاذى ولايمنع ذلك الطبيب الفاضل من رحمته والتعطف عليه ومناولته الدواء البشع إذا كانوا يرجون صلاحه <به> (٣)- وإن زاده ذلك بغتاً على أذاه، أما إلى هذه الغاية فقد كانت الربقة فى عنقك ستورة عن أكثر من عضر، أما الآن فقد أظهرت لآخر منهم غلاً وثيقاً قد ضم يدك إلى عنقك (لبعضهم) ستورة عن أكثر من حضر، فمايقدر لذلك أن يدنسه عن نفسك.

فقال رجل من تلا مذته للسائل: كنت يا فلان أسير

(١) ب و ك . فظهرت

(٢) غير موجودة فى ك

(٣) غير موجودة فى ب

شهوة خفية على من حضرك. هى دهتك إلى تطويل السؤال والحث على اكتساب المال فاستلبك من قبضها غضب عات هراك من ملا بسك التى سترت ربقة الشهوة ، فقال الرجل : مايكشف (١) لى معنى قوله إلى الآن. ثم قال معتذراً ألى الكندى : لعمرى لقد قلت مالا ينبغى فأنت أولى بالصفح و الإحتمال. فقال الكندى : ليس بصخيح (٢) حاجه إلى الدواء ولكن احتفظ بهذا الدواء فإنك إن احتفظت به نفعك وإن عتق.

١١- وقال أحمد من الغنب (٣) : كان الكندى يقول (٤) يانى انسخ كل ماتجده مكتوباً إذا اتسعت لك الجدة وامتدبك الزمان فإن ماتكتبه أسود من دفترك خير منه ابيض.

١٢- وقال : من صان لسانه أكثر أعوانه وجعل جميع الناس اخوانه.

١٣- وقال : المسترسل موتى والمحترس ملقى.

١٤- وقال أيضاً : العبد حر ما قنع و الحر عبد ماطمع.

(١) ك ـ تكشف

(٢) ك ـ با لصحيح

(٣) ك ـ احمد بن العنب و لعله احمد بن الطيب السرخسى تلميذ الكندى

(٤) ب ـ قال ، ك ـ تقول

١٥- وقال : ومن ملك نفسه ملك المملكة العظمى (ورقة ٦٢و) واستغنى عن المؤن. ومن ملك المملكة العظمى أمن الأمن الأعظم واستغنى عن المؤن) (١) فى ملكه، ارتفع عنه الذم والهرم، ومن ارتفع عنه الذم والهرم حمده كل احدٍ وطاب عيشه إلى الابد . فينبغى أن لايقصد (٢) فى الحمد عن (٣) كل أحدٍ وطيب عيش الابد إذ ليس أنفس منها مطلباً.

١٦- وقال : من انبع شيئاً اضطر اراً فهو متعبد له ومن تعبد لشئ فهو عبده.

١٧- وقال : غرض الشهوة اقتناء مشتهاها وغرض الهرب أن لا يوقع فيما يهرب منه والذى لايحظى غرض شهوته محظوظ والذى لايقع فيمايهرب منه سعيد

١٨- وقال : مع كل مصيبة ألم ومع كل حسرةٍ ندم .

١٩- وقال : من لم يكن حكيماً لم يزل سقيماً، من جهل رذل، العلم

(١) العبارة غير موجودة فى ب

(٢) ك ـ لقصر ـ يوجد شده فى فوق الصاد غير واضحة

(٣) ك ـ عند

غابر والجهل داثر، من أكثر المناكح (١) لم يسلم من الفضائح، من استشعر (٢) حلة العدل استكمل زينة الفضل.

هنا قلى رسالة الكندى إلى بعض اخوانه فى الامراض البلغمية العظام.

٢٠- وقال فى فصل يبطل (٣) به رأى من يرى عود النفس إلى هذا العالم من أصحاب التناسخ وإذا بطل دعوى من يدعى عود النفوس (٤) بطل (٥) عود ذوى النفس. قال هذا بمنزلة مايقولون أن رجلاً كان يشتاق إلى اللذات التى هى (٦) من ناحية الشهوات كالأ كل والشرب وكان يعد مها فلما وجدها عطف على علف الحمار ونور الجمل من التبن والحشيش والقت وماشبهه وهو على ذلك لايلتذ بها فعلى هذا كيف تشتاق النفس الناطقة فى حال تدبيرها البدن ومعاناتها لإعباء الطبيعة إلى المعارف وابحيرات، فلما تخلت من (٧) البدن (ورقة ٦٣ ظ) ومن الطبيعة عادت إلى أحوال

(١) ب ـ ذكر المناكح

(٢) ب ـ استسعد

(٣) ب ـ يطل

(٤) ك ـ النفس ولكن على هامش النفوس ،

(٥) ك ـ نبطل

(٦) غير موجودة فى ك

(٧) ب ـ هناك خط منحني بين تخلت والبدن غير واضح ولكن فى ك.. من

كانت لاتشتاق إليها ولاتنزع (١) نحرها ولاكفت من سجينها.

٢١- وقيل للكندى فلان غنى، فقال : اعلم أن له مالاً ولكنى لاأعلمه غنياً أم لا لأنى لاأدرى كيف يعمل فى ماله

٢٢- وقال : الحكمة ان كانت معطية كل شئٍ

حقاً فهى حق وهى أنفس الحق فمن أعطته ذاتها فقد أعطته أنفس الحق .

٢٣- وقال : ليس كل مطلوبٍ خارج عنا بموجود كلماطلب ولا موجود منه عقيب شئ منى فقد.

٢٤- وقال : رحمة العلماء إنماتكون من الشر وضحك الجهاّل بالذل وهاتان رذيلتان لأن الشر خاصة لكل رذيلة والذل لاحقة كل رذيلة

٢٥- وقال : أكمل ابحساسة قلة الاستحياء من النفس، ومن فاته الاستحياء من نفسه لم يفته (من) الزذايل ، ومن عدم الاستحياء <من نفسه > (٢) لم يعدم استحياء الناس من اخلاقه ومن لم يصحب الإستحياء (٣) من نفسه صحبنه الآفات ، ومن لزم الإستحياء من نفسه لزمته السلامة ومن لم يفته الإستحياء من نفسه لم يلحقه الذم

(١) ب ـ بنزع

(٢) غير موجودة فى ب و موجودة فى ك

(٣) ب ـ للاستحيا

لأن مع ركوب ما يستحي (١) منه الملامة والذم لكل من وجبت عليه (٢) الملامة فمن لم يلزمه الملامة لم يلحقه ذم .

٢٦- وقال العدل الموجود فى كل (٣) الأشياء هو خاصة الطبع الحقى لأن الاعراض إنماهي ابحروج عن العدل الحقى، فى، الاطراف اعنى الزيادة والنقص. فالعدل (٤) فى القوة المميزة ألانقصر (٥) عن الحق الانفع ولانحوز (٦) إلى الباطل أعنى المكرو الحيل (٧) وغير هما، والعدل فى الشهوة ألانقصر عن تناول مابه يبقى (٨) الإنسان وان لايعدوا ذلك ألى ما به اسقام بدنه ونفسه ومنعهاعن أفعالهاالشريفة ، والعدل فى الغضب ألانقصر (٩) عن النحدة أعنى الاستهانة بالمؤذيات البدنية والجد فى ذب المكاره عن ذاته وأن لايعدوا ذلك ألى تناول ماليس له ، والغضب والغشم والغيظ فالشئ

(١) ب و ك ـ يستحيا

(٢) ب ـ غلبه

(٣) ب و ك ـ كله

(٤) ك ـ و العدل

(٥) ب ـ يقصر ، فى ك لقصر

(٦) ب ـ بحوز

(٧) ب الحتل ، فى ك الحبل

(٨) ب ـ يبقا

(٩) ب و ك يقصر

الطبيعى أذا (١) لذواتنا الحكمة والعدل والعفة والنجدة واضداد هذه وإن كانت فى ذواتنا فهى عرض غير طبيعية لنا فنحن (٢) إذايجب (٣) أن يكون سعينا واجتهادنا في استحقاق هذا الشرف الذى قدمنا ذكره.

٢٨- وقال الرياضيات اعياد النفس لان فيها ومنها وبها يظهر (ورقة ٦٤ و) النفس العجائب المؤفقة (٤) لها والزين (٥) المعشوقة عندها وتناول (٦) اللذات الحقية (٧) لديها والتمتع بالراحة الحقية الصادقة فيها.

وهذه اقاويل موجزة مختصرة مبسوطة مكشفة عن الآفات العارضة فى سيل الفضائل المانعة من الاطنتهاء (٨) إلى (٩) الازواد والآلات المعينة على الانتهاء أليها.

٢٨- اثمن السلع الفضيلة ولاحرب اجحف من الرذيلة.

(١) ب ـ اذن

(٢) ك ـ فحق

(٣) ب ـ لحب ، ك ـ تجنب

(٤) ب ـ الموفقه

(٥) ب ـ والذين ، ك الدين

(٦) ب ـ يتناول

(٧) ب ـ الحقيقة

(٨) ك ـ الانها

(٩) ب ـ اليهاو

٢٩- من اتعبه الهرب من السيئات زماناً ألبسه دوام الراحة فى ظلال الحسنات اماناً.

٣٠- ومن هرب من تعب البدن الزائل لم ينج من تعب النفس اللازم القاتل.

٣١- من اتخذ العدل سنة كان له أحصن جنة .

٣٢- من اتخذ الحكمة لجاماً اتخذه الناس اماماً.

٣٣- العار عدم العفة والشره (١) ادنى حرفة .

٣٤ - من صبا إلى الشهوات اعقبته البليات

٣٥- من ظهر زهده اشتد ايده ولم يعصه عبده وسعد جده . ٣٦- الزاهد هو الواجد.

٣٧- من زهد فى الدنيا ملكها ومن اخرص عليها أهلكته (٢)

٣٨- من زهد فى الدنيا لم تفته (٣) ومن حرص عليها اتعبته.

٣٩- من اتخذ الحرص شعاراً جرعته الفوت مراراً.

٤٠- من حسن قنوعه دام ربيعه.

(١) ب ـ الشرة

(٢) ب و ك ـ اهلكها

(٣) ب ـ نقته

٤١- القنوع خير من ابحضوع.

٤٢- من باع الطمع بالبأس لم يستظل عليه الناس.

٤٣- من قل قنوعه كثر خضوعه

٤٤- من لم يكن قنعاً لم يزل جزءاً.

٤٥- من لزم الطمع لزمه الجزع.

٤٦- من لم يزل الطمع له راكباً لم يزل الفقر له صاحباً.

٤٧- من تولج ضيق مسلك الحلم افضى به ألى سعة اوطان الأمن

٤٨- من كان الحلم له وطناً كان له العز معقلاً

٤٩- من سكن عند الغضب لم يتحرك (١) له العطب

٥٠- من اطاع الغضب عصمة السلامة .

٥١- من عصا الحلم اطاع الذل.

٥٢- من فحش غضبه هدم حسبه .

٥٣- من تقحم الغضب اقتحم عليه الندم .

٥٤- خوف ما لا دفع له من اخلاق ما لا(٢) عقل له .

(١) ب . لحرك

(٢) غير موجودة فى ك

٥٥- شرب السم اهون من تضمن الهم.

٥٦- من اتبع الصبر اتبعه النصر.

٥٧- من حسن خلقه طاب رزقه ، ومن ساء حلقه قل رزقه

٥٨- من حسن رفقه عظم حقه.

٥٩- من رفق رفق، من خرق حمق.

٦٠- ابحرق فى الاعمال ادعى إلى الاملال (١).

٦١- الفخر أصغر القدر (٢) .

٦٢- (ورقة ٦٤ظ) من فخر فجر.

٦٢- من رضى بحظوظ (٣) الناس لم ينله اليأس .

٦٤- من رضى بحظ غيره لم ير النقص فى خيره .

٦٥- الحسد غاية الكمد.

٦٦- حزن الحاسد ابداً غير حامد.

٦٧- غيظ الحاسد إلى الابد.

٦٨- الحاسد غير واجد، فالحاسد ابداً فاقد

٦٩- الجود مودود غير موجود.

٧٠- ما اقبح البخل بكل ذى عقل.

(١) ك ـ الاقلال

(٢) ب و ك ، للقدر

(٣) ب ـ محفوظ

٧١- البخيل ابداً ذليل .

٧٢- البخيل غير اصيل .

٧٣- من اشتد بخله قل اكله .

٧٤- الامانة (١) ثوب الصيانة.

٧٥- خيانة الناس اقبح افلاس (٢).

٧٦- من لزم الوفاء لزمه الرضاء.

٧٧- من اطاع الوفاء لم يعصه الاخاء.

٧٨- من ساس نفسه بالصدق لم يجد لشئ فقداً.

٧٩- من صدقت لهجته ظهرت محجته .

٨٠- من صدق نفسه دام انسه.

٨١- من كذب ذهب .

٨٢- من استطال على الاخوان لم يصحبه انسان .

٨٣- من عدم الاخوان اكثر ذم الزمان ومن اكثر ذم الزمان لم بعدم الاحزان ومن كثر من الاحزان لم يعتبه الزمان ومن لم يعتبه الزمان لزمه الهوان .

٨٤- ومن حسن انسه كثر جنسه وأخص الاجناس جنس الايناس، ومن قلل جنسه اهان نفسه.

(١) ب ـ الابانه

(٢) ب و ك ـ افلاسا

٨٥- الصلف أنتن من الجيف (١) ، ومن ظهر صلفة بطل انفه.

٨٦- من حار عن القصد تاه فى الجهد.

٨٧- السرف ظماء (٢) والعجب عماء .

٨٨- من اعجبته (٣) نفسه فقد فسد حسه و من دخله العجب فقد لبسه الكذب .

٨٩- المعجب اكذب ومعرفة النفس اصوب .

٩٠- من لم يعجب بنفسه نصحها ومن اعجب بها فضحها.

٩١- خلق المعجب عنده انفس اعلاقه واحسن ما يرى فيه فقد اخلاقه.

٩٢- المعجب ابداً مغضب .

٩٣- من اقتحم الهزل ارتطم فى الجهل.

٩٤- من هذا اذى (٤)

٩٥- السعاية خزاية ، من سعى فقد هوى .

(١) غير موجودة فى ك

(٢) ب و ك ، طماء

(٣) ك ـ اعجب

(٤) الكلمة ـ غير واضحة و يبدو على الهامش بجانبها كلمة "اذا" وهى واضحة فى ك

٩٦- التشاغل بالمنى من افعال الصبا (١).

٩٧- من كسل هزل.

٩٨- وقال له قائل يوما : سمت فلانا ينقصك فغمني ذلك وعرفته نفسه ، فقال إنماينبغى ان نغتم (٢) إذا أنا تنقصت نفسى و تعرفنى عند ذلك نفسى فانى اولى منك بذلك لقديم المؤدة .

٩٩- وقال له قائل يوما : ان فلانا يتناولك (٣) يلسانه، فقال له : ان لم يتناولنى (٤) طبعى و نجري (٥) إلى لسانه لم يكن فى طبع لسانه ان ينالنى كما يناوله طبعه و اعفنى لسانى من تكلف تناوله .

١٠٠- وقال له قائل يوما ما : سمعت فلانا يفخر بكذا وكذا (ورقه ٦٥ و) فقال له : من لم يكن الفاخر له فعله لم يتزين له اهله .

١٠١- وقال له قائل : ان فلانا يزعم انك إنما تمسك عنه خوفا له

(١) فى المحطوطين ، الصبى

(٢) ب . يغتم

(٣) ب . ناولك

(٤) ب . تناولنى

(٥) فى المخطوطتين يخرى ويمكن "نجزى

فقال : لو خاف ما اخافنى منه كان نجداً حراً، فقال له الرجل : وكيف ذلك؟ فقال: لأن النجد لا يستأنس لا عدائه فلا يكون مر قوما. وقال له الرجل: ومن هؤلاء الاعداء الذين استأنس لهم؟ فقال: الجور (١) وجميع اتباعه. وقال له الرجل: ومن اتباعه؟ فقال له: الجهل و النفاق والسفه والتهور والجبن والحرص والحسد والشر (٢) و الخلاعة الموجبة لمن كان فى نفيها (٣) رحمة العقلاء واضحاك (٤) الحمقى. فقال له الرجل : هو عند نفسه النجد البطل. فقال له إذا القوى على نفسه الذى لا يصرفه عن فعل ما يوجبه الحق خوف الموت .

١٠٢- وقال له قائل يوما: من اقوى الناس؟ فقال: اقواهم على نفسه. فقال له: ومن اشدهم قوةَ عليها؟ فقال: من أمات شهوته وذلل غضبه حتى تصير له مركبا سلس القياد ينال به الحق ويدفع به الباطل، غير مكترث بالموت فى ذلك (٥) فقال: فمن احكم الناس؟ فقال: اعرفهم بنفسه واشدهم احتمالاً للادوية البشعة فى دفع اسقامها فقال له : ومن اعدل (اعدل) الناس؟ فقال : من لزم الحق فلم

(١) ك ـ الخور

(٢) ب ـ الشريد

(٣) ب ـ نصها، ك ـ نفسها

(٤) اصحال فى المخطوطتين

(٥) فى ذلك بالموت

يخرج عنه وعن العمل بما يوجبه الحق. فقال له : ومن اعف الناس؟ فقال: من عدل فى شهواته فلم يتناول منها شيئاً خارجاً عن ما به الضرورة إلى تناوله فى اقامة صورته الشخصية واثمار مثلها على شريطة قاموس العقل وناموس الوضع.

١٠٣- وقال له قائل يوماً : من اشقى الناس فى دنياه؟ فقال : من كانت ارادة نفسه اقتناء (١) ابحارجات عنه فانه فى كل حال يفوته به مطلوب ويعوزه به محبوب ومع كل فايت حسرة ومع كل مفقود مصيبة، وهذان ولدان الحزن والأسف اللذان هماضد الفرح والاغتباط، والاضداد لاتواقف فى شئ، فمتى كان انسان حزيناً آسفاً بطل فرحه واغتباطه ومن كان حزيناً آسفاً فهو نكد الحياة ومن نكدت حياته فهو شقى فى دنياه. فقال له : من الشقى فى الدار الآخرة؟ فقال : من لم يعرف خالقه وما يقرب منه والعمل بذلك .

١٠٤- وقال له قائل يوما. من احسن الناس (ورقة ٦٥ ظ) صورة؟ فقال له : البسهم للفضيلة (٢) الانسانية . فقال له : وما الفضيلة الانسانية؟ فقال له: الحكمة والعدل والعفة والنجدة فى كل <شئ>

(١) ل ـ اقناء

(٢) ب ـ الفضيله

١٠٥- وقال له قائل يوما: من ابخل الناس؟ فقال من بحل بما لا ينقصه جوده به على غيره ولا يخرجه من ملكه. فقال له: وما الذى لا يخرجه من ملكه ولا ينقصه جوده على غيره. فقال له : العلم، فإن الجود به غير ناقص منه ولا يخرجه من ملكه (١) بل يكثر به اثماره ويبغى آثاره بما لنا فى ذلك فى الدار الآخرة من جزيل الثواب فان من ثمر البحير خيرا وابحير . محمود المنقلب (٢) إلى دار القرار ومن حسنت أثاره فى دنياه محمود و المحمود مسرف الذكر، فثمرة الجود بالعلم مسرف الدنيا فى الآخرة (٣) فان حمد المنقلب (٤) ايضا مسرف فى المنقلب.

١٠٦- فقال له : من اجود الناس؟ قال : من جاد بما فيه التحصمن من جميع الآفات النفسانية والترقى إلى غاية شرف (٥) الفضيلة الانسانية. فقال له : وماذلك؟ فقال العلم الذى به الإحتراس من أفات الانفس والاجساد التى للانسان الإحتراس منها واقتناء الفضائل الانسانية التى كل ابحير فيها.

(١) ب ـ ملكنا، هكذا ايضا فى ك

(٢) ب ـ المتقلب

(٣) ك ـ الدنيا والآخرة

(٤) ب ـ المتقلب

(٥) ب سرف

١٠٧- وقيل له من اجهل الناس ؟ فقال من جهل انه لا يعلم لأن جهله مركب فماالذى يجهل ويعلم انه يجهل فجهله بسيط غير مركب .

١٠٨- وقيل له : ما احق الأشياء بالحمد هند ذوى العقول. فقال: مبدع الكل جل ثناؤه. جعله سبباً لثبات خلقه و وجدانه جل ثناؤه. فقال له : وما سبب ثبات خلقه؟ فقال : العدل ، لأن المعتدل ثابت وابحروج عن الاعتدال زايل فاصد والذى به وجدانه ، جل ثناؤه، العقل فإنا به وجدنا انا مبدعين فيوجب وجوه مبدع.

ENGLISH TRANSLATION

By

A. S. BAZMEE ANSARI

Signs and Abbreviations

B. ( ) Br. Mus. MS. 9033 Or., fols. 60 r—65 *v.*, on which the present is based.

K. ( ) Koprulu, Istanbul MS. 902 fols. 85 *r*—92 *v.*

[ ] Editor's additions or according to *K.*

( ) As in the original; may be deleted as it is our addition or is according to *K.*

Numbers of paragraphs and sayings are our own as well as the marks of punctuation and dots.

TEXT

1. (fol. 60 *r*) Abu Yusuf Ya'qub b. Ishaq al-Kindi. He was the first among the Muslims to acquire high proficiency in philosophy and all its branches; in mathematics and allied subjects in addition to his deep knowledge of the sciences of the Arabs and his excellence in humanities like grammar and poetry, astrology, medicine, various arts and sciences; qualities which are seldom united in a single individual. The list of his books exceeds one quire of paper (24 sheets) folded. He was the tutor to Ahmad b. Muhammad al-Mu'tasim and composed many of his works for him, and addressed to him most of his epistles (*rasa'il*) as well as the answers to his queries. He was the first [among the Muslims] to introduce this form of writing which was later followed by the succeeding generations of [scholars among] the Muslims. During the days of al-Ma'mun those who acquired name and fame before him were mostly Christians who had adopted in their works the old style of writing.

Due to the fame of his books and treatises and their being easily available at all places, I do not [intend to] exhaust [all] the [salient] points in his writings but would extract from them at random only a few (sayings) which are indispensable for embellishment this work.

2. (fol. 60 *v*). Among his sayings is : "As the First Cause, Most High, is connected with us through His emanation and as we are not connected with Him in any way except through His emanation, it is, therefore, possible for the receiver of His emanation to apprehend Him only to the extent of the powers bestowed on him. It becomes, therefore, obligatory for us not to meaning Him according to the degree of our apprehension of Him because His apprehension [of us] is most abundant, complete and all-pervading. So, when this is this he, who holds that the First Cause does not know particulars, is far from truth a great deal."

3. And he said: "The best speech is that which is

clear in meaning and spontaneous in expression. Such a speech, therefore, hits the bull's eye and is sweet in diction."

4. And he said: "The study of books of wisdom (philosophy) is the 'Id [occasion of festivity] of the rational souls."

5. And he said: "Plato likens the concupiscent faculty to a pig, the passionate faculty to a dog and the rational faculty to an angel. He says: 'He who is overwhelmed with concupiscence is [like] the swine; he who is over-whelmed with passion is [like] the dog, and he who is over-whelmed with reason is [like] the angel. Therefore, when one is [like] an angel, one is nearer God in likeness because of the things which are attributed to God the Almighty, namely, wisdom, might, justice, virtue, grace, remembrance (invocation), generosity, beneficence, bounty, and favour.

6. He said: "Man does not become a recipient of God's favours until he comes to possess these excellent qualities [mentioned in the preceding paragraph] with which he adorns himself, and which he comes to acquire and which [ultimately] dominate him. It is clear from this sentence that the ultimate fate of human beings depends on these virtues which are with them in [this world of] becoming and decay [and] which will accompany them to the Hereafter by way of provisions and outfit."

He said: "And due to this trichotomy some of those who believe in metampsychosis [say] that there are three [kinds of] souls, the possessing soul, the moving soul and decaying soul." He said: "The possessing soul would attain salvation, the moving soul is hopeful and decaying soul has no state worth mentioning."

7. He added: "In so far as Plato is concerned he too, like the ancient philosophers, maintains that the rational souls, after leaving the bodies, abide in the world of Divinity (Lordship) behind the heaven (*al-falak*) where pervades the Light of the Lord. But every soul, from the

very moment it leaves (fol.61 *r*) the body, does not attain to this station because there are souls which, when they leave the body, contain impurities and base matter. Consequently some of them go to the Sphere of Mercury and stay there for a while : and when they are purified and cleansed they ascend to the Sphere of the Stars, there they stay for a while, [and] then go up to the highest of the heavens; [here] they are purified to the highest degree and all the filth of the senses and [other] impurities are removed; they then ascend to the world of Reason and after crossing the Shade reach the greatest and the most noble station. They are then in such a state that no secret remains hidden from them and they come into contact with the Light of the Lord. They begin to contemplate things, whether small or great in number, [as clearly] as a man knows his finger(s). At this time all the things become manifest and exposed to them. The Lord then commits to them affairs relation to the administration of the world in whose performance and conduct they relish and take delight."

8. He said: "If a person either with his own hands or of his own wills damages even the most ordinary limb of his body he would be considered condemnable and bereft of reason; so what would be the fate of a person who damages the noblest limb [of his body] which actuates the faculties of sense-perception and the powers which govern his whole body, i.e. the brain. [It is so] because the definition of a live [organism] is that it is sensitive and moved by volition; and sensation in the body is diffused by the brain. And this is the case with all the psychical faculties such as reflection which gives birth to volition and thought."

9. And he said: "The users of intoxicants allow morbidity to enter their brains and as the body succumbs to intoxication, the brain becomes diseased, weakness grows and the faculty from which spring actions declines and is ultimately lost. So, who can be a bigger ill-wisher of his own self than he who is a cause of the destruction of his own life. It is surprising that they do so while thev

are keen on prolonging their life. So, when they are after reducing [their] life, it appears that they do not want [to do] what they are wont [to do].

10. A person whose grandfather was the governor of al-Kufah said to him: "How lazy you are in earning a living"! He said: "Had you known what it means to make a living, you would have [rather] blamed me for being exceedingly fond of it." The man said: "We do not find you at places where people seek a living, for instance, the courts of the Sultans, the meeting-places of traders (entrepots) and battle-grounds." He replied: "These are the places where you and your fellows surpass me in the achievement of the goal. But at the places of my seeking [a living] I overwhelm the adversaries in gaining my object. The man asked [fol. 61 *v*): "And who overwhelms these adversaries?" [He replied]: "He whom the hands of the adversaries do not reach (in order) to overwhelm him and to deprive him of his possessions although his servants and retainers are capable of dispossessing the adversaries of their gains."

The man [then] asked: "Where are the servants and retainers; neither do we see them nor they are visible to anyone else?" He replied: "They are very often seen hunting down, imprisoning, capturing and killing [both] men and animals. While you are talking to me you are [even] now in the clutches of one of them. And when he told the questioner that he was in the clutches of one of them, signs of anger appeared [on the latter's face] and he blurted out: "How closely these words [of yours] resemble nonsense! It was reported [that] al-Kindi smiled and said. "This is not unlikely that a truthful speech may appear absurd to a [sick] person whole illness has grown worse and whose reason has been clouded and who receives the kindly-disposed physician, who is very keen to cure him of his illness, with abuses and slaps and other insults. Nonetheless these acts of his would not prevent the learned physician from being kind and well-disposed towards him, neither would these deter him from administering to him [i.e. the patient] distasteful medicine [which] the people hope would cure him, although it might result in the patient's becoming more violent [towards the physician]'. So far the noose about your neck was concealed from most of those present here but now that you have exposed to one of them this strong collar, hidden from many of those present, [and] which had kept your hand fastened to your neck, he would not be able to rule it off your soul."

[Thereupon] one of the students of al-Kindi said to the questioner: "Ah! You (are) the captive of a burning desire, which you had kept hidden from those present and it was edging you on to prolonging the question and egging you on to acquiring wealth. Consequently unbridled anger made you discard this desire and tore off from you that garment, rendering you naked, which had kept concealed the noose of the burning desire." The person retorted: "I have not been able to understand his speech so far." Then apologising to al-Kindi he said: "By my age! [As] you are indulging in indiscreet speech, you deserve it more to be ignored and forgiven." Al-Kindi said: "[Although] a sound person does not need medicine, yet you keep this medicine carefully. If you take good care of it, it will do you good even if it becomes old."

11. And Ahmad b. al-Ghanab (?) said that al-Kindi used to say: "Oh Sonny! If you have the means and leisure, copy it out whatever written you come across because whatever of your note-book you leave black would be better than what you leave blank."

12. And he said: "He who minds his tongue will have many a supporter and all the people will become his helpers."

13. And he said: "The carefree remains unharmed while the careful meets with trouble."

14. And he also said: "A slave is [as good as] a free man if contented but a free man is [no more than] a slave if greedy."

15. And he said: "He who overcomes his self becomes the master of a large kingdom (fol. 62 *r*) and faces no difficulties. And he who becomes the master of such a great kingdom achieves the greatest peace and becomes free from regrets. And he who achieves the greatest peace remains free from regrets within his kingdom and is safe from blame and ruin. And he who is safe from blame and ruin every one praises him and life becomes pleasant for all time to come. He should, therefore, not expect praise from [each and] every one and a pleasant life throughout, for there is no object more valuable [to achieve] than these two."

16. And he said: "He who follows a thing involuntarily becomes deeply attached (devoted) to it, and he who is [fondly] devoted to a thing becomes [ultimately] its slave."

17. And he said: "The aim of desire is to get the thing desired, and to shun some thing is to avoid involvement in it. So he who does not miss the aim of his desire is happy and he who avoids to involve himself in it is lucky."

18. And he said: "Every misfortune is accompanied by sorrow and every disappointment by shame."

19. And he said: "He who is not wise will come to grief; he who is ignorant is abased; knowledge survives and ignorance perishes. He who takes too many wives will not escape censure (lit. disgrace, shame); he who dons the robes of justice, completes the decoration of excellence (nobility of character)."

[Here follows al-Kindi's Risalah *On Severe Phlegmatic Diseases* which he addressed to some of his friends.]

20. (fol. 63 *r*). In a chapter refuting the opinion of some of the believers in metempsychosis that the soul returns to this world, he said: "And when the premisses of those who claim the return of the soul [to this world] does not hold good, [the premiss of] the return of those

possessing the soul [also] does not hold good." He said: "This is [as they say] just like a person who was fond of pleasures which are a kind of appetite such as eating and drinking but he could not satisfy them. However, when he got the opportunity he did not spare [even] chaff, hay and trefoil (clover) etc., which are the food of an ass and the fodder of a camel. Yet, he could derive no pleasure from them. So, how it is possible for the rational soul when busy looking after the body and with the satisfaction of its urges (lit. abodes, halting-places) to turn naturally to the sciences and [the performance of] meritorious deeds. Therefore, when the rational soul is free from attending to the [need of the] body (fol. 63 *v*) and the [urges of] nature she returns to situations for which she had no desire, and was neither inclined towards them, nor was disposed to them.

21. It was reported to al-Kindi that such and such a person was wealthy. He said: "I know he has riches but I do not know whether he is free from want also, as I do not know how he spends his wealth."

22. He said: "Wisdom [is this] that every thing is given its due, [so] this is [in fact] *the* right and the most precious of rights. And to whomsoever wisdom surrenders herself [it is as if] she bestows on him the most precious of rights."

23. He said: "Every desired thing, external to us, is not present (i.e. available) when wanted, nor any desired thing can be called present when it is lost."

24. And he said: "The compassion of the *'ulama'* is on account of evil and the laughter of the ignorants is due to their meanness; and both these are vices, because evil is peculiar to every meanness and to every meanness is disgrace attached."

25. And he said: "The height of vileness is the want of modesty in the soul and he whose soul is bereft of modesty, vices never leave him. And he whose soul is shorn of modesty, people feel ashamed of his manners;

and he who does not possess modesty is always visited by misfortune. But he who sticks to modesty always enjoys safety and protection. He whose soul does not part with modesty, never faces condemnation, because the commission of shameful acts invites censure and condemnation; [and] he alone is upbraided who [in fact] deserves censure. So, he who does not deserve censure, never faces condemnation."

26. He said: "The equipoise (balance, justice) found in all things is peculiar to the natural instinct because deviation means turning away from the natural justice side-ways i.e. towards excess or want. Therefore equipoise in the discriminating faculty means that we should not be found wanting in [striving for] the most gainful truth and should not be attracted to vanity i.e. deceit and trickery etc. In the case of the concupiscent faculty justice means that no efforts should be spared in obtaining things on which depends the very existence of man and in this we should not go to the length of contracting both physical and psychical diseases which may prevent (the soul) from performing noble acts. [Similarly], in the case of the passionate faculty justice means that we should not be found wanting in fortitude i.e. belittling physical afflictions and making our best for removing all odium from ourselves. Even in this, however, we should not go to the extremes such as fury, tyranny and wrath. Therefore, what is innate with us is wisdom and equity, chastity, and fortitude. And their opposites, although present in ourselves, are accidentals which are not innate with us. It is, therefore, obligatory on us that [all] our efforts should be bent towards proving [ourselves] worthy of the honour which we have mentioned above."

27. And he said: "The exact sciences are the festivals of the soul because in them, from them and through them become manifest (fol. 64 *r*) fine wonders for the soul and lovely decorations through which she derives real pleasures and in which she finds genuine and true enjoyment."

Here are those short, pithy but comprehensive sayings (of al-Kindi) which remove those hurdles (lit. troubles) which block the pathways to excellence and the wherewithal (lit. kit and implements) which helps in reaching them. (i.e. excellences; nobility of character).

28. The most precious commodity is *fadilah* (excellence, virtue) and no war is more destructive than depravity.

29. He who is exhausted by eschewing evils for a long time, perpetual comfort and ease will afford him peace in the (cool) shade of virtues.

30. He who shirks [even] the temporary fatigue of the body, will not escape the inevitable mortal fatigue of the soul.

31. He who adopts justice as a habit, it becomes the strongest shield for him.

32. He who holds to wisdom as bridle [to control his passions], people hold him up as [their] leader.

33. Disgrace is absence of chastity; and cupidity is the meanest avocation.

34. He, who is deeply in love with sensual appetites, is pursued by calamities.

35. He, whose asceticism becomes known, gains in strength; his servant does not [dare] disobey him and he meets with luck in his efforts.

36. An ascetic is free from want (lit. rich, wealthy).

37. He who abstains from the world, obtains her; [but] he who covets her, she kills him.

38. He who shuns the world she does not overtake him, but he who covets her, she wearies him.

39. He who takes to avarice as a habit, tastes disappointment repeatedly.

40. He whose contentment is graceful, his spring knows no autumn.

41. Contentment is better than humiliation [and disgrace].

42. He who purchases avarice with disappointment, is not afforded shade (protection) by the people.

43. Whose contentment decreases, his humiliation increases.

44. He who loses contentment, always bewails.

45. He who is given up (lit. sticks) to greed, has to bewail.

46. He who is ridden by greed, is always accompanied by need (poverty).

47. He who enters on the narrow path of forbearance, reaches the extensive abodes of peace.

48. He who makes forbearance as his abode, honour becomes his haven (stronghold).

49. He who remains calm in the [face of] provocation, destruction never meets him.

50. He, who obeys anger, peace [and prosperity] never obey him.

51. He, who disobeys forbearance, yields to disgrace.

52. He, who exceeds [the limits] in anger, destroys his prestige.

53. He, who is overcome with anger, repentance befalls him.

54. Fearing the inevitable is the way of fools.

55. Taking poison is easier than undergoing anxiety.

56. He, who follows patience, is followed by success (lit. help).

57. Good habits bring prosperity; bad habits end in poverty.

58. He, who is polite, his share increases.

59. He who is skillful behaves civilly, he who is clumsy acts foolishly.

60. Clumsy acts (misbehaviour) invite disgust.

61. Pride lowers prestige.

62. (fol. 64 *v*). He, who becomes proud, commits a sin.

63. He, who is happy with other's lot, never suffers disappointment.

64. He, who is happy with the lot of others, suffers no loss in his (own) good.

65. Jealousy is the deepest sorrow.

66. The grief of a jealous person always goes in vain (lit. gets no praise).

67. The anger of a jealous person never cools off.

68. A jealous person never becomes rich, he is always in want.

69. Generosity is coveted, (but) is hardly available.

70. How exceedingly bad is miserliness to every sensible person.

71. A niggard is perpetually disgraced.

72. A niggard is not noble.

73. Whose stinginess increases, his food decreases.

74. Trustworthiness is the raiment of integrity.

75. Perfidy is the worst (form of) poverty.

76 He, who keeps his word, is always happy.

77. He, who is faithful, his brethren do not disobey him.

78. He, who deports himself with truth, never finds anything wanting.

79. He who speaks the truth, finds the middle or his way clear.

80. He who is true to himself, always endears himself.

81. He who speaks a lie is ruined.

82. He who is unfair (lit. overwhelms) to his brethren, finds no associates.

83. He who has no associates often blames the times; he who often blames the times, is never free from grief; he who is often in grief, is not favoured by the times; and he who is not favoured by the times is scorned at.

84. He who is highly sociable finds many friends (lit. fellows); and the best of the genera is sociality. And he whose genera (fellows) decrease debases himself.

85. Boasting smells fouler than a carcass; and he whose boasting is exposed, loses face.

86. He whose plans go awry, his labours go in vain.

87. Extravagance is thirst and pride is blindness.

88. He who becomes self-centred, loses all feeling, and he who succumbs to vanity is wrapped up in falsity.

89. A boastful person is the biggest liar, and knowledge of self is the best (thing to acquire).

90. He who is not vainglorious is his own well-wisher; and he who sounds his own trumpet, humiliates himself.

91. To a conceited person his morality is his most

precious possession and the best of what is seen in him is the loss of his morality.

92. A conceited person is always angry.

93. He who jests, ignorance befalls him.

94. He who talks idly, lands himself in trouble.

95. Slandering is a shame; he who slanders, debases himself.

96. Riding wishes is childish.

97. He who is lazy, becomes weak.

98. One day some one told him: "I heard a certain person slandering you; that pained me and I put him in his place." He said: "We should have felt pained had there occurred some defect in myself and you would have brought it to my notice because old friendship (between us) has a better claim on you."

99. Another person tole him one day: "Such and such a person slights you." He replied: "If my nature and my disposition do not bring me within the range of his (sharp) tongue and we mind what he says, his tongue would not, by nature, do to me what his [own] nature does to him because my tongue is above doing him what he has done [to me]."

100. Some one told him one day: "I heard such and such a person boasting of this and that" (fol. 65 *r*). He told him: "He, whose deeds bring him no credit, [would find] his own people a matter of no pride for him." "Who is the best ruler among men?" Al-Kindi replied: "He who knows his own self best and can best suffer even the most bitter and distasteful medicine for the treatment of his [psychical] ailments." The man then asked: "[And] who is the most just among the people?" He replied: "He who sticks to truth and does not veer from it or from doing what is demanded by Truth." The man [then] asked: "And who is the most continent among men?" He

replied: "He who maintains a balance in his carnal appetites and does not satisfy them for purposes other than those which are indispensable for maintaining the [outer] form of his individuality and bearing fruit in accordance with the rational laws and positive laws."

101. And some one told him one day: "Whose days are the most miserable (wretched) among the people?" He replied: "He whose self desires to possess what does not belong to him. Consequently he always misses what he is after; and what he loves, eludes him. And every thing missed is accompanied by grief, and every thing lost by misfortune. Both these are born of sadness and grief which are the opposites of cheerfulness and joy, and opposites never blend together in a thing. So, whenever a man is struck with grief and sorrow his cheerfulness and joy disappear. And he who is sad and grief-stricken his life becomes unhappy; and he whose life becomes unhappy his days become miserable." The man then asked: "Who is unlucky in the Hereafter?" Al-Kindi replied: "He who does not recognise his Creator and what brings him near Him and neither does he do anything to that effect."

102. And some one asked him one day: "Who is the most handsome (fol. 65 *v*) among men?" He told him: "He who wraps himself up with human excellences." The man then asked: "And what are human excellences?" He replied: "Wisdom, justice, chastity and chivalry in every [matter]."

103. He was asked one day: "Who is the most niggardly among men?" He said: "He who is mean [lit. miserly] with things which do not diminish by being given away to others and which [still] remain in his possession." He asked him: "And what is that which does not diminish by being given to others and still remains in one's possession?" Al-Kindi replied: "It is knowledge which does not diminish by use and does not go out of ones possession. On the other hand, in this way its fruits multiply and its vestiges remain, bringing

us in turn a generous reward in the life Hereafter because the fruit of virtue is [nothing but] virtue and the end of good up to the Lasting Abode remains laudable, and he who does good deeds, his worldly remains elicit praise and he who is worthy of praise is talked about often. Therefore, the fruit of generosity in knowledge will [be] project[ed] from this world into the next. Hence the praise-[worthiness] of the end reverts to the end itself."

104. He [the questioner] then asked: "Who is the most generous among men?" Al-Kindi replied: "He who gives away what may be a shield against all spiritual misfortunes and which may lead to [the attainment of] the highest degree of human excellence." He [then] asked: "And what is that?" He replied: "That is knowledge, which is a protection against the psychical and physical disasters which a man could guard himself against, and the attainment of those human virtues in which there is nothing but good [for a man]."

105. And he was asked: "Who is the most ignorant among men?" Al-Kindi replied: "He who even does not know that his ignorance is compound, but he who is ignorant and knows that he is ignorant, his ignorance is pure and simple."

106. And he was asked: "What is more deserving of praise in the eyes of the wise?" Al-Kindi replied: "The Creator of every thing, may His praise be great! Who made it [i.e. the Universe] the cause for the vindication of His Creation and His Existence; may His praise be great!" The man then asked: "And what is the reason for the vindication of His Creation?" Al-Kindi rejoined: "Balance (righteousness, justice), because anything that is balanced is firm [and strong] and deviation from balance leads to decay and corruption. And what is instrumental in making us know His Existence (may His praise be great!) is Intellect because it is through Intellect that we realise that we are (all) created beings; it therefore, makes the existence of a Creator necessary [and absolute]."

BIBLIOGRAPHY

'Abd al-Raziq, 'Ali — *Faylasuf al-'Arab wa' 1-Mu'allim al-Thani,* Cairo, Ihya' al-Kutub al-'Arabiyah Press, 1945.

al-Ahwani, A. Fu'ad — *Paraphrase du De Anima,* Cairo, 1950.

Aristotle — *De Anima,* translated by A. J. Smith, in *The Basic Works of Aristotle,* ed. R. Mckeon, New York, 1941.

Metaphysics, translated by W.D. Ross, vol. VIII in *The Works of Aristotle.* Translated into English under the editorship of W. D. Ross, Oxford, The Clarendon Press, 1928.

Physics, translated by R. P. Hardie and R. K. Gaye, in *The Works of Aristotle,* ed. W. D. Ross, Oxford, 1930.

Problemata, translated by E. S. Forestar, vol. VII in *The Works of Aristotle,* ed. W. D. Ross, Oxford 1927.

Awwad, Kurkis, — *Al-Kindi,* Baghdad, 1962.

Bacon, Roger, — *Opus Magnus,* ed. R. B. Burke, 2 vols., Philadelphia, 1928.

Badawi, 'A. (ed.), — *Aristu 'inda'l-'Arab* (Islamic

Studies No. 5), Cairo, al-Nahdah Press. 1947.

al-Bayhaqi, Zahir al-Din 'Ali, *Ta'rikh Hukama' al-Islam,* ed. M. Kurd 'Ali, Damascus, 1946; *Tatimma Siwan al-Hikmah,* ed. Muhammad Shafi', Lahore, 1935.

al-Biruni, Abu Rayhan, *Risalah li'l-Biruni fi Fihrist Kutub Muhammad Zakariyyah al-Razi,* ed. P. Kraus, Paris, 1936.

al-Mas'udi, *Muruj al-Dhahab,* ed. Barbier de Meynard and P. de Courteille, 9 vol., Paris, 1923.

al-Mawardi, Ab'ul-Hasan, *Adab al-Dunya wa'l-Din,* ed. M. Saqqa, Cairo, 1955.

Brockelmann, C. *Geschichte der Arabischen Litteratur,* 2 vols., Erster-dritter, Supplementband, 3 vols., Leiden, 1937-42.

Cicero, M. T., *On Divination,* translated by H. M. Poteat, Chicago, 1950.

On the Nature of the Gods, translated by H. M. Poteat, Chicago, 1950.

Corpus Hermeticum, Text established by A. D. Nock, and translated into French by A. J. Festugiere, 4 vols., Paris, 1945-54.

Cumont, Fr. *The Oriental Religions in Roman Paganism,* New York, 1956.

De Boer, T. J., "Al-Kindi wider die Trinitaet," in *Festschrift Theodor Noeldeke, ed.* C. Bezold, Giessen, Verlag Von Al-fred Toepelmann, 1906.

"Zu Kindi und seiner Schule," in *Archiv Fuer Geschiclte der Philosophie*, Bd. VI N. F., Berlin, 1900.

Duhem, P., *Le Systeme du monde;* histoire des doctrines cosmologiques de Platon a Copernic, 6 vols., new impression, Paris, 1954.

Fakhry, M., "The Classical Islamic Argument for the Existence of God," in *The Muslim World*, XLVII/2 (April, 1957). pp. 133-45.

Al-Kindi wa Suqat, in *al-Abhath*, vol. XVI (March 1963), pp. 23-34.

Dunlop, D. M., "Biographical Material" from the *"Siwan al-Hikmah,"* in *Journal of the Royal Asiatic Society*, (1957), pp. 82-9.

al-Farabi, *Ihsa' al-Ulum*, ed, Agel Gonzalez Palencia, 2nd ed., Madrid, 1953.

Farmer, H. G., "Clues for the Arabian Influence on Europeon Musical Theory," in *Journal of the Royal Asiatic Society*, (1925), pp. 61-80.

Finnegan, J. S. J., "Al-Farabi et le *Peri Nou* d'Alexandre d'Aphrodise," in *Mclanges Louis Masignon*, vol. 11. Damascus, 1957.

Flugel. V. G., "Al-Kindi gennat des philosoph der Araber," in *Abhandlugen fuer die Kunde des Morgenlandes*, 1, 2. Leipzig, 1858.

Gauthier, Leon, *Introduction a l'etude de la philosophie Musulmane*, Paris, 1923.

al-Ghazali, "Deliverance From Error" in *The Faith and Practice of al-Ghazali*, translated by W. M. Watt, London, 1953.

Gilson, E., "Les Sources Greco-Arabes de l'Augustinisme Avicennizant", in *Archives d'Historie Doctrinale et Litteraire du Moyen Age*, IV (1929-30), pp. 5-107.

Graf, G., *Geschichete der Christlischen Arabischen Litteratur*, 5 vols., Studi e Testi, 118, 133, 146-147, 172, Citta de Vaticano: Biblioteca Apostolica Vaticana, 1944-53.

Haskins, H., *Studies in the History of Medieval Science*, Cambridge, Mass, 1924.

Ibn Abi Usaybi'ah, *'Uyun al-Anba' fi Tabaqat al-Atibba'*, ed. Max A. Muller, 2 vols in one Cairo, 1882.

Ibn Nubatah al-Misri, *Sarh al-'Uyun Sharh Risalah ibn Zaydun*, Cairo, 1278/1861.

Ibn al Nadim, *Al-Fihrist*, Cairo, 1338/1929.

Ibn Fatik,al-Mubash shir, *Mukhtar al-Hikam wa Mahasim al-Kilam*, MS. in Ahmed III Library, Istanbul, No. 3249.

Ibn Juljul, *Tabaqat al-Atibba' wa'l-Hukama'*, ed. F. Sayyid, Cairo, 1955.

Ibn Sina, *Al-Najat*, ed. M. S. al-Kurdi, Cairo, 1333/1914.

"Fi Taqsim al-'Ulum al-'Aqliyah," in *Tis' Rasa'il*, Cairo, 1326/1908.

Ibn Rusud, *Ah-Kashf 'an Manahij al-Adillah*, Cairo, n.d.

Ikhwan al-Safa, *Rasa'il*, ed. Khyar al-Din al-Zirikli, 4 vols., Cairo, 1347/1928.

al-Izzmirly, I. Haqqi, *Faylasuf al-'Arab Ya'kub b. Ishaq al-Kindi*, transl. into Arabic from the Turkish by A. al-'Azzawi, Baghdad. 1962.

'Izzat, 'Abd al-'Aziz, *Ibn Miskawayhi, Falsafatuhu al-Akhlaqiyah wa Masadiruha*, Cairo, 1946.

Jaeger, W. W., *Aristotle*, Translated by R. Robinson, Oxford, 1948.

al-Jahiz, *Al-Bukhala,'* ed. Taha al-Hajiri, Cairo, 1948.

Jammer, Max, *Concepts of Force*, Cambridge, Mass. 1957.

Jourdian, Amable, *Recherches critiques sur l'age et l'origine des traductions latines D'Aristotle*, Paris, 1843.

al-Juwayni, *Kitab al-Irshad*, ed. M. Y. Musa and A. A. 'Abd al-Hamid, Cairo, 1950.

al-Kindi, *Rasa'il al-Kindi al-Falsafiyyah*, ed, M. A. Abu Ridah, 2 vols., Cairo, 1950-53.

Kraemer, Jorg, "Das arabische Original des Pseudo Aristotelische *Liber de*

Pomo", in *Studi Orientalistici in Onore di Giorgio Levi Della Vida,* 2 vols., Rome, 1956.

Lewin, B., "La Notion de *muhdath* dans le Kalam et dans la Philosophie." *Donum Natalicium H.S. Nyberg ablatum,* Uppsala, 1954.

idem, "Notes sur une texte de Proclus en traduction arabe", in *Orientalia Suecana,* IV (1955), pp. 101-8.

Madkour, I., *La Place d'Al-Farabi dans l'ecole philosophique musulmane,* Paris, 1934.

idem, *L'Organon d'Aristotle dans le monde arabe,* Paris, 1934.

Maimonides, *Guide For the Perplexed,* transl. M. Friedlaender, London, 1951.

Marmura, Michael E., and Rish, John M., "Al-Kindi's Discussion of Divine Existence and Oneness", in *Medieval Studies,* vol., XXV (1963), PP. 338-54.

Massignon, L., *Recueil des textes inedits concernant l'histoire de la mystique,* Paris, 1929.

Munk, S., *Melanges de Philosophie juive et arabe* Paris, 1955.

Nagy, A., "Die Philosophishce Abhandlungen des Ja'cub ben Ishaq al-Kindi," in *Beitraege zur Geschichte der Philosophic des Mittelatters,* Bd. II. Heft 5, ed. C. Baeumer and H. F. Hertig, Munster' 1897.

Nallino, C. N., *'Ilm al-Falak, Ta'rikhulu 'inda 'l-'Arab fi'l-Qurun al-Wusta,* Rome, 1911.

al-Nashshar, 'Ali Sami, *Les Methods chez les penseurs musulmans: et leur critique de la logique Aristotelicienue,* Cairo, 1947.

Plato, *Phaedrus,* transl. B. Jowett, in vol. I *The Dialogues of Plato,* New York, 1937.

al-Qifti, ibn Jamal al-Din, *Ta'rikh al-Hukama',* ed. J. Lippert, Leipzig, 1903.

Rahman, F., *Avicenna's Psychology,* London, 1952.

Al-Razi, Abu Bakr M., *Al-Sirah al-Falsafiyah,* ed. P. Kraus, in *Orientalia,* IV (1935), pp. 300-21.

Rescher, O., "Notizen ue ber enige Arab. Hss. aus Brussaer Bibliotheken," in *ZDMG,* 68, Band I (1914), pp. 47-63.

Rescher, Nicholas, *Al-Kindi: An AnnotatedBibliography,* University of Pittsburgh Press, 1965.

idem, "Al-Kindi's Sketch of Aristotle's Organ," in *The New Scholasticism,* XXXVII, (Jan. 1963), pp. 44-58.

idem, "Al-Kindi's Treatise on Platonic Solids," in *Medieval and Renaissance Studies,* ed., R. Hunt, R. Klibansky and L. Labowsky, London, 1965.

-and Haig, Katchadourian — "Al-Kindi Epistle on the Finitude of the Universe," in *ISIS*, Vol. 56 (1965).

idem, — "Al-Kindi's Treatise on the Distinctiveness of the Celestial Sphere", in *Islamic Studies*, Karachi, IV/2 (1965), pp. 45-54.

idem, — "Al-Kindi's Epistle on the Concentric Structure of the Universe," in *ISIS*, vol. 56 (1965).

Ritter, H. and Plessner, M., — "Shriften Ja'qubibn Ishaq al-Kindi in Stambuler Bibliotheken," in *Archiv Orientalni*, IV (1931), PP. 363-72.

Rosenthal, F., — *Ahmad ibn al-Tayyib al-Sarakhsi*, Publications of the American Oriental Society, New Haven, 1943.

idems, — "Al-Kindi and Ptolemy," in *Studi Orientalistici in Onore di Giorgio Della Vida*, Rome, 1956.

Ross, W. D., — *Aristotle*, London, 1956.

Sa'id al-Andalusi, Abu'l-Qasim, — *Tabaqat al-Umam*, ed. Luis Cheikho, Beirut, 1911.

Sambursky, S., — *The Physical World of the Greeks*, transl. M. Dagut, New York, 1956.

al-Shahrastani, — *Al-Milal wa'l-Nihal*, ed. A. F. Muhammad. 3 vols., Cairo, 1948.

Sarton, G., — *Introduction to the History of Science*, 3 vols. in 5 parts, Baltimore, 1927.

al-Shahrazuri, *Rawdat al-Afrah wa Nuzhat al-Arwah,* MS. in Ragheb, Istanbul, No. 990, fols. 219-21.

al-Sijistani, Abu Sulayman, *al-Muntakhab Siwan al-Hikmah,* Ms. in Br. Museum, Or. Ms. 9033, fols. 60r-65v. ; MS. Koprulu, Istanbul, 902, fols. 85v-92v.

Steinschneider, M. "Uber die Mondstationem (Naxatra) and das Buch Arcandam," in *ZDMG* (1864), pp. 157-60, 181-85.

idem, *Die Europeische Ubersetzungen aus dem Arabischen bis* Mitte des *17,* Jahrhunderts, vol. CLI of the Sitzungeberichte der Akademie der Wissenschaften. Wien, 1906, new impression, 1957.

al-Tawhidi, Abu Hayyan, *Al-Imta' wa'l-Mu' anasah,* ed. by A. Amin and A. al-Zein, 3 vols, Cairo, 1939.

Taylor, A. E., *Aristotle,* New York, 1955.

Thery, G., *Authour de Decret de 1210 : II-Alexandre d'Aphrodise,* Bibilotheque Thomiste VII, Le Soulchoir, Kain. 1927.

Thillet, Pierre, "Sagesse Grecque at Philosophie Musulmane," in *Les Mardis de Dar al-Salam,* Sommaire MCMLV (1958) Paris, 1958.

Tritton, A. S., *Muslim Theology,* London, 1947.

al-Turayhi, M. Qasim, *Al-Kindi Faylasuf al-'Arab al-Awwal,* Beirut, 1962.

Uberweg, F., *Grundriss der Geschichte de Philosophie*, ed. K. Praechter Basel, 1953.

Al-'Umari, Shihab al-Din Ibn Fadl Allah, *Masalik al-Absar fi-Mamalik al-Amsar*, vol. 5, part 2, MS. in Aya Sophia, fols. 291-93.

Walzer, R., "Islamic Philosophy" in *History of Philosophy : Eastern and Western*, ed. S. Radhakrishnan, London, 1953.

idem, "New Studies on al-Kindi," in *Oriens* X (1957), pp. 203-32.

idem, "Un frammento nuovodi Aristotle," *Studi Italiani di Filologic Classica*, (New Series), XIV (1937) pp. 125-37.

Wensinck, A. J., "Les preuves de l'exitence de Dieu dans *la theologie musulmane*" in *Mededeelingen, der Kronik, Akadamie Van Wetenshappen*, Deel 81, Sirie A, No. 2, Amsterdam, 1936.

al-Ya'qubi, *Ta'rikh,* Beirut, 1960.

al-Zanjani, 'Abd al-Karim *al-Kindi* (in Arabic), al-Najaf 1382/1962.

Since the book was sent to the press, Professor Martin Levey edited and translated the Medical Formulary of *Aqrahadhun* of al-Kindi (Madison : the University of Winconsin, Press, 1965).